THAILAND, MALAYSIA & SINGAPORE BY RAIL

THAILAND, MALAYSIA & SINGAPORE BY RAIL

by Brian McPhee

BRADT PUBLICATIONS, UK
HUNTER PUBLISHING, USA

First published in 1993 by Bradt Publications, 41 Nortoft Rd, Chalfont St Peter, Bucks SL9 0LA, England.

Distributed in the USA by Hunter Publishing Inc., 300 Raritan Center Parkway, CN94, Edison, NJ 08810.

Distributed in Asia by Sun Tree Publishing Ltd, 1 Newton Road 03-17, Goldhill Plaza (Podium Block), Singapore 1130.

British Library Cataloguing in Publication data

A catalogue record for this book is
available from the British Library

ISBN 0-946983-75-5

Cover photos: Front — paddy fields (Marc J. Boettcher), Sprinter train in Thailand (Brel Ltd). Back — Lisu girl (John Davies).
Photos by the author
Maps by Patti Taylor
Typeset by Patti Taylor, London NW10 3BX
Printed by Guernsey Press

CONTENTS

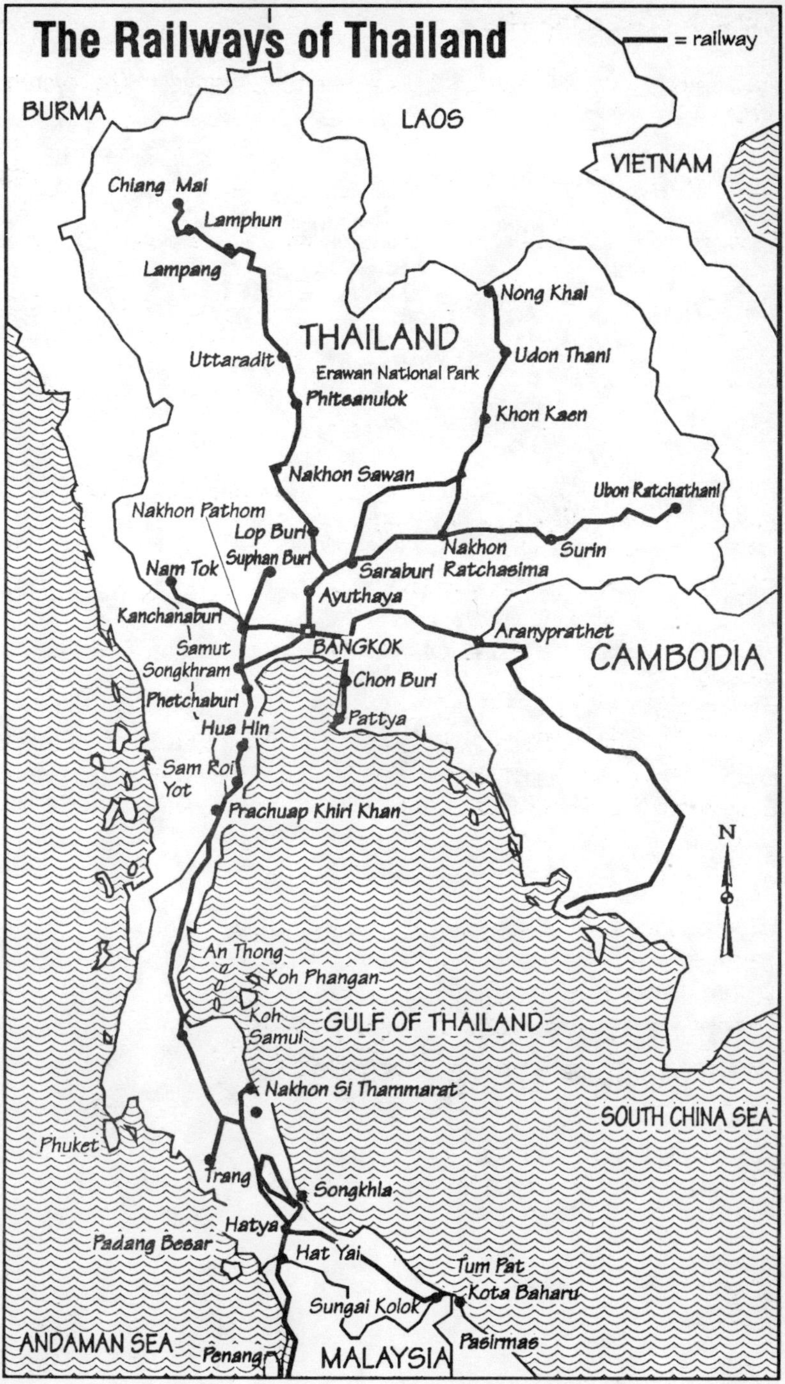
The Railways of Thailand
= railway
BURMA
LAOS
VIETNAM
Chiang Mai
Lamphun
Lampang
Nong Khai
THAILAND
Uttaradit
Udon Thani
Erawan National Park
Phitsanulok
Khon Kaen
Nakhon Sawan
Ubon Ratchathani
Nakhon Pathom
Lop Buri
Nakhon
Ratchasima
Surin
Suphan Buri
Nam Tok
Saraburi
Ayuthaya
Kanchanaburi
Aranyprathet
Samut
Songkhram
BANGKOK
CAMBODIA
Chon Buri
Phetchaburi
Pattya
Hua Hin
Sam Roi
Yot
Prachuap Khiri Khan
N
An Thong
Koh Phangan
Koh
Samui
GULF OF THAILAND
Nakhon Si Thammarat
SOUTH CHINA SEA
Phuket
Trang
Songkhla
Hatya
Padang Besar
Hat Yai
Tum Pat
Kota Baharu
Sungai Kolok
ANDAMAN SEA
Penang
MALAYSIA
Pasirmas

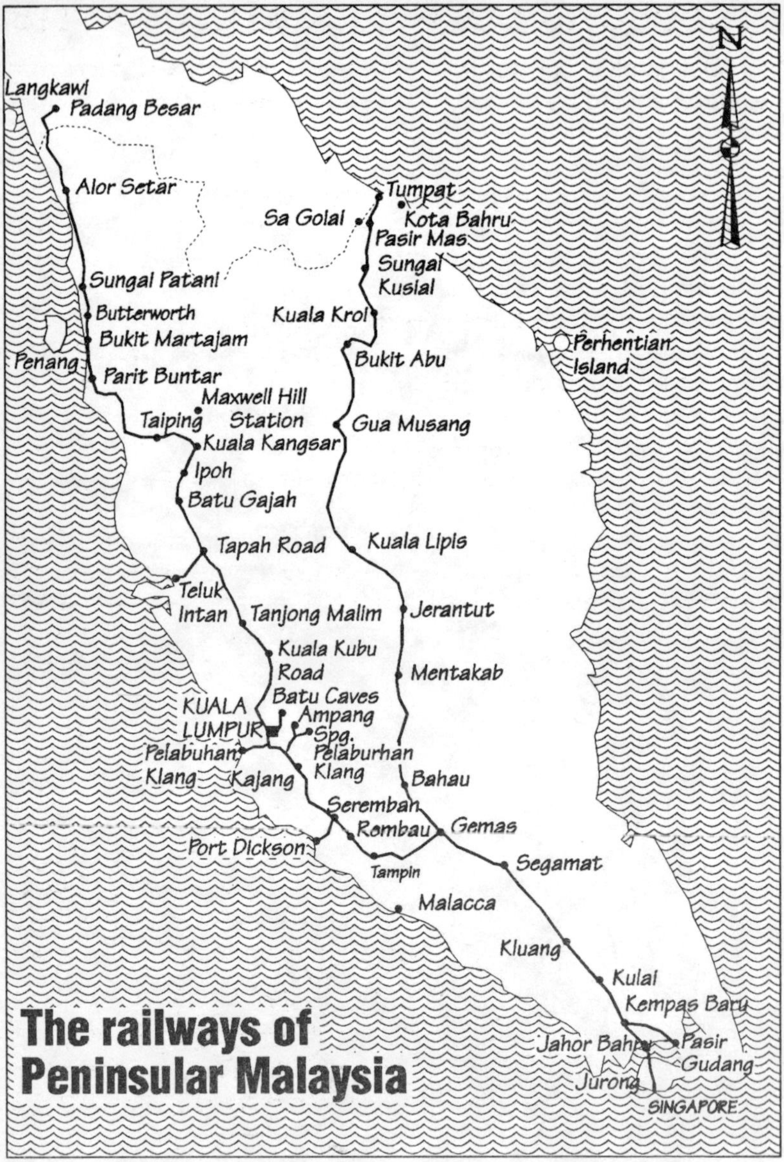

The railways of Peninsular Malaysia

INTRODUCTION AND ACKNOWLEDGEMENTS

This book is obviously for train travellers; but it doesn't mean that the reader should be entirely committed to the rails. It is hoped that advice on such matters as health, what to bring, etc. will be of general assistance.

Things change. Sometimes the change is without notice. Despite recent timetables, alterations are expected. In any event corrections, criticisms and suggestions are very welcome and will be acknowledged in the next edition.

Apart from the tourist agencies and railway authorities and staff, my particular thanks to the following: Tom Bishop who contributed two pieces and helped to correct the text, Pairuch Rogarerngam, Sanong Jut, Ikasthira, Martin Hindle, Naa Clearwan, Ian Holbrook, Kanchana Pongnoy, Joanna Drake, Chalermlap Ganachera Na Ayuchaya, Rafa Abdul Hamid B Raja Osman, Azizah Ujang, Othman Bin Hj Mohd Sharif.

Much assistance was gained from strangers on the trains, some of whom, particularly in Malaysia, possessed names so long as to be beyond instant memory. Surely there are few regions in the world where the local people and fellow travellers are so agreeably helpful.

Retired locomotive at Phitsanolok station

Old locomotive at Butterworth station

Chapter 1

Discovering Thailand, Malaysia & Singapore by Rail

These three countries operate and are joined by excellent railway systems. Naturally enough the Singapore section is miniscule — the island is only 600 square kilometres in area — so it's generally included under the Malaysian heading.

It is *Peninsular* Malaysia we are concerned with here. Apart from a small stretch in Sabah this is the only section of the country that provides a passenger rail service. This is also where the overwhelming majority of travellers find the greatest number of attractions.

Any visitor to the region is in the happy position of journeying with ease through all or part of it. You can take the train from Bangkok to Singapore or vice versa. You can restrict yourself to travelling in one country exclusively — there is an enormous amount to see — or alternatively you can stay at home and read this book and wish you were there.

The assumption is that the visitor will travel south from Bangkok (except for the eastern — central — line in Malaysia which assumes you are going north) but many, particularly Australians, will go mainly in the reverse direction. For them there is no need to read the following account backwards but in sections.

WHY THAILAND?

Exotic? Beautiful? Friendly? A living culture? Yes, all three descriptions flaunted in the brochures are true. It is difficult to encounter anyone who has travelled in this country who has had anything but an enjoyable experience. Of course there is a negative aspect. Word has got around. The hordes are coming. So far the country's strong and individual character — it has never been colonised like its neighbours — has resisted the impact. But like many parts of the world it will not remain the same for long. So hurry before other foreigners — or *farangs* — get there.

Where you go in Thailand depends on your interests. If you are an admirer of eastern art, architecture and archaeology, particularly temples or *wats* then there are an abundance in the central and northern regions, not to mention Bangkok. Many are of great beauty and antiquity. If it's beaches then Thailand's compare with the Caribbean's and are far less crowded. Sometimes there's no one there. You will also find splendid hill treks in the north, national parks, rice paddies, fishing villages and much more. If by chance you are impelled to study 'night life' combined with traffic pollution then there's no need to move further than Bangkok. I have even met people who have come to Thailand just to eat. At least this is what they seem to do exclusively. One can hardly blame them. The cuisine, now gaining popularity in the west, though generally spicy, is of world renown and inexpensive. The sea food is special indeed.

If a Thai loses his temper he loses face. This makes for serene travelling and one never encounters the noise and confusion and red tape that you might find in India, for example. This 'serenity' can lead to some frustrations however. One has just got to be patient. Problems are usually those of communication.

Courtesy then is the thing and smiles are the norm (except on the faces of speeding lorry drivers should you venture on the roads). It is also true to say that Thais are helpful and efficient (but not when driving lorries).

Facilities for the traveller at all levels are first rate and in popular areas probably better than those in the west. There is little difficulty involved in buying tickets, changing money, etc. unless of course you're in a remote area. Even a shoe seller or barber may have half his shop devoted to a travel agency. Some can organise your train ticket and all seem to be able to organise anything else.

Hotels are numerous and available as is budget accommodation and superb value (though not so much as in the past). Budget travellers can obtain a bed for 100 baht (approximately £2.25) for two people and really basic accommodation can be half this amount.

In fact everything in Thailand is inexpensive by western standards, except beer. But never mind. The enormous variety of fresh tropical fruit juices and milk shakes would even bring comfort to a dipsomaniac.

WHY MALAYSIA AND SINGAPORE?

The stunning variety found in Malaysia not only applies to the terrain but to the populace as well. There are three distinct and harmonious ethnic groups: the Malays, the Chinese and the Indians, most of whom are Tamils. This creates different cultures that must operate together and to some degree blend. The Chinese are to be found in the built up areas and are usually working if not eating. The rural landscape is populated by the more relaxed Malays mainly in *kampongs* or villages. In remoter areas the indigenous people are encountered such as the Orang Asli, some groups of which wear clothes only to go swimming.

Although the railways have existed a long time in Malaysia and have a fascinating history the country has not long been a tourist destination. There still remains a slow and relaxed atmosphere which is perhaps just as well considering the heat.

All ethnic groups, but especially the Malays, are more conservative than their Thai neighbours. The Islamic influence, which is not nearly as strong as in the Arab countries (because of the religion's late arrival) is nevertheless very evident in dress, conduct and architecture. But the friendliness is real and in some regions the helpfulness is so pronounced as to be almost embarrassing. (On my first visit to Kota Bharu in the northeast an old man addressed me with these words: "Dear Sir or Madam" — I am, I believe, a sir — "Could I be of sufficient assistance to you?" With great enthusiasm and expertise he guided me around the town.)

For many, myself included, the most fascinating parts of the country are the extensive, dense rain forests with an extraordinary variety of flora and bird life. There are also splendid white sand beaches, some of which unfortunately are off the railway route on the east coast — but Penang with its brilliant coastline is on the rails, or nearly. The slow moving rural towns (*kampongs*) provide a contrast to bright glossy sky-scrapered Kuala Lumpur. And there are towns and cities such as Malacca that express an exciting history involving European invaders and colonisers.

Facilities for the traveller are good and transport is remarkably inexpensive. Accommodation, even at budget level, however, can be two or three times as high as Thailand's but is still cheap by European standards. The old budget 'doss houses' are gradually disappearing.

And then there's Singapore, claimed by some — particularly the Singaporeans — to be the shopping and feasting centre of the east. But of course there is more to see in Singapore than the modern spick and span city.

THE RAILWAY EXPERIENCE

Many travellers do not consider journeys by trains — at least not at the outset. This is not because they've weighed the pros and cons but precisely because they haven't. Rail in this region is by general consensus the best way to travel, particularly long distances. The trains run on time. They are clean and comfortable and even third class, though basic, is acceptable.

There are, of course, the standard reasons for taking a train instead of using the road. You can relax and stretch out and walk about. You can stroll through the carriages. There are (usually) clean toilet and wash basin facilities. You can store your luggage within view (there is a limitation here on Thai 'Sprinter' trains).

There are restaurant cars and you can sit there if needing a different location. There are no bumps or swerves. (One traveller claims to have read a considerable part of Joyce's *Finnegan's Wake* on a Malaysian train, a tribute both to the railways and the reader.) There is an excellent and verifiable safety record. Not so road transport in Thailand: the accident rate here is a matter of deep public concern.

Where the railways really outshine the roads, however, are in location. The tracks are more remote than the roads. The terrain in many parts holds an additional degree of interest: jungles and forests, distant vistas of mountains, coffee coloured rivers, flat distances of green paddy fields, rural villages, rubber and palm oil plantations. Sometimes one catches a view of working elephants and everywhere are the placid plodding water buffaloes, the very sight of which would cause Somerset Maugham to burst into tears.

Thais and Malays make excellent travelling companions. Not for them the restraint shown in some European countries. For them a train journey is an outing. (In southern Thailand on one occasion the majority of the third class passengers seemed to be selling food to each other or comparing the contents of their shopping bags.)

No matter what age you are or whatever your economic status trains are ideal meeting places and information is passed on freely. Many Thais speak some English and nearly all Malays do. On a long haul there will be a large contingent of travellers from more countries than you ever thought existed. The vast majority are young and are living on a budget, or at least trying to.

If travelling first or second class you can usually obtain a comfortable sleeper for little extra cost. This will save the price of a hotel. However, not surprisingly you will miss the view because (1) it's dark outside and (2) you are asleep. (Sleepers are now not available on the east coast Malaysian line.)

Of course one disappointing feature is that the train may not reach the destination you require. This applies to the north of Thailand above Chiang Mai although a line to Chiang Rai is proposed. It also applies to the east coast of Malaysia. Interesting towns such as Malacca in Malaysia are more conveniently reached by bus but the train/bus combination here provides a much more scenic alternative.

In Thailand the rail network stretches to the Burmese (Burma is now officially called the Union of Myanmar), Laotian and Cambodian borders. Some time soon the lines may continue over these frontiers as the political position changes. And Malaysian Railways (KTM) joins Singapore with Thailand along two routes that stretch through the whole of the country.

THE RAILWAYS OF MALAYSIA AND THAILAND — A SHORT HISTORY

by Tom Bishop

The great railway builders of Europe and, more particularly, those of industrial revolution Britain, strongly influenced railway development in Southeast Asia during the late 1800s.

In the cases of Thailand (then Siam) and Malaysia (then Malaya) these influences took two totally different guises yet ended with the same result — a one metre gauge railway system linking Singapore in the far south with Chiang Mai in the northern Golden Triangle area, a distance of 1567 miles.

Colonisation of the region by the British, French and Dutch meant the mining of minerals and appropriate transportation to the ports. In Malaysia, the first line was built from Taiping to Port Weld (now Kuala Sepetang) for the exportation of tin from the Larut tin mining area. Under the administration of Sir Frank Swettenham, this and other new 'mine to port' lines were designated metre gauge track width with a future view to linking them on a north-south route. This would allow for the exploitation of the inland agricultural regions.

Two Pioneer Corps divisions from Ceylon completed the initial eight mile route on February 12 1885 and it opened for both passenger and goods traffic on June 1 of the same year, to coincide with the 60th anniversary of the world's first railway — the Stockton and Darlington railway in England.

The first passengers from Port Weld to Taiping arrived late — because the short trip had first been made without attaching the carriages full of railway officials and VIPs! With appropriate British originality, the first locomotive on this auspicious occasion bore the plate 'No 1'. The line was destined for failure and within 10 years tin production had declined with the new state port of Teluk Anson (now Teluk Intan) taking over.

Rubber became the main Port Weld export by 1920 and the original line was to suffer the indignity of having its rails removed by the Japanese for use in the building of the infamous Burma Death Railway during World War II (see page 158). Rails were replaced after the war to carry a daily charcoal and livestock train. The line finally closed in the 1970s.

Even after closure, Malaysia's first railway was abused. The line was removed to build a sewage tank and further buildings for the King Edward VII school which occupies the old station building.

In 1909 Malaya already boasted a through route from Prai (now Butterworth) to Johore with ferry links at either end of the line, to Penang and Singapore respectively. A replacement causeway to Singapore was built in 1923, yet to this day a frequent ferry service links Penang to the mainland station.

The next 10 years saw the completion of a rail link from Prai through those newly acquired northern states to Padang Besar. This provided a link with the Royal State Railways of Thailand through Hat Yai. Thus, the British had succeeded in opening up the ports of Malaya (Penang, Teluk Anson, Malacca) and Singapore with a rail network and linking with the Siamese rail system, an idea it had instigated some 60 years before. The one major missing link was that Thailand was not colonised thanks to the efforts of three successive kings and the Royal Siam Engineers.

In later years a Malaysia East Coast line was built linking Sungai Kolak and Kota Bharu at the border. This line extended down the eastern peninsula to meet the western route at Gemas en route for Singapore. The topography presented a bigger obstacle than the Padang Besar to Kuala Lumpur route. With mountains and rainforest to overcome, the 327 mile line was not opened until 1931. Today it provides one of the most scenic railway trips in Asia with a single daily service in each direction, the train aptly named *The Golden Blowpipe*.

In the 1970s the escalating prices of petroleum provided a big swing to rail travel and Thailand Railways benefited enormously. So much so that it is now constructing further track mileage; no longer to protect its borders, but to serve the development of its eastern seaboard at Sri Racha and Khao Chi Chan plus, the construction of a route from Khirirat Nikhom to the tourist resort of Phuket in the south. A Chiang Mai to Chiang Rai route was included in the original railway plans of 1887 but this is still 'pending construction'.

As Thai Railways approaches the centenary of the first passenger service it is again importing trains from that once influential colonial giant, Britain, in the form of ten luxury railcar sets, nicknamed 'Sprinters'. Not such a far cry from the original purchase of ten steam locomotives from Messrs Dubbs and Co of Glasgow in 1893, following King Rama V's decision to protect his borders by building rail links from Bangkok. Whether it was his admiration of British engineering or the potential possible colonisation of his country, but his decision had certainly been British inspired. In 1855 Queen Victoria had presented his predecessor, Rama IV, with a gift of a model steam train such as that used in Britain. Presented by a diplomatic delegation from Britain led by the highly respected Harry Smith Parks, it was hoped to convince the king of the need for new trade routes between Burma and Malaysia, i.e. Thailand colonisation through British built railways.

At that time the Siamese treasury was too weak to support such a venture, but later the pressing need to bring outlying areas within easier reach of the capital meant the establishment of a railway department in 1887. There was a rather rapid completion of the first 45 miles of track from Bangkok to Ayutthaya by March 26 1896. However, this was slow compared to the laying of the next 120 miles of track to Nakhon Ratchasima by 1900!

There was little German colonial interest in the area at this time, which suited independently-minded Siam. British management was replaced with German contractors in these early years, from 1896 to 1917.

From Nakhon Ratchasima two lines were constructed to meet the natural border of the Mekhong river in the north and Khong Chiam in the east, although the latter ends short of the border at Ubon Ratchathani. A further line was constructed to Aranyaprathet connecting with the Cambodian line to Phnom Penh. Today, this through route is under reconstruction.

Siam's late entry into railway engineering was boosted further by the efforts of Rama VI after his coronation in 1910. The metre gauge was adopted to allow links with Indochina, Malaysia and Burma). This replaced the original 4ft 8½in track width introduced by the British contractors assigned to the construction of the first railway.

Rama VI ensured completion of the major route to Chiang Mai by 1919. The leap forward continued with the consolidation of various railway departments and track mileage totalling 2350 miles by World War II.

Emphasising its commitment to railway transport, Thailand took delivery of its first two diesel locomotives from Switzerland as early as 1928, upstaging its southern neighbour by 20 years. Passenger service diesels were not introduced into Malaysia until 1957.

FACTS ABOUT THAI RAIL (SRT)

- The system was taken over by the government in 1890.
- It is controlled by a Board of Commissioners
- The length of the main track is 3,861 kilometres.
- There were 85.3 million passengers carried in 1990, 81.6 million being third class passengers.
- There are 437 stations throughout the country.
- The system is single track except for 90km double tracked between Bangkok and Ban Pachi. (Further double tracking is taking place.)
- There are 2,480 bridges. Many of the wooden ones are being replaced by metal structures.
- Forty one provinces out of seventy three are connected by rail.
- There are seven steam locomotives, 279 diesel locomotives, 181 diesel railcars, 1,555 passenger cars. (The figures are for 1990 and do not take into account the purchase of new diesel main line locomotives and 'Sprinter' rail car additions.)
- The average speed of a main line passenger train is 51km per hour and the top speed of a 'Sprinter' 120km per hour.

FACTS ABOUT MALAYSIAN RAIL (KTM)

- The railway is wholly owned by the Malaysian Federal Government. KTM is a public corporation coming under the portfolio of the minister for transport.
- The first stretch of track was laid in 1885.
- In 1990 over eight million passengers were carried.
- There are 1658 kilometres of main line track.
- The Sinaran Express and Express Rabyat originate in Kuala Lumpur and travel north and south.
- Serandung Malam has no third class. But first and second class provide sleeping berths.
- KTM administers the service to Singapore in cooperation with the Singapore government.

Station amenities

There are two stations in Bangkok each distinguished by the fact that it takes a sterling effort to pronounce its name. Hualamphong is the main station and is the one you'll be almost exclusively concerned with. Thonburi on the other side of the Chao Phrya River serves just one line.

The Malaysian main station is Kuala Lumpur and is deservedly world famous and Singapore station, part of KTM, contains all amenities.

At all main and branch line stations there are toilets, mainly Asian style and washing facilities which normally are clean. There are left luggage offices, food and drink vendors, information bureaux and at the stations in the capitals there are money exchanges. Not often are there restaurants attached, nor in Thailand many rest rooms (ie rooms to rest as distinct from toilets). In Malaysia in main stations there are rest rooms and prayer rooms for Muslims.

Right throughout the region shops, restaurants, guest houses and hotels are a stone's throw from the station. (This does not apply to the more remote parts of Malaysian Eastern line.) Cheap transport to and from the station is in plentiful supply.

It is not surprising that there is a shortage of station restaurants, apart from the presence of cafes outside. Passengers seem to eat an enormous amount when travelling; snacks are usually purchased from hawkers who don't harass you. Presumably on arrival passengers have had a surfeit.

LINES

Thailand

There are five main lines: Northern to Chiang Mai, Southern to Hat Yai and Padang Besar (and Sungai Kolak) and thence Malaysia, eastern to Aranyaprathet — for obvious reasons referred to as 'Aran' — to the Cambodian border; east to Ubon Ratchathani and north eastern to Nong Khai on the Laotian border near Vientiane.

There are short side routes, eg Thong Sung to the town of Trang and on to Kan Tang — but you wouldn't want to go there; Thong Sung to Nakhon Si Thammarat; Nam Tok by way of Kanchanaburi provides a real rail experience heading to the Burmese border and takes in the 'death' railway but is probably best managed by weekend excursion.

The northern line to Chiang Mai is the most popular and agreeable route and arguably the most scenic, at least after Phitsanulok. The line to the Cambodian frontier provides no highlights and would be of little interest to the international traveller unless he had a compulsive need to view rice paddies. It will however come into its own if the border opens up and you can continue on to Phnom Penh and beyond.

You can of course travel down from Bangkok to Singapore in one go, changing at Butterworth. The whole trip takes two days and two nights.

Malaysia

There are two main lines running down the western and eastern (or central) side to Singapore.

Arau is the terminus for the western line on the Thai border but the international traveller must change trains much earlier (or later) at Butterworth which adjoins the popular destination of Penang.

The eastern line originates at Lumpat but effectively at Pasir Mas which is the station nearest the Thai border. Now that the highway along this route has been completed the passenger demand has withered away resulting in a reduced service of one main train a day. However all is not lost. KTM, despite everything, intend to upgrade this line making it suitable for faster trains. Also there are vague plans to construct an east west connection. We will wait and see.

There are a few small branch lines usually serviced by *relbus* (railbus). Some of these lines were built for industrial purposes, eg for the transport of tin and some have now been closed to passenger traffic, eg Port Dixon and Port Weld lines. The fast bumpy little trip from Kuala Lumpur to Port Kelang provides a pleasant excursion.

THE EASTERN & ORIENTAL EXPRESS

There are three hotels in the region that in varying degrees serve as nostalgic reminders of an elegant and privileged past: the Oriental in Bangkok, the Eastern and Oriental in Penang and the revamped Raffles in Singapore. Now, a luxury train service is due to come along to complete the picture.

It is due to start in autumn 1993 making one return trip a week between Singapore, Kuala Lumpur and Bangkok, stopping at Butterworth for Penang and Surat Thani for Phuket. (This latter excursion involves a fairly lengthy bus trip.) The whole journey will take 41 hours, a long time on a train but with such luxury who can complain? In fact there will only be one full day travelling as two nights are spent in slumber. The distance covered is 1,943 kilometres (1,200 miles) and thus there will be a fair sampling of the contrasting scenery of the region.

In addition to the main route there will be an overnight excursion from Singapore to Malacca in Malaysia and from Bangkok to Phitsanulok for Sukhothai — probably the two most outstanding historical sites in the region. These excursions can be taken independently or added on to the main route.

So what can a passenger who has paid £650 (sharing a private cabin) expect? Apparently sumptuous luxury and first rate service.

Route: The Eastern & Oriental Express

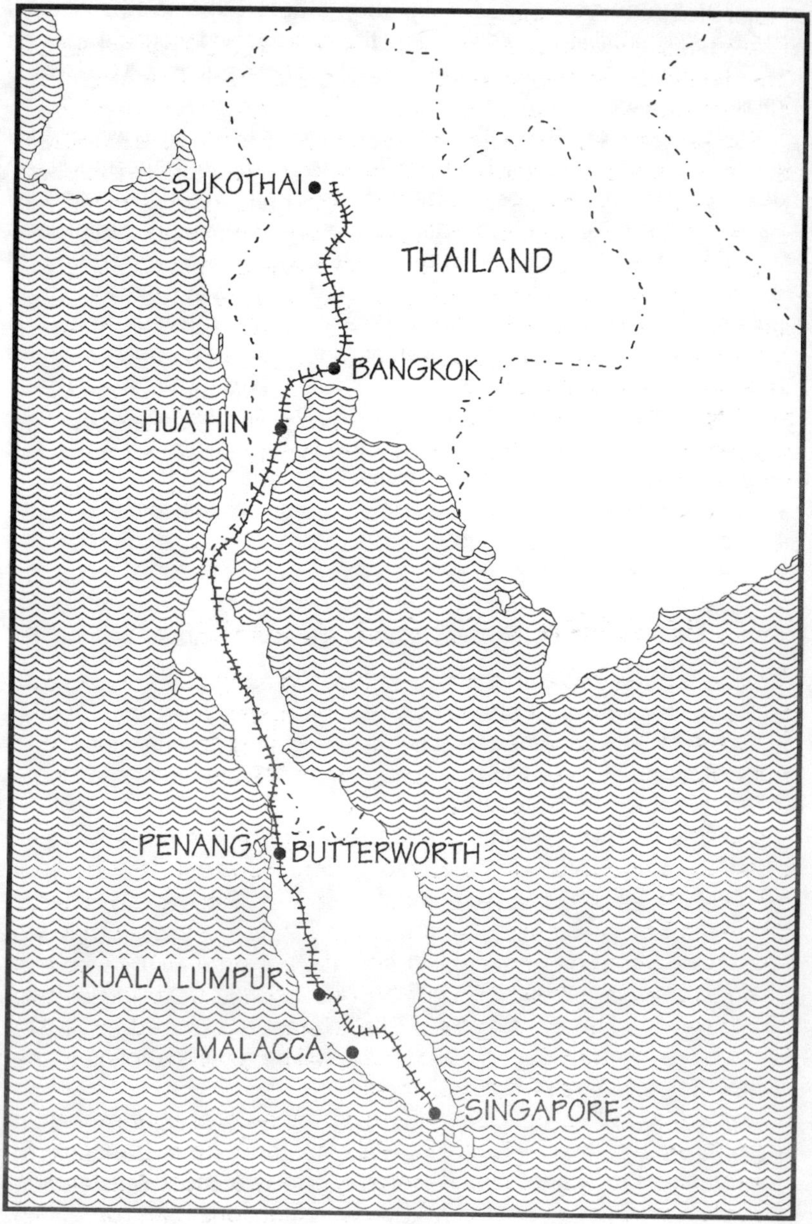

The original carriages, from New Zealand, have undergone substantial modification. The designer responsible for the restoration of the interiors of the Venice-Simplon Orient Express has used a 1920-1930 motif which also reflects the cultural and artistic traditions of Southeast Asia. The eventual cost of the conversion will be US$20 million — quite a sum.

The 22 carriage rake with capacity for 132 passengers will be fully air-conditioned. There will be 13 sleeping cars (each attended by a cabin steward), and two classes of accommodation: standard cabins, and the larger state cabins, both with private washing and toilet facilities and showers. There will also be a richly appointed and spacious Presidential car with two bedroom and dressing room suites. The rest of the rake will be made up of two restaurant cars, one bar car, one Pullman/restaurant car with boutique, an observation/bar car (at the rear of the train), and three service cars.

'A new travel experience' is promised. Should this trip live up to its claims it will certainly be that: a relaxing luxurious journey with more than a whiff of nostalgia. But it doesn't come cheap. Apart from the fare already mentioned one can take a more expensive cabin or the Presidential suite, this for £900 (US$1,550).

Reservations can be made in London (071) 928 6000.

Further information can be obtained from Caroline Rathbone, Press Office, Orient Express Hotels, Sea Containers House, 20 Upper Ground, London SE1 9PF, UK. Tel (071) 620 0003.

There are more than 27,000 temples in Thailand. The Thai name *wat* refers to all buildings within the temple compound which form a kind of community centre.

SCHEDULE
(Subject to confirmation)

Northbound from Singapore			
SINGAPORE (Keppel)	Sun		1500
KUALA LUMPUR	Sun	2200	2300
Tapah Road	Mon		0530
Ipoh	Mon	0630	0645
BUTTERWORTH (for Penang)	Mon	1030	1230
Surat Thani	Tues	2050	2105
Hua Hin	Tues	0509	0538
BANGKOK (Hualampong)	Tues	0920	
Sukhothai Excursion			
BANGKOK (Hualampong)	Tues		1955
Phitsanulok	Wed	0650	
(Coach transfer to Sukhothai)			
Phitsanulok	Wed		1200
BANGKOK (Hualampong)	Wed	1740	

Southbound from Bangkok			
BANGKOK (Hualampong)	Wed		1955
Hua Hin	Wed	2320	2330
Surat Thani	Thur	0617	0627
BUTTERWORTH (for Penang)	Thur	1625	1830
Ipoh	Thur	2150	2200
KUALA LUMPUR	Fri	0200	0230
SINGAPORE (Keppel)	Fri	1030	
Malacca Excursion			
SINGAPORE (Keppel)	Fri		1830
Tampin	Sat	0650	0710
(Coach transfer to Malacca)			
KUALA LUMPUR	Sat	1010	1045
Tebong	Sat	1400	1415
(Return coach from Malacca)			
SINGAPORE (Keppel)	Sat	1850	

Chapter 2

The experience

THAILAND: A JOURNEY — A LONG HAUL

It is 7.51pm on a Friday evening at Hua Hin, or as Mr Chunchai Mee would have it, it is 19.51 *exactly*. This station master is both youthful and precise. His neat khaki uniform is pressed daily. There is a proud display of ribbons. He is possessed of short black hair and impassive good manners. His English is more than workmanlike. His peak cap sits *exactly* as it should. And the train, number 43 diesel, pulling an impossible number of dusty carriages, bound for Hat Yai via Surat Thani — number 43, as usual is right on time.

But Mr Chunchai Mee is not himself. There is not the well known shine to him. His voice is oddly dead. He has told me that he has been promoted and this means moving to another, bigger, station. He doesn't want to go but what can he do? Promotion is promotion. Orders are orders. He loves Hua Hin. He relishes his work here. This little patch has become part of him.

Hua Hin station is indeed a delight. It is the home to a number of garden gnomes, a small pond and carefully tended flower beds. There is also the cosy tiny temple house that is a waiting room and used to be the exclusive preserve of the king. An ancient steam locomotive is on display. Minutes away are the beaches and the famous Sofitel Railway Hotel.

Outside, in the quiet forecourt, a host of eager trishaw operators with over-muscled legs and insistent offers wait for customers. There will not be many. Most of the foreign tourists arrive by bus, a three hour trip from Bangkok, unaware of the overriding pleasures of rail travel.

Mr Chunchai Mee's assistant rings the brass bell that would be more appropriate on a sailing ship. Like the station itself it is polished to perfection. We clamber aboard. The carriages are crowded: middle class Thais escaping the lethal traffic of Bangkok, workers visiting relatives, rubber tappers returning to their jobs and, of course, an enormous number of *farangs*. Nearly all the *farangs* are young. They are travelling south with their rucksacks and eager expectations. They will be heading for Koh Samui or Koh Phangan, gleaming islands that are referred to with some respect by young internationalists.

Second class non air conditioned — that is the way to travel on a long haul, with a sleeper, of course. 'Experts' will tell you that third class is hard and uncomfortable and that first class is twice as expensive as second class and not much different and certainly less sociable. Personally, for shorter trips during the day, I feel that third class is fine.

It doesn't take long for that special Thai service to make itself felt. I have only just found my seat and put my small bag in the rack when a formally attired waiter with a bow tie and an engaging smile is there. He wants to know if I want a beer — a large cold Singha. I do. I certainly do. The smile broadens. And why shouldn't it? After all he obtains a commission on every bottle he sells. The *farang* sitting opposite me places no objection as he is asleep. He awakens slowly, sees the beer, matches the waiter's happy smile with his own. '*Bier Sing koo-ut nung, kup*,' he orders.

Even amongst the country's visitors *sanuk* (having a good time) seems to prevail on trains. Perhaps it's catching.

My companion is Swiss. He is not young. He visits Thailand every year and he loves the place. This time he has been to Bangkok, Chiang Mai and Chiang Rai in the north and has spent a few days in Khao Yai National Park. He reels off like a check list the animals he has seen: gibbons, elephants, wild pig and civets but complains that the place is being destroyed by its development: the heavy traffic, the overused trails, the litter and the hordes of visitors. He is going south to the water fowl sanctuary at Khu Khut where he hopes there are *not* hordes of tourists. I inform him that when I was there I virtually had the place to myself — it is relatively unknown and is not a listed national park. This news cheers him immensely and we order another beer.

The carriage is brimming over with *farangs*. They examine guide books, gaze at portentous maps, swig at water bottles, munch hawkers' food, spoon railway delicacies and their enthusiasm is infectious. *They have plans.*

"This guy told me that you could rent a bungalow in Koh Phangan for 50 baht a day for two ... That's not bad ... They say you can buy huge crabs from the fishermen ... Yes, but how do you *cook* 'em? I want to hang out a month ... No ... I'm only there a couple of days. Have to get down to Singapore ... We did a four day hike up north ..." and so on.

As is my habit, I wander down to the third class. Here there are insufficient seats. People are sprawling in the corridors, sitting on insubstantial cases and awkward bags. All the windows are open and the fans are whirring above the noise of busy conversation. We pull into Chumphon. Night has fallen with tropical abruptness.

There are half a dozen young *farangs* in the carriage with their trusty water bottles, adjusting easily, it seems, to the hard straight backed seats. Four head shaven saffron robed monks occupy one corner. The youngest is no older than twelve, the oldest, with his creviced gnarled features and weak spindly legs, is sleeping. The others are engaged in an earnest dialogue. A policeman, tight uniformed in olive green, his gun in a holster at his hip, smokes happily. So do many more in the carriage. On every second window is a well illustrated sign declaring in English that it is prohibited to smoke.

Those who are not smoking appear to be eating. From all sorts of packages and bags emerge chicken and pork and rice and noodles and fruit. In a timber crate on the floor a number of hens cluck with apparent contentment but maybe they sound like this whatever. At Chumphon even more food is at hand: hordes of eager children and a sprinkling of adults board the train or press their wares to the windows. There are papaya salads, barbecued red chicken on bamboo sticks, bags of rice, sugared spaghetti, fruit of all description, chewing gum, coca cola ... and then we're off again. While the hawkers head fast for the exits Thai parents unnecessarily silence their dutiful children by putting even more food into their mouths.

It's somewhat of an anticlimax to be back in second class after the even greater amiability of third. But now dinner is served. This is the first time I've tried the new all-in *farang* Thai meal: soup, a roll, a main course — I settle for *plaa priaw wa'an* — (sweet and sour fish) with rice, of course. This is followed by fruit. At 100 baht however this is not nearly as good value as the individual dishes that are listed on menu number two and which — unless you're Thai — has to be prized from the waiter. My companion has chosen *goong thawt* (fried prawns). He confirms that they are as delicious as they look.

Along the carriage people are discussing food, discussing costs, making new friends, making new plans, hurling clichés and laughter into the air.

It is time for sleep. It is ten o'clock. Beds are made up, a light woollen rug is provided, curtains are pulled across ... a quiet descends. I insert ear plugs and put on an eye mask — courtesy of an airline — and go to sleep on the bottom bunk, undisturbed until daybreak.

Early morning is the best time on a train in this region. We are clackitty clackitting across a silent ghostly plain. Golden sunlight pierces misty distances. There are rubber and fruit plantations and later there will be limestone outcrops strewn around like pieces of odd old discarded machinery; and in the villages and in the countryside people are already going about their business. Thais rise early. This is a sensible habit in the tropics.

We arrive in Surat Thani where most of the *farangs*, like a huge team, dismount and crowd the station and move off in the gathering light. Another three hours and they'll be on the beach in Koh Samui. By 8.15am, *right on time*, we reach our destination: Hat Yai.

I understand Mr Chunchai Mee's sadness. I will miss his smiling welcome. Before I return he will have moved away. Perhaps later on I will see him at another station. But what if he is promoted *here*, to this busy purpose built town that presents to you only a bare bland face? Maybe there'd be one consolation: outside the impersonal station stands a small ancient steam locomotive, a sturdy little work horse. He'd appreciate that. It's surrounded by a tiny walled lawn with a few plants. It wouldn't take Mr Chunchai Mee long to create a lot more flower beds. And what about some garden gnomes?

MALAYSIA: A SHORT RUN

The Express Langkawi for Kuala Lumpur is due in at 1.25 stopping only at Tapah Road which provides a connection to the cool misty Cameron Highlands. The whole trip will take only four hours. This station, Ipoh, is usually in a rumbustious mood; but not today. At weekends it is overwhelmed by passengers but now there is a mere trickle. Some are engaged in a challenging pastime: crossing and recrossing the rails, apparently oblivious to the danger of an approaching train.

On the next platform an object has engaged the attention of a huddled group. It is an old stately restored box carriage. A Malay woman dressed in a *baju karong* — a long sleeved tunic worn over a sarong — shows it to her tiny olive eyed daughter but the girl is too young to see anything in the relic. Her eyes are elsewhere. A throng of Chinese youths, their heads thrust forward like inquisitive turtles, all dressed in T-shirts, jeans and plimsolls — worn like a uniform — examine it with delicate interest. An old Malay woman, traditionally attired, broom in hand and ruefully preoccupied, sweeps around them.

This is the station for Malaysia's second largest city: Ipoh is a big bustling metropolis that unfortunately fails to present a cogent spectacle of its exciting past. It is a city built on tin. Indeed tin holds sway today. It is thoroughly Chinese though it is true that on the station all the staff are Malay and so are some of the passengers. It is not on the regular tourist route. The colonial station and adjoining hotel — the whole structure is referred to by the locals as 'the Taj Mahal' — represent its major attraction. Last night I stayed in the hotel. It is all but falling to pieces. Crowned by a large dome it has a troubled mix of various architectural styles. Neo classical, colonial with Islamic influence? It defies definition. Perhaps this is its attraction. Its columns are badly cracked and haphazardly repaired. Paint peels everywhere. The white building is about to die. But let's be fair. With its spacious airy rooms with high ceilings, its improbable colonnades, its lush wine coloured threadbare carpets and its dust it retains an odd and shabby gentility. One somehow feels sorry for its fall from grace; and flanking this outrageous structure is a delightful flower filled *padang* (park).

Now the train, a sturdy powerful diesel with its complement of once glittering carriages, slowly eases its way into the station and bells ring.

I find a seat in a third class carriage. These compartments are as a rule more comfortable than their Thai counterparts. Generally they have padded adjustable seats (some, it is true, needing repair) and carpets — yes, *carpets*. It seems that nearly everyone here is Hokkien Chinese. The strange, brittle quacking dialect fills the carriage. Soon no doubt they will be eating. Eating here is a very regular practice, almost a religion.

The countryside has been ransacked. Tin is the culprit. In the distance occasionally you can see the intense wooden scaffolding of a mining operation; but there is also the relief of rivers and large towns, the palm oil and rubber plantations, the imminence of heavily wooded hills and the green swathes of jungle. The west coast line has not nearly the visual excitement of that on the eastern side, but never mind; at least there is more scenic variety here.

'You are pushing it this way sir ... *this* way'. A Tamil Indian passenger is helping me to adjust my aeroplane style seat with its badly torn fabric. 'It is easy when you are knowing how ... you see' he exclaims with a glow of pride as the seat collapses with a shudder, nearly sending me sprawling backwards. 'Too far' he unnecessarily adds. 'It seems it is a little problem in parts.' We again adjust it. 'You must be knowing how sir. It is easy when you are knowing how.'

My companion is very dark skinned, about thirty five years of age and seems to be full of flashing white teeth and long winded advice. He has a predilection for the present tense. He runs a shop in Penang with his brother. He is going to Kuala Lumpur and adds somewhat mysteriously 'on urgent business'. I impertinently ask him what sort of business but he repeats 'urgent business ... *very* urgent'. He shows me a photograph. It is of his family. The patriarch hovers smilingly in the background. There is a plump wife in a sari and four small children. 'Six children. I am a very lucky man. Three girls and three boys.' When I point out that there is only one boy in the picture he says, 'But two are coming later. We pray for it. Three boys, three girls. This is a big family, is it not?'

He offers me some pineapple but I am replete with papaya. Hawkers at the stations are armed with all sorts of food and drink. Chicken and mutton satay, tropical fruit, *nasi goreng* (fried rice), noodles, Coca-Cola ...

We stop at Tapah Road. Up above are the famous Cameron Highlands with their lush forests and unbounded fertility and quasi English style cottages. There you can indulge in strawberries and cream, even though out of season. It is not pointed out to you that the strawberries are deep frozen.

A group of Malay school girls joins the carriage. Their bright bashful faces are bound tight by white *chadors* like young nuns. They sit quietly, hardly talking.

We pull into Kuala Lumpur station, the best in Southeast Asia. It is cool and organised and efficient. A gleaming rail car surges out at some speed — no crossing of the lines by passengers here. My Indian friend wishes me a fond farewell. He is tightly grasping a small battered suitcase. 'I must be going fast,' he says. 'Very urgent business I am having here. My family is waiting for me in Penang.' I expect him to make a mad dash for the barrier but he saunters off. Even here in the capital, miles from the *kampongs*, people move slowly; and even those on 'urgent business' seem to have succumbed to this entirely agreeable practice.

SO, WHAT DO WE SEE FROM THE TRAIN?

In this region rail travel can be relatively slow. It is easy to be overcome by an urge to stop the train because a scene to be cherished is about to escape you. It might be water-buffaloes languidly bathing themselves in a still reed filled pond, or a straw hatted young woman, handsome in profile, up to her knees in mud; or an ancient Khmer temple that looms up right next to the tracks; or a distant dark teak forest; or an enormous golden Buddha sitting solemnly on a hillside; or a sleepy Malaysian village or *kampong* surrounded by oil palms planted in serried rows with their tall branchless trunks crowned with clusters of large sweeping fronds; or a group of children searching for frogs on the banks of a coffee coloured river; or a sunset on the plains — a smear of crimson across the sky; or a railway crossing where more than a hundred motor cyclists, revving their engines, wait until the train goes by; or a huge limestone outcrop poking out of the coastal plain like a giant's finger; or a crude railway line, still in operation, seemingly cut out of a cliff face; or a glistening golden tower (*chedi*) rising gently into the sky ...

However, there are three features that surely dominate the view: rice, rubber and jungles.

In Thailand, particularly in the central region and the north-east, the green swathes of rice paddies stretch out endlessly into a flat distance. You will see this in Malaysia as well, particularly in the northern states of Perlis and Kedah; but of course the scene will dramatically change, depending on the time of year and where you are. The rice will be glorious golden for a brief period at harvest time but when cut all you'll see is a monotonous brown stubble. A patchwork effect is sometimes created, the result of some fields being irrigated and others not or some fields lying fallow.

Then there's the rubber that covers three quarters of the cultivated Malay Peninsula and much of southern Thailand as well. The plantations seem to have no beginning or end. The white-trunked slender trees are laid out in neat orderly rows as if in a fruit orchard. Their leaves turn into a russet colour during the dry season and then fall off leaving a ghostly skeletal landscape. Whereas the rice paddies are occupied for much of the year by workers involved in their back breaking tasks, the rubber plantations viewed from the train appear to be completely abandoned. There is a simple explanation for this.

And, particularly in Malaysia in the central eastern region, you are constantly in the company of a green wall of lush forest, a veritable riot of shapes. This is the world's oldest jungle.

THE STORY BEHIND THE PICTURE

Rice

Rice, rice and more rice. It stares at you from your plate; it is your persistent companion viewed from the train. The Thai word for it '*kow*' means 'food'.

It is consumed by millions three or more times a day in one form or another (sticky rice is the favourite in the north). Thailand is the rice bowl of Asia. The country *lives* on rice. It is an integral part of its culture, part of the spirituality. In a way it symbolises life itself.

It is produced in the greatest quantities in the central plains. One could be forgiven for thinking that the soil in this vast region is eminently suitable for the growing of this cereal; but it is not. Many countries have a significantly higher per acre yield. They do not have, however, the extent of paddies in production, nor the immense hardworking labour force. At certain times of the year the paddies are positively bristling with human heads. Everyone joins in, even the small children.

For every ten inhabitants there is one water buffalo. They are the silent partners in the agricultural world. These slow, gentle, patient creatures are well suited to their allotted tasks. They almost look as if they enjoy ploughing; certainly they don't object to mud. (In the wet season their life style is much more relaxed.) They possess a grand passion for water: sitting in it, rolling in it or just simply walking in it. The reason for this is the absence of sweat pores — they need water to keep cool. They are easy to keep and seem to have no objection to children riding on their backs. They confer on their owners a status. To possess more than one will earn great respect.

Assuming that there is a single rice harvest a year — and in the central plains there are usually two — the season starts early in May. This is symbolically represented by the Royal Ploughing Ceremony (see page 56). It is the water buffalo which accomplishes this task. The plough is usually a simple single blade. The 'operator' will treat the buffalo as an old friend which, of course, he is. The monsoon may come in June depending on your location. Where irrigation exists the paddies are flooded. Where it doesn't the farmer just hopes for sufficient rain. The water is retained by the surrounding earth walls. Rice seeds are then planted by hand and four months later the young plants are uprooted and transplanted in adjoining muddy fields. This is the really back-breaking task. The land greens and then after three to five months produces a sea of golden stalks. Now the rice is harvested by hand with a sickle and is taken for threshing and winnowing.

As with rubber growing the work in the rice paddies is spasmodic, intense at times when everyone slaves from dawn to dusk and more relaxed at others.

Perhaps the most culturally interesting part of the region is the northeastern or *Issan* area with its significant Laotian influences. Here life is a struggle. There is only one crop a year and most people cannot afford the pumps for irrigation. The monsoon is at best irregular.

Lek — this is her Thai nickname — described her way of life to me as we sat by a tiny creek adjoining her family's small holding thirty miles from Ubon Ratchathani. I had known her two years before in Bangkok where she held down a good job as a children's nanny for a rich family. The family were kind to her and she loved them. She could eat whatever she wanted and could purchase good clothes. They gave her plenty of time off. But she had returned to the rice paddies. There she sat in her simple sarong and flat straw hat under the ferocious gaze of the summer sun. Why?

Here the average weekly wage is ten American dollars, there is no irrigation and sometimes the whole harvest fails. (1992 produced the worst drought in forty years.) Furthermore the problem of river pollution is immense. Only recently a factory discharged molasses into the River Mun which runs nearby. It killed nearly everything in its wake and even this tiny creek may be affected. Such a happening would produce stunned incomprehension or anger to westerners but Lek, with an acceptable touch of fatalism, lets nothing get her down. She is a beautiful, graceful woman who holds her head high; and always there is the flashing smile.

'Food better here,' she says. 'Mud crab and what you call?' (She illustrates. It is grasshopper.) 'It good too and little fish and shrimp and bamboo shoot. We eat even when time bad. And when we not have food then friends bring. Everyone exchange. Not pay money.'

She lives in a tiny fragile house consisting of two rooms. Nine members of her family share this simple accommodation. Her father is pleased that last year he paid off the money he'd borrowed to purchase the water buffalo. Later she tries to explain to me the nuances of the community life they lead, their hard but cheerful existence which Lek seems to prefer above others; but it is a difficult task. This flat timeless land withholds its secrets from strangers.

'*Farang* not understand,' she says softly, wistfully, looking away.

She is right.

Rubber

What is the reason for the apparently dark, deserted rubber plantations? Why is it that while we pass in the train the tappers are in the *kampongs* relaxing or asleep? The reason is that tapping normally takes place *before sunrise*. The best time is at about 2am when acetylene torches are used, for then the sap runs freely. During the heat of the day tapping is ineffective and in the hot dry season it cannot take place at all.

Rubber trees take seven years to mature. This means an awfully long wait. What is done during this interminable time? How can the tappers survive? They sometimes themselves have difficulty in explaining this but survive they do by growing ordinary crops, perhaps maize, vegetables, mace, fruit and nuts, and of course, all trees aren't planted at the same time. For the first three years these crops are grown between the infant rubber trees as their roots are not yet long enough to be disturbed by ploughing. The grower may invest in oil palms, also planted in orderly rows. At present it is Malaysia's major agricultural export. The fruit is used for the making of soap, margarine and other products and the residue from the kernels provides livestock feed.

The tapper's life is not an easy one. Apart from the unsocial hours the tool of trade is a razor sharp scraper. One slip and a finger could go missing; so for safety reasons alone two hands are used.

The tree is divided into three sections. Cutting starts from above shoulder height. A central channel is made and the cuts are at thirty degrees. The sap, which is below the bark, eventually runs into a small cup or container which is put on the ground or wired to the tree. The latex is collected from the cup after two hours.

'Bleeding' each section may take up to two years; then the next section is dealt with, leaving the used area to grow another layer of bark. The cuts are close together. Only a finger nail width divides them. The latex is then mixed with a catalyst. It is now ready for further processing and transport to a middle man or direct to the factory. (The trees are productive for twenty years or more.)

The story of the rubber industry in Malaysia has its dramatic moments. In the mid 19th century the trade, with its dark history of human exploitation, was the exclusive preserve of Brazil. The penalty for smuggling rubber seeds out of the country was death; but eventually some reached Kew Gardens in London from where they were sent to Singapore. Then a legendary figure appeared on the scene. 'Rubber' Ridley was the director of the Botanic Gardens in Singapore. He patiently demonstrated to the unconvinced British planters that plantation rubber could be grown. He was in luck. It was 1890. Soon the motor car industry was to boom and the demand for rubber become huge. To this day the main buyers are tyre manufacturers.

Vast sums of money have been made but that's not to say there haven't been severe slumps. The present one has lasted three years and would have been worse except for the demand for latex — the result of the AIDS epidemic.

To the rail traveller these plantations often appear to be endless. It is true that those owned by the large combines and tyre companies are indeed extensive; but some are as small as ten acres. Whatever the size the working period is spasmodic as mentioned. No work can be carried out in the three month dry season. There is no sap, and the trees conserve moisture by shedding their leaves, which cover the earth with a gold and russet crust. Nor can tapping take place in the wet. When the bark is damp the trunks can be damaged.

It is said that a prudent plantation owner working solidly with skilled workers may become relatively well off after twenty five years, but this is a long time to wait.

There is a current note of ecological optimism in the rubber growing world which previously had a bad reputation in this area since the cutting down of the jungle and the clearing of undergrowth removes most of the animal, bird and insect life that existed there. Now a Sri Lankan engineer with the improbable name of Hope Todd has made one of the most significant conservation contributions to the modern world. His process for treating old rubber trees, 'Borwood', means that this timber, which previously was unsuitable for making furniture, can be turned into the equivalent of teak. Hitherto old rubber trees were of no significance. They were either used for charcoal or left to rot. Now this vast reservoir of timber can be employed for the making of furniture and the building of houses. Mr Hope Todd deserves a thousand accolades.

The rain forest

For those on a tight schedule the rain forest may seem less than fascinating. From the train window one is enveloped in a sea of green, a confused configuration of shapes, and initial enthusiasm for this scene may, after a few hours, become clouded. The extravagant bird life that normally exists here is driven away by the noise of the train. Sensibly, animals, apart from the ubiquitous domestic water buffalo, fail to put in an appearance.

The huge Peninsular Malaysian rain forest — and this is the one that far outshines any other in the region — can be amply observed on the eastern (or central) line. You will have the jungle with you for most of the time; but the only way truly to experience it is to be *enveloped* in it. You must get off. Remaining on the train will give you only a modicum of its atmosphere. Much of it, in any event, is missed: the single train from both directions travels mainly at night.

There are huge, soaring, smooth-trunked trees of which there are 2000 varieties containing the more recognisable oaks, chestnuts and palms. There are dense tree canopies through which the sun filters; there are jungle ferns, spinous rattan vines, wild orchids — of orchids alone there are 800 different species. Insects are numerous and noisy. Snakes are present including enormous pythons and venomous cobras (but keep their distances) and leeches can be at times a nuisance.

It is the ornithologist who is most happy here. The bird life is a wonder. At times you seem to be in a vast wooded aviary and you wonder if your ear drums could be affected by the cacophony in the early morning. (In Singapore, these species can be identified at close quarters at the newly expanded Juron Bird Park.) Amongst many others you may see the colourful hornbill, kingfishers, osprey, fishing eagles, brown doves, the common mynah birds, woodpeckers and pheasants.

Unfortunately the larger animal life is becoming part of the country's mythology. Tigers are rarely observed, nor are elephants. The Malaysian two tone tapir is more common and monkeys and gibbons exist in large numbers in the tree canopies. Barking deer, civets and forest cattle are often seen but of course are not nearly as interesting; but barking frogs are.

Taman Negara (which means National Park), covers part of the states of Terengganu, Kelantan and Pahang (see page 181) and provides probably the best rain forest experience.

One must not forget the human occupants. They are referred to under the umbrella name of 'Orang Asli' or Original People. This classification covers a large number of tribal and racial groups and some certainly aren't 'original'. The life style and religion (mainly animistic) varies from group to group: some are hunters, others are fishers and others still cut patches out of the jungle for cultivation (mainly hill rice). You can see Orang Asli settlements on the Tembeling River on the way in to Taman Negara.

From the train the endless vistas of jungle are broken at intervals by brown rivers, big and small, tiny sleepy *kampongs*, numerous exiguous railway stations and the odd large town.

Although the problem of logging is more prevalent in other parts of Malaysia, with its pernicious effect on indigenous people, it is nevertheless carried out in certain parts of the peninsula, a matter of grave concern for the conservationists. The government maintains that the destruction of the rain forests is only its business and no one else's. A pity. International pressure may eventually have some effect.

OFF THE RAILS

Islands and beaches — Thailand

The tireless search to find a place in which to do nothing at all can take time and energy. It is not, of course, the normal rail traveller's consuming passion; but a break from the journey can be beneficial and the surprising fact about the country is that many outstanding islands and beaches, some free of tourists, have easy rail or rail and boat access. It is true that *some* islands that once were havens have been 'discovered'. The result is that travellers trying to 'get away from it all' encounter hundreds of others trying to 'get away from it all'. Koh Phangan in southern Thailand is a case in point. It has recently attracted more backpackers than you even knew existed; but surprisingly — or perhaps not — most report, as if in one vociferous voice, having a joyful experience.

In the past the attraction of Thailand's islands and beaches have been underestimated. The Caribbean has received most of the accolades but this region has better climatic conditions and many of the islands are less developed and some of the coconut palm fringed beaches equivalently idyllic. But commercialism, even in northeastern Malaysia, will eventually have its day.

THAILAND	
Beach or Island	Rail access
Hua Hin	Hua Hin
Koh Chao	Surat Thani
Koh Hai (and other islands)	Trang
Koh Phangan	Surat Thani
Koh Samui	Surat Thani
Pattaya	Pattaya (but very limited service)
Phuket	Surat Thani (plus 6 hour bus trip)
Prachuap Khiri Khan	Prachuap Khiri Khan
Songhkla	Hat Yai
Trang (south of)	Trang

There is no rail connection to the top of the Gulf of Thailand and therefore by sticking to the train you will miss Koh Samet and Koh Chang, the latter an undeveloped island near the Cambodian border. It is also fair to say that the famous or infamous resort of Pattaya, though possessing a pleasant beach, doesn't present you with a pleasant opportunity to swim, the sea being highly polluted here.

Going south one comes to Hua Hin which is on the coast and although not possessing the ambience or quality of light of the southern islands is highly agreeable because the crowds here are Thai. The sea shore is of white sand but there are rocky outcrops so you can only swim in certain parts. There are a few good deserted beaches near Prachuap Khiri Khan. The beach at Ao Manao is used exclusively by the Thai military. Further south again we come to Surat Thani which is the gateway to the 'paradise' islands of Koh Samui, Koh Phangan and Koh Tao. Samui is a 'bungalow' island with the glorious long white sand beach (with clear water) at Chaweng, and Lamai and numerous other beaches and sandy stretches where you can swim alone. The superb beach at Haad Rin on Koh Phangan can be full of people sleeping off a hard night. There are other more solitary spots around the island. Koh Tao is not noted for its beaches but for its 'away from it all' atmosphere. But the nearby island of Nang Yuang possesses three sand bars or beaches which form the subject of a popular postcard.

For the rail traveller Surat Thani is also the improbable connection for the west coast including the international resort island of Phuket with its splendid scenery and excellent beaches. This is 'hotel country', however. Nearby is the lovely island of Phi Phi, a national park, but the daily invasion of sightseers here is like a mass migration.

Songhkla is on the mainland backed by casuarina trees possessing a long, clear sandy beach, and is relatively peaceful and certainly pleasant.

South of Trang, the last beach and island region on the itinerary, there are some wide sandy beaches (but closer to the town two or three suffer from litter). From Pak Meng pier you can get a boat to Koh Hai, a tiny and beautiful island. There are other 'isolated' islands, tourist free, nearby.

Malaysia

The best beaches are in the north on both coasts. Train travel will exclude the popular and fairly spectacular east coast island of Tioman which like the exquisite unspoilt island of Paulau Kapas (near Marang) is off the main route. But perhaps the gem of the whole region is the Perhentian Island group on the east coast near the Thai border. Here peace reigns supreme, the waters are crystal clear and the beaches quite enchanting: a beachcomber's delight.

On the west coast up north is the well known island of Penang, 'the Pearl of the Orient', with its capital Georgetown. There are a number of golden sand beaches, Batu Ferringhi being the best known. There are many hotels here but things get quieter and better the further out you go. Even here the beaches don't *quite* match the allure of the east coast variety. Finally, for those who want something different, the Langkawi island group up near the Thai border — only the one island is visited — has good beaches and an agreeable quiet and unique atmosphere, although becoming more and more of a Malay holiday destination. (Two beaches with fair rail access, Port Dickson south of Kuala Lumpur and the Beach of Passionate Love near Kota Bharu, are not recommended.)

MALAYSIA	
Beach or Island	Rail access
Langkawi	Alor Star Padang Besar Butterworth
Penang	Butterworth
Perhentian Island	Khota Bharu (station is Wakaf Bharu) Pasir Mas

National parks — Thailand

The Karen tribesmen who live north of Chiang Mai are not at all happy. They demonstrate this condition with expressions of the utmost mournfulness. The previous week they'd received a visit from a government officer. It was certainly not news to them that they lived within the borders of a national park. But they and their forebears were there long before the park; for 200 years in fact and in all that time they have not altered their way of life one little bit — except for a change in religion. (My friend's parents were animists but he had been converted to Buddhism.) They grow rice. That is harmless enough. There are no opium poppies in the region. Their crime is to do what they have always done: to practise shifting agriculture. When their paddies become temporarily exhausted then they take another piece of the forest by the 'slash and burn' method. They also hunt game — monkey and deer — but there is very little game left. Now the government is telling them to mend their ways. Why should they? No one 'owns' land and whatever they take from the soil is for their own meagre survival. There are no cash crops; and for generations this tribe has lived here contentedly. They are happy people. They are all friends. They have to be. They love their hard working isolated existence. Who could say they are doing anything wrong?

Of course the problem is a difficult one. Here, as in so many places, the degeneration of the forest is not caused by the usurpers such as loggers and prawn farmers but by the indigenous population itself.

Some of the more popular national parks in Thailand are being damaged by tourist visits but efforts are being made to abate this and the country is not without its heroic conservationists.

More than eight million people will visit the parks annually — but take heart in that only a few areas are seriously affected. Thailand has over sixty — yes, *over sixty* — national parks, not to mention a number of wild life sanctuaries. Here there are some of the richest and most fascinating varieties of flora and fauna as can be found anywhere in the world. Many of the less well known national parks remain almost undisturbed.

Expect to experience dense rain forest vistas of thickly forested hills and mountains, occasional tribal villages, brown rivers and clear streams and sightings of the smaller varieties of wild life. In some places elephants put in an appearance — and again in some places hordes of other tourists do as well. It is true that some *farangs* report disappointment, almost disillusionment, having fully expected to observe huge lumbering bears, snarling tigers and elephants, preferably charging (at someone else). For nature lovers however taking the trails in some of these parks, content with the sight of deer, monkeys etc. and the sight and sound of an enormous variety of birds, the experience can be unforgettable. *The atmosphere* is the thing here.

There is a small charge for entering the parks. Accommodation is available at nearly all. Camping is possible at all the parks which also have basic facilities. Usually food is available. At most places guides can be hired. TAT (Tourist Authority of Thailand) will advise you in these circumstances but better still contact the Royal Forestry Department Phahonyothin Road, Bangkhen, Bangkok 10900, Tel: 579-1151/60. The 'bible' for *farang* nature lovers published as recently as 1991 is *National Parks of Thailand* by Denis Gray, Colin Piprell and Mark Graham: beautifully produced, economically priced with a clear, helpful yet scholarly text and breathtaking photography. Something to treasure. Published in Bangkok by Communications Resources (Thailand) Ltd.

The list below of Thai national parks with easy rail access is, of course, selective.

National Park	Rail Access	Highlights
Doi Inthanon	Chiang Mai	Thailand's highest mountain, misty views, waterfall, tribal villages, bird life, spectacular vegetation including wild orchids

National Park	Rail Access	Highlights
Doi Khun Tan	Tankhuntan	Limited animal life, good bird life, excellent hikes and superb camping; absence of motor traffic. Some bungalow accommodation. The main trail leaves from the station where information on the park is available.
Erawan	Kanchanaburi	Waterfall, caves, smaller mammal species, raft lodge excursions, modern conveniences. (Avoid holidays and weekends.)
Khao Sam Roi	Hua Hin	Splendid views of coastline, caves, good trails, superb bird life.
Khao Yai	Prachin Buri	Nominated World Heritage site, thick forests, many trails, much bird life, sightings of elephant, gibbons, bats, etc. (Avoid holidays and weekends.)
Sai Yok	Nam Tok	Waterfall, rivers, streams, caves, smaller mammals, river rafting.
Thale Ban	Hat Yai	Dense rainforest, monkeys, deer, immense variety of bird life, frogs, splendid accommodation on lake.

National Parks — Malaysia

Endau Rompin, straddling the boundary between Johor and Penang, has no rail access and not much other access either. Special tours can be arranged with permits etc. to this remote region where the Sumatran rhinoceros is reputed to roam. Never mind, the huge national park of Taman Negara which *does* have rail access is the king of the whole region. (It is dealt with in detail on page 181.) Originally named the King George V Park, it's new name simply means 'National Park'. It came into existence in 1925, is as big as a nation and spans parts of three states: Pahang, Terengganu and Kelantan. This is in effect the peninsular Malaysia National Park system although a smaller and far less interesting 'leisure park' exists with rail access at Kuala Lipis, namely Kenong.

A nature lover somewhat disturbed by the human intrusion in

some Thai parks will be initially upset here. There are plenty of trippers and leisure holiday folk but they don't wander far from headquarters. Here you can really 'get away from it all', taking a ten day jungle trek combined with mountain climbing. At the far salt licks and further afield you have that enervating experience, particularly at night, of being utterly alone in a true jungle. This, after all, is the world's oldest. The further out you go and as long as you are patient then you may well see rare wild life such as tapirs and elephants; but even if disappointingly you don't then the huge variety and cacophony of bird life combined with the eerie atmosphere will keep you happy.

Taman Negara is considered to be an angler's paradise. The rivers contain over 300 varieties of fresh water fish, some weighing up to 20lbs.

The rail connection here is at Tembeling and Jerantut and there is a three to four hour river trip into the park. All types of accommodation are available and tents and equipment are for hire. On the longer treks it is mandatory to take a guide. You should be physically fit as the walks are quite demanding, not because of the terrain but because of the heat. From mid November to mid January, which is the wet season, the park is closed.

Chapter 3

Where to go

The following are suggested destinations on the lines together with a few that might require a bus trip for a short distance from the station or a boat connection to an island. One exception is the popular tourist resort of Phuket on the west coast — from the rails a spectacular six hour bus trip is required here. A few destinations, e.g. Khao Yai National Park and the River Kwai, are probably better reached by special SRT weekend excursions. There is no line through the so called 'Golden Triangle' of northern Thailand so extensive bus trips would be necessary from the rail terminus of Chiang Mai.

In Malaysia the eastern (or central) line is more central than eastern and cuts through the remote jungle. The east *coast* is thus almost entirely missed and with it the popular island of Tioman. A decision will have to be made as to whether to take the 'jungle train' and miss Penang or the western line and miss the jungle. The decision is a difficult one.

THAILAND: A-Z OF DESTINATIONS

An Thong National Marine Park

This 'park' consists of 40 islands nearly all uninhabited except by colonies of leaf eating monkeys. The rail access is from **Surat Thani** but most visitors take the trip from the island of **Koh Samui**. The coral reefs and marine life cannot be compared with that on the west coast of Thailand in the Andaman Sea but nevertheless, with its isolated forested limestone outcrops, the area is quite spectacular. Accommodation is available on Koh Wua Talab and tents can be hired here.

Aranyprathet (Aran)

This small, raw town will come into its own if the political problems of Cambodia are settled. In Pranchinburi province, a rail terminus for the eastern line, it has not yet dispelled its vaguely tense atmosphere. The refugee camps are nearby but many Cambodians are now returning to their own country. The town itself, a quiet place that indulges in shops of all descriptions, is the scene of much activity in the weekends. Thousands cross the frontier. A huge market sells smuggled goods of suspect quality. Already there is a rail connection into Cambodia and on to Phnom Penh, at present used only by the returning refugees. When the tourist can travel through to Phnom Penh this place will become a large trading outpost and a tourist objective. The only westerners one sees here at the moment are aid workers in huddles.

Ayutthaya

The ancient city, beloved by Thais and tourists alike, is 72km north of Bangkok and was the country's capital for over 400 years when it was one of the most magnificent cities in the east. It even outstripped its counterparts in Europe. It is now an atmospheric relic. The gold and glitter is no more but with imagination one can summon up its glorious past. Old temples abound and some have been partly restored. The city is set on the banks of the Chao Phraya river and there are well tended lawns and gardens.

Ban Chiang

See Udon Thani.

Bang Pa In

This charming conglomeration of architectural styles — mainly European — lies placidly on the banks of the Chao Phrya River 14km from Ayutthaya, so a short bus journey is necessary. It has been compared with Versailles with its ornate gardens, its topiary and ornamental ponds. Once a royal retreat, it now seems sadly uninhabited except by hordes of tourists who, despite their swarming presence, fail to intrude on the delicacy of the surroundings. But Bang Pa In has got little to do with classical Thailand and purists may find the spectacle somewhat artificial. For others it is a quiet delight.

Chiang Mai

This is the northern rail terminus and provides, as Thailand's second city, a welcome relief from the steamy touch of Bangkok. For a start it's only a fraction of Bangkok's size. Traffic conditions are positively idyllic (though getting worse). It is, however, or has become, a busy commercial and tourist centre. It is set more or less on the River Ping with its colourful flame trees and is overlooked by Doi Suthep Mountain, itself a splendid sight with its heavily wooded surrounds and its improbable *chedi*. There are, it is true, a host of modern hotels and everywhere you look there seems to be a guest house or a travel agent. But there are also innumerable teak shop houses and glistening temples. A splendid restored old city wall surrounds it. But Chiang Mai is not there for itself: it serves the Golden Triangle and the innumerable tourist sites of the north and northwest such as Mae Hong Son, Chiang Rai, Chiang Saen, Mae Sai etc. You will certainly catch a glimpse of hill tribe people, the women in their beautifully embroidered hand-woven garments. This is, after all, the centre for hill trekking.

Doi Inthanon National Park

Doi Inthanon is at 2565m the highest mountain in Thailand and forms part of the very scenic national park. It is a short distance from the northern city of **Chiang Mai** and is a must for ornithologists and those who enjoy distant misty views or rain forests, waterfalls, taking forest trails or admiring wild orchids. It is not noted for its animal life but makes up for this in many other ways.

Erawan National Park

In Kanchanaburi province 190km west of Bangkok it is a mountainous, heavily forested area close to the Burmese border. The waterfalls here are famous and draw huge crowds, perhaps too many. They are best observed between June and November. The larger mammals exist here but are very rarely seen. There are slow loris, stump tailed macaque, rhesus monkeys and more than 80 bird species. There are limestone caves to explore. This park, like Sai Yok, is not the place to seek peace and isolation or to wait patiently for wild life. It is too popular for that.

Hat Yai

This is a purpose built town, clean and comfortable, and is considered a terminus for the south bound train to Malaysia. It is the principal centre in the province of Songkhla and, because of its youth, displays little Thai character — except at Wat Haad Yai Nai where an enormous reclining Buddha is on display. Its reputation for cheap contraband goods is overstated. There are a large number of modern hotels very reasonably priced. The main source of revenue — male tourists from Malaysia — has disappeared due to the AIDS problem. The town remains however a night life centre and there are products galore to buy though not necessarily bargains. Despite its empty past and lost source of income the city grows and grows.

Hua Hin

Though a small town, part of which is a forlorn and decaying village (but nevertheless with character) it is now a peaceful though crowded resort southwest of Bangkok. It is one of the best places in the country to indulge in a variety of delicious sea foods. It is the traditional royal resort once much favoured by the rich because of its proximity to Bangkok. It is on the Gulf of Thailand. The beach, though rocky, is extensive and swimming is good but not in the harbour which is polluted. A huge new hotel overlooking the village has affected the atmosphere. The rich have departed. Only the Sofitel (Railway) Hotel gives any clue to its privileged past.

Kanchanaburi

The main town of Kanchanaburi province set in a boundlessly fertile valley is 130km west of Bangkok. It is near the infamous **Bridge over the River Kwai** and contains war cemeteries and the Jeath Museum. This area and the Death Railway are dealt with in detail on page 158.

Khao Sam Roi Yot National Park

Located on the east coast of the southern peninsula, with rail connections at Hua Hin and Prachuap Khiri Kahn, it is 'the Mountain of Three Hundred Peaks'. It is noted for the enchanting views of the coast and its limestone outcrops and caves. Its marshes are a habitat for innumerable migratory birds. However, there has been serious ecological damage caused by prawn farming.

Khao Yai National Park

This is not strictly a rail destination but is included because the SRT run a one day excursion here with bus connection. It is one of the world's leading parks and is hugely popular and thus under grave environmental threat. It is situated in central Thailand and covers parts of four provinces. There are excellent jungle walks, thickly forested valleys, panoramic hill top views, waterfalls and, regrettably, a golf course. Larger animal life is more observable here than most other parks in the region but you need to be lucky and patient. It is best known for its elephants, gibbons and hornbills but also contains the Malayan sunbear, barking deer, mongoose, badger, tiger, clouded leopard, sambur, wild pig and other elusive creatures. There are 318 species of migrant and resident birds. Bats in the evening are in abundance. Butterflies are everywhere.

The excursion provided by SRT is excellent value: the drawback is that much wild life can only be observed in the early morning or evening. In any event, because of the mounting traffic and the large numbers of visitors that help to scare away the animals, the right to stay overnight has been abolished. (There are lodges and bungalows and camping facilities on the edge of the park.) This decision has aroused a furore in the kingdom. Nevertheless, for conservation purposes, it may be necessary.

Korat (Nakhon Ratchasima)

The gateway to the northeast region 260km from Bangkok and the provincial capital, it provides the first introduction to the *Issan* people. It came into being during the Ayutthaya period (1688). The much revered statue of Lady Mo, the Joan of Arc of Thailand, who defeated the invading Laotian forces in the early part of the 19th Century, stands in the centre of town. There is not much here, however, to attract the tourist and over the years the city has become somewhat frowzy. It serves as a jumping off point to the splendid Khmer site of Phimai.

Khu Khut Water Fowl Sanctuary

Asia's largest bird sanctuary is 80km from **Hat Yai** by bus. Rarely visited by international tourists, a trip here is a real experience. Thailand's largest lake (really a collection of lagoons), Thale Luang, is the breeding ground for over 140 species of birds. Best observed from November to February and March to June, especially at dawn and sunset one can hire a flat bottomed boat and glide over the shallow waters whilst observing huge flocks of egrets, herons, grebes, cormorants, ducks, etc. It is not only the waterfowl that are of interest; the boat trip itself through the reed beds is a unique experience. There is an atmosphere of peace and everywhere, except for the flapping of wings, there is absolute silence. Regrettably there is little published information in English about the fascinating bird life here.

Koh Hai

This small paradise island can be reached from the rail connection at Trang. The water here is particularly clear and the sands glistening white. It is however only one of a group of islands and one can take a choice. It is virtually free of western tourists and accommodation is relatively expensive.

Koh Samui

This together with Koh Phangan and Koh Tao form a group of stunningly beautiful islands studded with coconut palms and picturesque beaches of white sand. They are accessible from Surat Thani by ferry. The two main tourist spots and the best beaches are at Chaweng and Lamai and naturally enough this is where nearly everyone goes. The result is a lack of Thai atmosphere. But despite the swarms of tourists, mainly backpackers and the huge number of new bungalow developments, the place hasn't lost all its charm and there are still undisturbed spots around the coast. Phangan, an hour further on, is even less developed and is thick with young and old hippies. Koh Tao is even further out and more primitive and is popular with divers. There is an idyllic marine natural park that can be reached from the islands (An Thong see page 33).

Lamphung

Pronounced 'Lampoon' this quiet northern town near Chiang Mai has some gratifying temple complexes of extraordinary antiquity. It is also noted for its longan (like lychees) and its garlic with the attendant aroma. It is a handicraft centre.

Lopburi

This archaeological site with its town 154km north of Bangkok seems almost as if it is embracing the railway line. An old Khmer capital, it flourished in the 17th century. The Phra Prang Sam Yod (the Sacred Three Spires) gives you some indication of the grandeur of Angkor Wat in Cambodia. The great dark towers are particularly impressive in the evening light.

Nakhon Pathom

The town here is famous for its *chedi*, the world's tallest Buddhist monument. It was built in 1860 by Rama IV and has the grandeur of a St Pauls or Chartres cathedral. It is one of the great spectacles of the country. Like a huge bell it seems to rise forever into the sky. The roof is of splendid brown tiles.

Nakhon Ratchasima

See Korat.

Nakhon Si Thammarat

This is the second largest city in the south, 860km from Bangkok. It is a clean, sprawling town and is Thailand's 'gangster centre' though you would hardly know it. Rarely visited by western tourists, it nevertheless is the site of the south's most imposing temple complex: Wat Mahathat. The *chedi* here has been recently restored.

Nong Khai

This town, which time seems to have fixed into place, is the terminus for the northeastern railway line and is about to boom again. Its present lethargy is the result of the isolation of Laos just across the swirling chocolate-hued Mekong River. When the new bridge is complete — construction commenced at the end of 1991 — then the place will lose its 'end of the line' ambience. Provision is made on the bridge (a gift from the Australian government) for the construction of a single track railway line and eventually one will be able to travel from Bangkok to Vientiane 20km northwest. With the possibility of briefly visiting Laos (visas are obtainable in Bangkok and Nong Khai itself) much interest has been aroused in this town.

Padang Besar

This is where Thai and Malaysian railways meet on the western side. Immigration formalities take place on the station here. The town itself has a market and not much else. It is only a border settlement but even at this it presents a sad and shabby spectacle.

Pattaya

This is a resort and is world famous (or infamous) and is 147km southeast of Bangkok. It has very limited rail access. It contains everything for the holiday maker but is unlikely to overwhelm the train traveller wanting to see as much as possible with limited time. The once sleepy fishing village has been transformed at hectic pace into a brash hotel and night club zone. Although it hardly competes with most of Thailand's beautiful beaches there *are* palm fringed sands and many pleasant hotels and guest houses. The sea is badly polluted, so you can't swim. The paradox is that hordes of tourists, mainly middle aged single men, prove that this is still a very popular tourist destination. But perhaps this isn't a paradox.

Phangan

See under Koh Samui

Phimai

Located 48km from the railway connection at Korat is this fascinating archaeological site. The buildings here of brick and stone are 1000 years old and resemble those at Angkor Wat. Although the temples are dedicated to Mahayana Buddhism there is a strong Hindu influence. There is nowhere better in Thailand to see a display of ancient Khmer monuments. Some of the restoration work however is a little haphazard.

Phitsanulok

Half way between Bangkok and Chiang Mai on the rails this provincial capital is not a real tourist destination but is nevertheless a thoroughly agreeable town. It is the gateway to **Sukhothai** and is a pleasant and convenient place for an overnight stay. As the wonders of Sukhothai await one then there's little point in seeking enchantment here except at Wat Phra Si Rattana Mahathat where the 14th century Buddha image is considered Thailand's finest. In the evening here everyone seems to be in a restaurant. There are hundreds of them along the Nan River serving interesting and delightfully inexpensive food in an enjoyable atmosphere.

Phuket

This popular tourist resort is situated 900km south of Bangkok on the west coast and is an island joined by a bridge. The railway, however, at this stage follows the *east* coast so going by train and bus is certainly not the fastest method. Railway access however is available at Surat Thani, the same station that serves Koh Samui. There is, naturally enough, an enormous amount of tourist development on Phuket with luxury hotels by the score. But there are a number of fine, white, sparsely populated beaches and other exceptionally beautiful natural attractions. The less well known Krabi is not far away and the internationally famous island paradise Phi Phi can be reached by boat or plane in the company of thousands of other tourists.

Prachuap Khiri Khan

Formerly a hideaway for bandits it is 278km south of Bangkok on the Nang Rom Canal bank overlooked by the Mirror Mountain. The half moon shaped bay has been compared with that at Rio de Janeiro, presumably by those who have never been to Brazil, but it is serenely beautiful in its own right with vistas of lush plains and jagged peaks and tall limestone outcrops. **Khao Sam Roi Yod** National Park is not far away. As yet there are few western visitors.

Sai Yok National Park

Reached from the terminus of the western line at **Nam Tok** near the Burmese border, this park bears resemblance to Erawan which is part of the group of national parks that form a sanctuary along the border. It does not quite possess the spectacular waterfall of its neighbour though its own is certainly worth seeing and is at its best between May and December. Limited accommodation is available.

A better place to observe wild life than Erawan it is also far less crowded. There are barking deer, Malayan porcupine, sambar, wild pig and a very minimal possibility of seeing elephants. There are also colonies of bats. The limestone caves here are worth visiting. There are plenty of rivers and creeks and you can raft down the Kwai Noi River for days on end.

Sala Maetha

This tiny town on the northern line in the foothills 45km south of Chiang Mai is certainly *not* worth a visit but the station for railway buffs *is*. It is a microcosmic delight of palm trees and well ordered gardens and splendid rose bushes. Less than ten tickets a day are sold here yet there is a staff of four who appear to spend most of their time in repose. There is a minuscule timber and tile ticket office. The staff are uniformed in a style that befits a prize winning station.

Samut Songkhram

On the shore of the Mae Klong Bay 74km south west of Bangkok this interesting, heavily populated town is rarely visited by western tourists — but it gives an authentic picture of town life in Thailand, warts and all. The bay itself is thick with all sorts of craft and boat building is one of the main industries. Salt production fields and shrimp farms — both environmental hazards — can be seen nearby. There are several floating markets which are frustratingly held at very infrequent intervals depending on the moon. Don Hoi Lot, a bar of worm shells at the mouth of the river which can be observed in April and May only, is very worthwhile. This is also an excellent place for sea food dinners and odd odours.

Songkhla

This involves a forty minute taxi or bus trip from Hat Yai and is a huge fishing port on the Gulf of Siam. The lazy, long crescent beach here is pleasant without being spectacular or remote with facilities for picnics and numerous restaurants. Odd, old Chinese tile buildings oozing with character present themselves along the waterfront as do the spiky casuarina pines. The salt water lake

(Thailand's biggest inland sea) of Thale Sap is the home of **Khu Khut Waterfowl Park** where 140 species of birds can be observed and a boat trip here is a never to be forgotten experience for nature lovers.

Sukhothai

This town is situated at the end of a one hour bus trip from Phitsanulok railway station. It is the birthplace of the Thai nation. It is 427km north of Bangkok and this former capital flourished from the mid 13th century for two hundred glorious years. This was the Golden Age of Thai civilisation and the enormous number of temple complexes in the Historical Park supports this. These extensive ruins are atmospheric indeed with lovely hyacinth filled ponds, extraordinary Buddha statues and images and splendid *chedis*. But it is a long day here and under the weight of the tropical sun it can be exhausting.

Sungai Kolak

On the banks of a river of the same name this town is on the Malaysian border on the eastern side. Somewhat ramshackle but with plenty of hotels, no traveller would want to stay here unless waiting for the border to open.

Surin

On the northeastern line this town, 200km from Korat, does not demand a visit except in late November when the famous elephant round up takes place. The main events are in the third week. The people here obtained their expertise in the logging industry. The event is well presented and is a great spectacle.

Surat Thani

This is the capital of the largest province in the south and is 700km south of Bangkok and although would be in many ways an agreeable place to live — it is inexpensive for one — it is nevertheless a huge commercial centre for rubber, seafoods, coconuts and various manufactured products. It serves as the railway (and bus) connecting point to the ports for the islands of **Koh Samui** and **Koh Phangan**.

Thale Ban National Park

The rail access here is **Hat Yai** and the park is not all that far from the Malaysian border. Perhaps more of an attraction to wild life specialists, but the layman will get a better perspective of undisturbed rainforest than at many other parks that attract hordes of visitors. There is also more varied wild life here than elsewhere but tigers and bears are, as everywhere else, a very rare sight. There are over 200 species of birds. This region is picturesque and there is also a touch of that elusive feeling that an adventure may be in store for you. Staying in the limited accommodation in the form of lakeside bungalows is itself a hugely enjoyable experience.

Trang

Referred to also as Tab Liang Town, it is located 828km south of Bangkok and is on the branch line that leaves the main line at Tung Song. An historically important trading town it is now a major exporter of rubber. A neat, clean provincial place it is located near two minor national parks and a beautiful coast line with white sand beaches (some of which unfortunately are quite dirty). Not far away are the jetties from which one can take a boat to the attractive islands nearby including **Koh Hai**.

Ubon Ratchathani

This town sits quietly and remotely amongst the rice paddies on the banks of the River Mun. It is the railway terminus for the eastern line. It is also the place where one can experience the real *Issan* culture. It is a poverty-stricken infertile region with a strong Laotian influence. Many can barely scratch a living from tiny rice paddies that are subject to frequent droughts and floods. This doesn't appear to worry the local inhabitants unduly who smilingly work through the piercing heat of day as if nothing was more natural. The town itself is remarkably modern but tends towards dullness. *Issan* food is capable of outraging the throat. There are some splendid temples within striking distance, nearly all demonstrating a Khmer influence and also tours as far as the Mekong River on the Laotian border.

Udon Thani

This town south of Nong Khai is the rail connection for Ban Chiang. The place itself, a moderate sized development, was an American military base during the Vietnam War but seems to have been abandoned and left to itself. As such it is a town of unperforated dullness; but not so **Ban Chiang** 50km away. This friendly, sleepy settlement on the plains is the site of the dawn of civilisation, its bronze age preceding that in the middle east. Two burial pits are on display. The museum provides an excellent account but much of the finds here have been smuggled away. Some are exhibited in the

National Museum of Bangkok. Despite the paucity of material 'in situ', this quiet, torpid site possesses its own individual atmosphere.

MALAYSIA: A-Z OF DESTINATIONS

Alor Star (Alor Setar)

The old and endearing state of Kedah in the northwest of the country adjoining Thailand with Perlis is the rice bowl of Malaysia. Its capital is Alor Star, a town that has been awakened by a dam. This reservoir on the Muda River which — surprising for dams — has provided an irrigation system that has enormously increased rice production. The railway here serves as an outlet to the Kuala Perlis ferry to Langkawi island. Very few tourists stay which is a pity because although there are no overwhelming attractions the town is traditionally Malay. It is also acceptably torpid. Furthermore Kuala Keday, a 'quaint' fishing village, is only 12km away and the fort on the other side of the bay is a spectacle.

Batu Caves

The best time to visit here is during *Thaipusam* (see page 63) when Hindus collect in a great colourful mass to pay homage and atone for past sins by self inflicted 'injuries' — spikes through the skin and slashed tongues and other forms of self mutilation. Buried deep within a huge limestone outcrop there is a 270 step climb to the entrance or you can take a tiny rail car for most of the way. There are a number of somewhat frightening looking statues of legendary significance. The cathedral cave is particularly impressive with numerous stalactites and dust filled shafts of light. Dampness and other visitors are all around you.

Butterworth

The only magic in this town is in the name and the fact that it is the rail (and road) link to the former island of Penang. You can go by ferry to Penang or by the splendid new car bridge built as recently as 1985 and the longest in Asia. Uncomfortably looking over the North Strait to Georgetown, Butterworth seems unable to present any reason for a traveller to stay. It is flat and heavily populated despite its size and its industries is made to appear somewhat shabby beside its flamboyant neighbour. There is a huge air force presence here; however this is being reduced.

Cameron Highlands

This hill resort, 1524 metres above sea level and reached by a brilliantly engineered road up through the jungle, presents a cool face to the visitor and not only climatically. It was a hill station during the British 'presence'. People make astonishing comments (for the tropics) such as 'Isn't it chilly!' It is misty as well and picturesque with green hills coursed by lush valleys and many think it is a consoling presence. It is certainly a contrast to what is below. The solid and neatly constructed English style houses, some with rose gardens, seem only to lack an owner with a Harris Tweed jacket, pipe and labrador. The atmosphere is settled, the people, Malays and Indians, a little stand-offish. This is perhaps what the cold does to you. Somewhat touristy with a golf course and much top level accommodation, it possesses unbound fertility. There are tea plantations, huge vegetable farms, butterfly farms, 'jungle' walks and strawberries are available in season. The three charming villages here are Ringlet, Tanah Rata and Brinchang and the area is reached by bus or taxi from Tapah Road railway station.

Gemas

This town has the distinction of being avoided by tourists. There is nothing there nor is there meant to be. It simply forms the rail junction between the western and eastern (or central) lines.

Georgetown

See Penang.

Kelang Port (Klang)

This is Kuala Lumpur's sea port and a hectic, busy, overcrowded place it is. Not on the tourist map, it can be reached by a rather unspectacular train ride from the capital. But it has something. It is free of tourists for a start.

Ipoh

This is the second largest city in Malaysia with wide well planned thoroughfares, a colonial past and a history of tin and war. It is the capital of Perak state, a Chinese city with regrettably little to interest the tourist unless he is a ravenous consumer of Chinese food for which it has a reputation; though some say the reputation was gained for the *quantity* of restaurants. It has an interesting but now dead railway past, a railway station of colonial variety and an old and elegant railway hotel: an enormous mock neoclassical Islamic construction that is decomposing with dignity and dust. One can reach somewhat circuitously **Batu Gajah** from here where the remains of the famous Kellies castle can be seen: a tower with ramparts, it was the most palatial planters' building in the country, a 'folly', and never completed.

Jerantut

This town — as well as Tembeling — provides rail access to **Taman Negara** (National Park). An agreeable and friendly place, it possesses good cheap restaurants, some hotels and information on the park. It usually provides a stopover when *returning* from a visit to Taman Negara.

Johore Bahru (Johor Baru)

This most southerly of Malaysia towns is largely ignored by travellers because of its proximity to Singapore which stands across the causeway at the south of the island in all its glistening modernity. Johore Bahru, a sprawling ramshackle place, thick with street stalls, balefully examines its neighbour from a safe distance. Immigration formalities are carried out here — on the train — and there's no reason and probably no desire for the international traveller to dismount.

Kenon Recreation Park

Near Kuala Lipis, this is an area of 128 sq km with a variety of flora and fauna, waterfalls, limestone caves, mountain streams. There is good trail walking and camping but this is more of a 'picnic' area than a 'wilderness park', at least in comparison with its huge dominant neighbour, the Taman Negara.

Kota Bahru (Kota Baru)

This is the capital of Kelantan, at the top of the state near the Thai border. Here, if you are travelling from the north, the full face of Islam presents itself: the mosques, the muezzin, the traditionally dressed women, the different time for weekends; and with all this Kota Bahru is a quiet, neat, well ordered town with modern mosques and spruce city squares and parks. Its markets are some of the best in the country — but it has been isolated and it shows. The place is brazenly traditional. Perhaps the real Malaysia. It holds a famous bird singing contest in June each year. 'The Beach of Passionate Love' is nearby but is somewhat disappointing and is littered. It doesn't compare with Thai beaches nor most of the Malay beaches. However, from here one can visit the idyllic unspoiled **Perhentian Islands** which perhaps outshine all others in Malaysia and Thailand depending on what you're looking for. If it's isolation and utter peace of mind and beautiful white sand beaches then this may be the answer to your dreams. Budget travellers should note however that even living primitively here it is more expensive than on a Thai island.

Kuala Perlis

This tiny busy town, with its air of seaside simplicity and muddle of fishing craft, is the port for the 'paradise' islands of Langkawi and is an hour by bus from the railway station at **Alor Star**. The jetty is very crowded but a new one is to be built. If you miss the ferry your enthusiasm for the place might trickle away as there's nothing much to see apart from two streets crammed with shops and cafes. The ferry is modern and comfortable and the trip across is a thoroughly agreeable experience.

Langkawi

The rail access to this group of islands of which Langkawi is one is from Alor Star through Kuala Perlis. It is a restful place, interesting in that it is a large 'working' island with an abundance of paddy fields and rubber plantations. The beaches are picturesque but not quite up to the high standard of the east coast or southern Thailand, though there are plenty of palm trees and bright days, and silence has a pleasant habit of settling all around you. This is a favourite holiday destination for Malay middle class families. Pantai Cenang seems to be a good place to stay and is not too busy. The waterfalls on the island are certainly worth a visit.

Malacca (Melaka)

This town, reached by bus from the railway station at **Tampin**, possesses an authentic depth of history. For many, a visit here is indeed an enhancing experience. For the Malays themselves the place, which is quite small, possesses a deep significance. It was where Islam was brought ashore by the Moorish traders of Sumatra. It has been under the control of the Malays, the Dutch, the Portuguese and the British and this mosaic of its past is displayed in architecture, food and language. (An old form of Portuguese is spoken by some.) A trip along the splendidly muddy, filthy river, flanked by clusters of faceless hovels and unkempt boats, is indeed an experience as somehow the occupants of this derelict region live peacefully enough with the refuse, the rats, the lizards, the litter and the crocodiles. Elsewhere the town brightens up and proudly displays its chequered antiquity.

Maxwell Hill (Bukit Larut)

This cool, damp hideaway, Malaysia's oldest hill station, doesn't compare with the Cameron Highlands; but it also has more than a touch of cosy 'Englishness' about it with its neat cottages and bungalows and log fires. Jungle walks are available and there are some distant misty views of the Malacca Straits. It is 40 minutes by road from near the railway station at **Taiping**. Its new and official name is now 'Bukit Larut'.

Pasir Mas

This is in effect the terminus of the eastern line for those going to Thailand. There is little point in walking around let alone staying here but it is also the nearest access station to Kota Bharu, which is very worthwhile.

Penang

In 1985 this ceased to exist as an island as it was joined to the mainland by a long bridge. Busy ferries from Butterworth, the rail connection, ply their way across the straits to Georgetown, the capital, also often referred to as 'Penang' but the Malays call it 'Tanjong' — an abbreviation of Tanjong Penang. It is a heady mixture of old and new and is thoroughly Chinese. That is not to deny the Indian presence — mainly Tamils — with their glittering temples and curry houses. There are huge edifices of concrete of course but also suitably ageing timber and tile shop houses and narrow meandering streets and alleys chock full of traders and hawkers and the locals who love to eat. The beaches of Penang, except those far out, are 'touristified' with modern hotels and facilities. Batu Ferringhi is the well known beach here.

Perhentian Islands

Mentioned in very few guide books, these islands are a real find for the traveller seeking a day or two (or a month or two) of back to nature tranquillity. They seem to possess everything that tropical islands *should* possess and more: idyllic white beaches, green waters, dense rain forests criss-crossed by trails, coconut palms, coral reefs, brilliant sunsets. There is diving, snorkelling and fishing to be had but it is by no means commercial. Quarters are primitive except for one chalet resort. They are reached from **Kota Bharu** via the small port of Kuala Beset. The islands are 21km offshore and the boats there are quite regular.

Taiping

The Taiping to Port Weld was the first railway line in the country (see page 5). A Chinese town founded on tin, it has a raucous past and a somewhat uninteresting present. It is wet and like Ipoh has its fair share of retired people. There are some misty views but the best site is the Lake Gardens. It provides access to Maxwell Hill (Bukit Larut).

Taman Negara

This is Peninsular Malaysia's prime national park, an enormous expanse of lush jungle. Here there is a whiff of adventure. The railway connection is with Tembeling or alternatively Jerantut. There is no point in going there if you're not 'an outdoor person' but jungle aficionados will find much that is gratifying. Stretching over parts of three states in 'the green heart' of the country you reach the entrance by boat along the shallow Tembeling River. There are minor rapids to negotiate and the **Orang Asli** settlements appear on either side. Visitors arrive at Kuala Tahan where there is accommodation and restaurants to suit all pockets, or you can camp on the edge of the jungle, an enjoyable experience. The real attraction, apart from the almost impenetrable forest, is the cacophonous bird life: eagles, kingfishers, woodpeckers, osprey, hornbills and many more can be readily observed but the more spectacular animal life is secretive indeed. You would be lucky to see a tiger or elephant or tapir. There are treehouses overlooking saltlicks for this purpose. The further you go from Kuala Tahan the more wildlife you'll see, but you may have to be satisfied with civet cats and barking deer, not to mention the odd cheeky rat. There is plenty of fishing, boating and short and not so short jungle walks. On a trek in the early morning you may think you're listening to a giant orchestra tuning up. (Closed in wet season mid November to mid January.)

Tapah Road

This is the town that provides rail access to the Cameron Highlands. This is about all it does do.

Tembeling

This small scatter of houses next to the station is the rail outlet to the Taman Negara. There is nowhere to stay here and as the only train arrives in the dark there's nothing to see either.

River Kwai station

A section of the "Death Railway", Kanchanaburi

Chapter 4

Taking in the holidays and festivals

NATIONAL HOLIDAYS — THAILAND

Special care should be taken to avoid if possible travelling on national holidays unless you book in advance. There are sometimes crowds at weekends at popular departure times but usually you can get on the train if a bit more uncomfortably.

January 1	New Year's Day
February (full moon day)	Makha Bucha
April 6	Chakri Day
Mid April	Songkran
May 5	Coronation Day
May (full moon day)	Wisakha Bucha
July (full moon day)	Asanaha Bucha
August 12	H.M. The Queen's Birthday
October 23	Chulalongkorn Day
December 5	H.M. The King's Birthday
December 10	Constitution Day
December 31	New Year's Eve

FESTIVALS ACCESSIBLE BY RAIL — THAILAND

Without a doubt the best time to be in a specific region is when a festival is in full swing. You can observe the real meaning of *sanuk* — fun, pleasure, having a good time, living it up. Festivals are *not* concoctions for tourists: they present an essential ingredient of Thai culture. The drawback is that it is the worst time to travel and trains should be booked. In some parts, but not often, there is a shortage of accommodation. Those 'roughing it', however, should have no trouble; even sitting on the floor in a crowded third class carriage is no real hardship.

The vast majority of festivals are calculated on the lunar calendar. The following particulars have been supplied by the Tourist Authority of Thailand (TAT), who publish annually a very helpful booklet entitled *Major events and festivals*. You are advised to get a copy before planning a trip.

All destinations have easy rail access but some may also require a short bus trip. (Phuket requires a longer bus trip from Surat Thani.)

Bo Sang Umbrella Fair
Bo Sang, Chiang Mai
Third week in January

Almost everyone in the small village of Bo Sang, near Chiang Mai, derives a livelihood from making gaily painted paper umbrellas. This fair, held on the main street, celebrates their traditional skill and features contests, exhibitions, stalls selling umbrellas and other handicrafts, and the selection of Miss Bo Sang.

Phra Buddha Chinaraj Fair
Phitsanulok
January

This fair honours the Phra Buddha Chinaraj, one of Thailand's most sacred Buddha images which is now enshrined at Wat Mahathat in Phitsanulok. Festive as well as religious, it features assorted kinds of entertainment such as folk theatre and *rumwong* dancing, as well as stalls selling local products.

Don Chedi Memorial Fair
Suphanburi
January

In 1592 at Don Chedi, King Naresuan the Great of Ayutthaya won a famous duel on elephant back with the leader of an enemy force, thus liberating the Thai kingdom. This fair commemorates the momentous event with historical exhibitions, outdoor entertainments, and the high spirits characteristic of all Thai festivals.

Flower Festival
Chiang Mai
2nd weekend (Fri-Sun) in February

The north is noted for its rich variety of flowering plants, particularly temperate-zone specimens which are at their best during this cool month. Spectacular floral floats are a memorable feature of this annual event held in Chiang Mai, together with displays of flowers, handicraft sales, and beauty contests.

Bang Sai Arts & Crafts Fair
Bang Sai Arts & Crafts Centre, Ayutthaya
January or February

The annual fair shows products of H.M. the Queen's SUPPORT programme. Visitors will enjoy shopping, and viewing exhibitions and demonstrations of local products from each district of Ayutthaya province. Folk entertainment performances enliven the fair.

Straw Bird Fair
Chai Nat
January or February

Straw is a plentiful by-product in rice farming, and local villagers construct large, brightly coloured straw birds reflecting the more than 85 species contained in the Chai Nat Bird Park. The straw birds are paraded in a fair which also features local handicrafts and culinary delicacies.

King Narai Reign Fair
Lopburi
Third weekend in February

The fair celebrates the reign of King Narai the Great, the Ayutthayan monarch best known for his promotion of diplomatic relations with European powers during the mid 1600s. The fair is largely staged at King Narai's Lopburi palace, and features homage-paying ceremonies, colourful processions, folk entertainment and native bazaars.

Phra Nakhon Khiri Fair
Phetchaburi
February

The old city of Phetchaburi, about two hours drive from Bangkok, is overlooked by Phra Nakhon Khiri (City on the Mount), a hill on which are located a number of religious structures and a palace built in the mid-19th Century. A historical light and sound presentation is one of the attractions of this popular fair.

Hae Pha Khun That (Homage Paying Fair)
Nakhon Si Thammarat
February

During this three-day event, the people of Nakhon Si Thammarat pay homage to locally enshrined relics of the Buddha. There are a number of religious ceremonies, among them a traditional merit-making procession which brings a Phra Bot — a cloth painting of the Buddha's life story — to be placed over the relics.

Kite Fighting & Traditional Thai Sports Fair
Sanam Luang, Bangkok
February

Flying kites is a popular Thai sport. It becomes a fascinating spectacle when opposing teams skilfully fly male and female kites in a surrogate 'Battle of the Sexes'. The cumbersome male *Chula* kite tries to ensnare and drag the smaller, more agile female *Pakpao* kite back to male territory, while the female kite tries to evade capture and fell its male opponent. Other activities will include *sepak* and *loop takro*, Thai chess, *krabi krabong* (swordfighting contest).

Chao Mae Lim Ko Nieo Fair
Pattani
February

Chao Mae Lim Ko Nieo, a goddess believed to possess potent magic powers, is revered in Pattani and other provinces of the far south. This annual fair pays homage to her and features ascetics able to perform extraordinary feats of endurance as well as a lively procession of devotees through the provincial capital.

Asean Barred Ground Dove Festival
Yala
Early March

Dove-lovers from all over Thailand, as well as from other countries in the region like Singapore, Malaysia and Indonesia, come to Yala for this event. The highlight is a dove-cooing contest involving more than 1,400 competitors; young prize doves are on sale along with local products and sports contests are held.

Phra Buddha Fair
Saraburi
Early March

Phra Buddha Bat, the Holy Foot Print enshrined in a hill temple near Saraburi, is one of the most sacred places in Thailand, and this fair is held annually to pay homage. Large numbers of Buddhist pilgrims come to the shrine during the event, which also features performances of folk music and a handicraft bazaar.

Pattaya Festival
Pattaya City, Chon Buri
Early April

Thailand's world-famous seaside resort puts on its most festive face for this annual event, held at the height of the summer season. Food and floral floats, beauty contests, stalls selling local delicacies, and a spectacular display of fireworks on the beach are only a few of the highlights that attract merry-makers.

Sweet Grape Fair
Damnoen Saduak, Ratchaburi
Second weekend in April

Succulent sweet grapes grow plentifully in the area around the famous floating market at Damnoen Saduak in Ratchaburi Province. While they are the main feature of this fair, along with a Miss Grape competition, other local fruits such as pomelo, papaya and guava are also on sale, as well as handicrafts of the area.

Songkran
Nationwide
Mid April

The old Thai New Year is an occasion for merrymaking in Bangkok as well as in other parts of the country, with religious ceremonies as well as public festivities. Anyone who ventures out on the streets is likely to get a thorough soaking but all in a spirit of fun and welcome at the peak of the hot season. Songkran, the traditional Thai New Year, is celebrated all over the country but nowhere with more enthusiasm than in Chiang Mai. Part of the celebration is religious, marked by merit-making ceremonies at local temples, and part is pure pleasure, with good-natured water throwing, parades and beauty contests.

Wisutkasat Songkran Festival
Bangkok
April

People in Wisutkasat organise this festival to preserve and promote Thai culture. The first day features sprinkling water on revered Buddha images, freeing captive birds and fishes, sprinkling water on adults' hands to bless and honour elders. The second day features alms-giving to monks, a Miss Songkran contest and several forms of entertainment.

Visakha Bucha
Nationwide
Full-moon day, May

This is the holiest of all Buddhist days during the year, marking the birth, enlightenment and death of the Buddha. As on Makha Bucha, temples throughout the country are crowded with people who listen to sermons by revered monks, and in the evening there is a solemn candlelit procession around the main monastery building.

Royal Ploughing Ceremony
Bangkok
Usually early May, at Bangkok's Sanam Luang

An ancient Brahman ritual, this celebrates the official commencement of the rice-planting season and is held at Sanam Luang, the large field across from the Grand Palace. Colourful costumes are worn by the participants who perform various ceremonies which are believed to forecast the abundance of the coming rice crop.

Candle Festival
Ubon Ratchathani
July

The commencement of Phansa, or Buddhist Lent (known in Thai as Khao Phansa), is observed in the northeastern city of Ubon Ratchathani with this lovely festival that displays artistic skill as well as piety. Beautifully carved beeswax candles, some of them several metres tall, are exhibited in colourful parades before being presented to local temples.

Tak Bat Dok Mai
Saraburi
July

This impressive merit-making ceremony coincides with the start of the annual three-month Rains Retreat, when Buddhist monks must remain in their monasteries. Devotees offer flowers and incense to a procession of monks who then ascend to the Shrine of the Holy Footprint where they present the offerings as tribute.

HM The Queen's Birthday Celebration
Nationwide
August 12, national holiday

Throughout Thailand, public buildings are decorated to honour Her Majesty Queen Sirikit on the occasion of her birthday. The most splendid are to be seen in Bangkok, particularly along Ratchadamnern Avenue and in the area around the Grand Palace, where both government offices and streets are garlanded with coloured lights.

Food and Fruits Fair
Nakhon Pathom
September

Site of Thailand's largest Buddhist monument, the 127-metre Phra Pathom Chedi, Nakhon Pathom also holds this annual fair to display the wide range of fruits that grow in the province. In addition, there are demonstrations of Thai and Chinese food preparation, floral floats, and numerous other entertainments.

Phichit Boat Races
Phichit
September

Phichit is located in one of the most beautiful parts of Thailand, with green valleys and picturesque wooded hills. This annual regatta takes place on the Nan River which runs through the provincial capital and features numerous low-slung wooden boats racing with great gusto to the cheers of spectators.

Vegetarian Festival
Phuket and Trang
October

This annual festival originated among immigrant workers in the 19th Century and is one of the major events of Phuket's year. Residents of Chinese ancestry go on a ten-day vegetarian diet and there are ceremonies at local Chinese temples as well as parades that feature remarkable feats by ascetic believers.

Festival of the Tenth Lunar Month
Nakhon Si Thammarat
October

This ceremony is celebrated locally during the fifteen nights of the waning moon period in the tenth lunar month to bring merit to the souls of ancestors. Buddhists offer a variety of foods and other gifts to monks, and there are also numerous cultural performances, exhibitions, contests, and other entertainments.

Chinese Lunar Festival
Songkhla
October

Thais of Chinese ancestry make offerings to the moon or Queen of the Heavens in gratitude for past and future fortune. Traditional festivities include lion and dragon dances, lantern processions and contests, displays and folk entertainment.

Chon Buri Buffalo Races
Chon Buri
October

The water buffalo is one of the mainstays in the life of a Thai farmer, but in this annual event it is put to more amusing uses than ploughing the local fields, such as buffalo races and contests pitting buffalo and man. Beauty contests add to the fun of a festival that attracts crowds from nearby seaside resorts.

Chak Phra and Thot Phapa Festival
Surat Thani
October/November

Chak Phra means 'to pull a sacred Buddha image', an activity occurring on the same day as the Thot Phapa ceremony, a form of merit-making when Buddhists offer saffron robes to monks and donate money to temples, at the end of the Buddhist Rains Retreat. Thot Phapa occurs at dawn, before Chak Phra, the ceremony when Buddha images on elaborately decorated carriages are pulled by local people in land and waterborne processions. There are also traditional forms of evening entertainment.

Phimai Boat Races
Nakhon Ratchasima (Korat)
November

These popular races take place on the Mun River near the old Khmer city of Phimai, a fascinating archaeological site that can be visited at the same time. Besides the regatta there will be a competition of boats decorated to resemble the famous Royal Barges, entertainments, and stalls selling local produce.

Loi Krathong and Candle Festival
Sukhothai
Full moon night of November

According to tradition, Loi Krathong originated in Sukhothai, the first Thai capital, and so it is appropriate to hold this memorable festival in the atmospheric ruins of the ancient city. Highlights include displays of lighted candles and fireworks, folk dancing, and a spectacular light and sound demonstration.

Yi Peng Loi Krathong
Chiang Mai
Full moon night of November

In Chiang Mai, an unusual part of the Loi Krathong celebration is the Yi Peng Festival of the ritual of the lighted balloon. After a day of merit-making, the people launch colourful hot air paper balloons into the sky, bearing the troubles away. In the evening, all homes and shops are decorated with beautiful lanterns. Later, traditional *krathongs* are also floated in the river and other waterways.

Surin Elephant Round-up
Surin
Third week of November

Internationally famous, this annual event brings crowds of visitors to the provincial capital of Surin, where over 100 trained elephants are assembled. Among the spectacular features are wild elephant hunts, tugs of war, demonstrations of log pulling skills and a parade of elephants outfitted for medieval war.

Bang Sai Loi Krathong
Ayutthaya
November

Celebrations include traditional float (*krathong*) and beauty contests, handicrafts demonstrations and exhibitions, special events, and *krathong*-launching beneath the full moon.

Thailand Long-boat Races
Phichit
November

Traditional long-boat racing is popular in many provinces. TAT and other sectors organise these races to select Thailand's fastest long boat crews to send them to compete in international regattas. Other activities include tourism exhibitions and local handicrafts stalls.

River Kwai Bridge Week
Kanchanaburi
Late November, early December

(See page 158)
Celebrated in the movie of the same name, the Bridge on the River Kwai is the setting for this week-long series of events in a province that also has other interesting attractions. Highlights include a light and sound presentation at the bridge, archaeological and historical exhibitions, and rides on vintage trains.

Silk Fair
Khon Kaen
November/December

Everybody has heard of Thailand's lustrous silks, and Khon Kaen is one of the major centres of production. Many shops will be offering the beautiful fabric at this fair, which is combined with the traditional Phuk Sieo (friendship-making) ritual. Festival processions and cultural shows add to the atmosphere.

Trooping the Colours
Bangkok
December 3

Their Majesties the King and Queen preside over this impressive annual event, held in the Royal Plaza near the equestrian statue of King Chulalongkorn. Dressed in colourful uniforms, amid much pomp and ceremony, members of the elite Royal Guards swear allegiance to the King and march past members of the Royal family.

HM The King's Birthday Celebrations
Nationwide
December 5, national holiday

This is celebrated by all Thais for their King and is perhaps unique in the modern world, and his birthday provides an annual occasion for public expression. Government buildings, businesses, and homes all over the country are elaborately decorated and the area around the Grand Palace is spectacularly illuminated.

Phuket King's Cup Regatta
Phuket
December

This is an annual event in the blue waters of the Andaman Sea off the island of Phuket, sponsored by the Phuket Yacht Club and other groups. Competitors come from Malaysia, Singapore, and other countries as well as Thailand and trophies are awarded in several different categories.

NATIONAL HOLIDAYS — MALAYSIA

There is an annual variation of dates due to the difference of the Chinese and Hindu calendars and the Muslim year which consists of 354 days.

January 1	New Year's Day except in traditional Islamic states
February	Chinese New Year
April	Hari Raya Puasa (The end of Ramadan)
May 1	Labour Day
May 9	Vesak Day
June 6	King's Birthday
July 2	Maal Hijrah
August 31	National Day
October 26	Deepavali Hindu festival
December 25	Christmas Day

Some states have particular holidays that are not celebrated throughout the country. They are:

January 1	Kedah
February 1	Federal Territory of Kuala Lumpur
February 8	Selangor, Perak, Negri Sembilan, Penang
February 12	Johore
March 5	Kedah and Negri Sembilan
March 8	Selangor
March 10	Terengganu
March 11	Selangor
April 8	Johor
April 19	Perak
May 7	Pahang
June 14	Malacca
July 16	Penang
July 16	Negri Sembilan
July 31	Kelantan
August 23	Perlis
October 26	Pahang

Many of these dates are variable and should be checked.

FESTIVALS ACCESSIBLE BY RAIL — MALAYSIA

Because of the three ethnic groups there is much to be experienced. Malays, Chinese and Indians all take their festivals seriously. In some cases there are spectacular and colourful displays and some are engagingly loud and even wild such as Thaipusam. Virtually all the dates will vary from year to year. Most of the information on major festivals has been provided by the Tourist Development Corporation of Malaysia who should be consulted for more up to date advice. Monthly bulletins are issued.

Thai Pongal
January (14)

This is a Hindu festival celebrating the harvest and the start of the Hindu month of Thai.

Thaipusam
January (20)

Thaipusam is a South Indian Hindu festival which has long been celebrated in this country. It is named after the Tamil month of Thai (January/February) when the Hindu constellation Pusam is in its ascendancy. Thaipusam is a celebration or rather a day of penance and atonement.

On this day Hindu devotees seek absolution and pardon through self mortification. They skewer themselves with steel spikes and spears and dance their way to the temples carrying kavadies (wooden or steel yokes of varying sizes, shapes and colours) accompanied by a retinue of friends and relatives who sing devotional songs backed by traditional Hindu drums and clarinets. The penitents apparently feel no pain as they enter into a state of trance and contemplation.

Hindu temples throughout the nation hold this celebration. However, Batu Caves in Kuala Lumpur and the waterfalls temple in Penang are the major focal points with their mammoth crowds, chariot processions and mystical pageantry.

Chinese New Year
February

This is a loud and joyous festival. It is celebrated by Malaysians of Chinese origin. The celebration itself lasts for 15 days. It climaxes on the 15th day with a loud and noisy beat with the clamour of Oriental Chinese drums, the sound of firecrackers, and the antics of the lion and dragon dancers. The eve of Chinese New Year is an auspicious day. The evening meal on this day is participated by all members of the family who come from near and far. It is called the reunion dinner. Chinese New Year is also a time to fulfil traditional obligations such as the offering of gifts to the Gods, appeasing of the souls of departed loved ones and giving away of *Ang Pow* (gift of money packed in red packets). And the all day fun and merriment hardly tapers off till long after the 15th day which is called Chap Goh Meh.

Birthday of the Jade Emperor
February

A special offering at temples to the Supreme Ruler of Heaven.

Chap Goh Meh
February

Chap Goh Meh is celebrated as a culmination to the Chinese New Year. It is celebrated on the 15th day after Chinese New Year with prayers and offerings. The celebration is similar to Chinese New Year itself with the loud clamour of firecrackers, together with the inevitable lion and dragon dancers. On this day Chinese virgins will also cast oranges into the sea, for they believe that in doing so they will be blessed with compatible spouses in the future.

Hari Raya Puasa (Idul Fitri)
April

Hari Raya Puasa is the most prominent of all Muslim festivals. It is celebrated as a culmination to a month of fasting and prayer. Hari Raya falls on the first day of Syawal, which is the 10th month in the Muslim calendar.

Celebrations start with prayers in the morning of the festive day. Muslims also pay a visit to the graves of their departed loved ones after prayers at the mosque. Hari Raya is a time for family get-together, community fellowship and also a time to forgive, forget and make merry. It is a time to hold 'open-houses', to welcome and treat relatives and friends with special festive dishes such as *rendang* and *ketupat*. The Prime Minister and Muslim Cabinet Ministers will hold their annual open houses. Guests are welcome to partake in this festive jollity and to wish them the greetings of the season — *Selamat Hari Raya*.

Wesak Day (Vesak Day)
May

A Buddhist festival, it is the most important of all Buddhist celebrations. It is a day of prayers, offerings, chanting and alms-giving. The festival highlights the three significant events in the life of Lord Buddha. They are: his birthday, his enlightenment and his entry into the perfect state of peace known as Nirvana.

Hari Raya Haji (Idul Adha)
June

Hari Raya Haji is celebrated as a sequel to Hari Raya Puasa. It is a day of thanksgiving and sacrifice. It is celebrated by Muslims and the festival also marks the tenth day of Zulhijjah which is the twelfth month of the Islamic calendar. It is at this time when Muslims perform their *haj* or pilgrimage to Mecca, the Holy Land. This festival is quite similar to Hari Raya Puasa where Muslims invite guests to their homes for feasting and fellowship. Muslims who could afford it present an entire head of goat or a bull as a sacrificial offering to the less fortunate. The morning of the festival day commences with prayers at the mosques and visits to the grave sites of loved ones.

Maal Hijrah
July

This is a significant festival which marks the start of the Muslim calendar. The Muslim calendar commenced when Prophet Muhammad journeyed from Mecca to Medina on the first of Muharam in 622 AD. On this day Muslims partake in religious discussions, fraternal fellowships, seminars and attend *ceramahs* (lectures) as a sign of affirming their faith. The singing of *nasyids* (hymns) is an important aspect of this festival.

Merdeka Day
August 31

On the 31 August 1957, Malaysia gained its independence from British rule. Annually on this day the nation's citizens celebrate Merdeka (which means independence). Merdeka Day celebrations in Malaysia are participated by one and all, the old and the young, with a great sense of patriotism to the King and the country. It is a gala affair, filled with pomp and pageantry. Grand celebrations are held all over the nation, marked by parades, processions, stage performances, competitions and fascinating fireworks display. In Kuala Lumpur, where the major events of the celebrations take place, the Merdeka Square becomes the focal point where the various races, corporate citizens, government bodies and other communities join hands with the King, the Prime Minister and his Cabinet members in a show of solidarity and national unity.

Prophet Muhammad's Birthday (Muharram) September 9

The Prophet Muhammad was born in 571 AD. All over the Muslim world the Prophet's birthday is celebrated on a large scale. However, the festival is not celebrated with merriment and feasting but rather on a solemn note and a spiritual tone. Verses from the Holy Koran are recited. It is a day of obligation for Muslims to worship at the mosques, attend sermons and to partake in religious discussions, procession, and lectures as in the festival of Maal Hijrah.

Mooncake Festival September

This festival is celebrated to mark the successful victory of the Chinese peasants in overthrowing their autocratic Mongolian overlords in ancient China. The festival falls on the 15th day of the Chinese Lunar Calendar.

The festival is synonymous with mooncakes and lanterns. There are a variety of mooncakes made of varying flavours and ingredients. These can be purchased from the local shops and supermarkets. In Malaysia the festival is celebrated extensively by the Chinese community. The highlight of the festival is on the night of the festival, when children and sometimes adults march out from their homes holding gaily lit lanterns of different sizes and shapes.

Deepavali October 24

This is the Hindu festival of lights and symbolises the triumph of good over evil, and of light over darkness. The morning of the festival commences with the customary oil bath. Following this, Hindus dressed in their festival best offer prayers in their household altars and at temples. This is followed by the Malaysian 'open-house' concept of festive fun and gaiety. Deepavali, like most other Malaysian festivals, is a nationwide community celebration where neighbours, friends and relatives visit one another to exchange good wishes and to share in the festive feasting.

Christmas Day
December 25

Christmas is celebrated in Malaysia by the Roman Catholics, Anglicans, Protestants and also the other smaller Christian communities. But like most festivals in Malaysia, the whole nation partakes in the festivity, unlike the western nations where Christmas is usually a private family affair. The homes of Christians on Christmas Day are thrown open to a continuous stream of guests, relatives and neighbours. Christmas carollers do make house visits long before Christmas Day itself. On the eve of Christmas Day, Christians all over the nation attend their traditional midnight mass at the grandly decorated churches. The fun begins after mass and usually tapers off towards dawn, only to pick up again before the forenoon. The festive mood continues right through until New Year.

NATIONAL HOLIDAYS — SINGAPORE

Dates are for 1992 and those in brackets are variable.

January 1	New Year's Day
(February 4 & 5)	Chinese New Year
(April 5)	Hari Raya Puasa
April 17	Good Friday
May 1	Labour Day
(June 11)	Hari Raya Haji
August 9	National Day
(October 24)	Deepavali
December 25	Christmas

FESTIVALS — SINGAPORE

Somewhat surprisingly, Singapore celebrates a large number of festivals involving the three ethnic groups. The Chinese celebrations dominate but there are also very worthwhile Indian and Buddhist events. Here again the dates will vary in most cases year by year and should be checked. There are a number of international events, sporting and otherwise, held here and the Singapore Tourist Promotion Board will provide the dates. Many of the festivals are similar to those held in Malaysia.

Ponggal, The Harvest Festival
January

Celebrated by the Southern Indians, Ponggal is a time for thanksgiving. In an early morning ritual, rice is cooked in a new pot and allowed to boil over, symbolising prosperity.

Later, rice is prepared in Hindu temples while prayers are chanted to the accompaniment of bells, drum beats, clarinets and the blowing of huge conch shells. Rice, vegetables, sugar cane and spices are offered to the gods. The festival is celebrated at the Sri Perumal Temple in Serangoon Road and visitors are welcome.

Thaipusam
January

This Hindu festival is an awesome spectacle of mind over matter.

Entranced devotees, carrying enormous steel arches called *kavadis*, with their bodies pierced by spikes, hooks and skewers, join a three kilometre procession. Yet they appear to feel no pain. Amazingly there is also no blood to be seen even from the tongues and cheeks which have been pierced by sharp skewers.

This deeply religious festival is celebrated by Hindus everywhere but has taken on a more ornate form in multi-cultured Singapore.

The procession, which follows days of fasting and prayer, can be observed in the afternoon along a three kilometre route from the Sri Perumal Temple in Serangoon Road to the Chettan Temple in Tank Road. Procession times, and the route map, are published in the daily newspapers. Spectators are welcome, but care should be taken not to obstruct the procession. Shoes should not be worn into the temples.

Lunar New Year
February

Lunar New Year is one of the most vibrant, entertaining and colourful of all the festivals on the singapore calendar. While the official public holidays fall on two days, the celebration will go on for 15 days as the Chinese community rolls out the red carpet to welcome the year according to the Chinese zodiac.

Chinatown is ablaze with colour and light from hundreds of Chinese lanterns and other decorations which form the Lunar New Year light-up, organised to add a special dimension to the holiday mood.

The Lunar New Year is also a special time for visiting family and friends and for experiencing the many ethnic delights prepared for the festive season.

Chingay 20 February

The word 'Chingay' refers to a Chinese-style decorated float. Essentially religious in origin, such floats with all their artistry, glitter and brilliance, are the centrepiece of an excitingly memorable parade celebrating Singapore's multi-cultural heritage.

The length of Orchard Road from Scotts Road to Dhoby Ghaut is closed off for this annual spectacle and spectators line the route early to catch the best view. You can watch the antics of the lion and dragon dancers, stilt walkers and big-headed dolls, and enjoy other aspects of Singaporean culture including Indian dancers, a Malay bridal entourage, bands, pugilists and acrobats.

Hari Raya Puasa April

Hari Raya Puasa signifies the end of the fasting month of Ramadan. It is a time for renewing family ties; households prepare days in advance for this important festival.

Special cakes and other delicacies are prepared and homes are decorated. On the day itself, Muslims don their new traditional finery and visit friends and relatives.

To mark the occasion, the traditional Malay area of Geylang is brilliantly lit and decorated from March 14 to April 12. A bustling bazaar springs up to cater for shoppers in search of delicacies, new clothing, household goods and other seasonal items. It's an ideal opportunity for visitors to experience the camaraderie for which the Malay community is renowned. Malay homes are decorated with lights to welcome in the festival.

Birthday of The Third Prince May

The Third Prince is a child god who rides 'wheels of wind and fire' and bears with him a magic bracelet and spear.

To celebrate his birthday, mediums go into a trance, cutting themselves with swords or spikes. Their blood is smeared on yellow paper charms, eagerly sought by devotees. The rituals can be observed at various Chinese temples or at outdoor make-shift sites.

Vesak Day May

An important festival for the Buddhist community, Vesak Day commemorates Lord Buddha's birth, enlightenment and entry into the perfect state of peace known as Nirvana.

The festival begins as saffron-robed monks chant the holy *sutras* (scriptures) and devotees visit the temples to pray and meditate.

During the day caged birds are set free and when night falls candlelight processions mark the end of the celebrations.

The festival is celebrated at all Buddhist temples including the Buddhist Lodge in River Valley Road, the Thai Buddhist Temple in Jalan Bukut Merah and the Tibetan Buddha Sasana Temple in Jalan Toa Payoh.

Dragon Boat Festival
June

The Dragon Boat Festival honours an ancient Chinese poet and statesman, the honest and upright Qu Yuan, who committed suicide by throwing himself into the Mi Luo River as a protest against political corruption and injustice during his time. Legend has it that fishermen tried to save him. They beat furiously on drums, gongs and cymbals, thrashed the water with their paddles, and threw rice into the waves in an attempt to prevent the fish from devouring him.

Festival of Hungry Ghosts
July-August

According to Chinese belief, the gates of hell are thrown open throughout the seventh month of the lunar year and for 30 days the spirits of the dead are set free to roam our 'world of light'.

To appease any straying, destitute spirits, an initial offering is usually made on the evening of the first day of the seventh month. Candles and joss-sticks are lit in a row in front of Chinese homes, and incense papers are burned.

Throughout the festival, celebrations are going on almost everywhere. Huge incense sticks burn and vast marquees are erected at venues for celebratory dinners. Outdoor concerts and colourful *wayangs* (Chinese operas) can be seen at street corners in Chinatown and other venues.

National Day
August

National Day itself is marked by a parade that becomes more impressive each year. Colourful contingents use every ounce of creativity in order to surpass the efforts of the previous year.

Mooncake Festival
September

Colourful lanterns, glowing with candlelight, make a memorable sight during this special Chinese festival, celebrated when the moon is at its fullest.

One of the more popular legends explains the festival. It tells how Chinese patriots conveyed secret messages hidden in mooncakes and thus gathered support for a revolt against the tyranny of the Yuan dynasty.

Mooncakes have become a special delicacy for this season. They can be bought at hotel pastry shops, supermarkets and in Chinatown.

Through September to October, the Chinese Garden at Jurong features magnificent displays of traditional lanterns in all shapes, sizes and colours. The best time to view the display is in the evenings when the beauty of the lanterns is most evident.

Birthday of the Monkey God
September

The birthday of the Monkey God, one of the most famous Chinese mythological characters, is celebrated at the Monkey God Temple in Seng Poh Road opposite Tiong Bahru Market.

A sedan chair, carried shoulder high, rocks and jerks as if possessed by the spirit of the crafty but loyal Monkey God.

It heads a dramatic procession of mediums who, apparently in a trance, cut themselves before distributing paper charms to devotees.

Festival of the Nine Emperor Gods
September-October

This Chinese festival is marked by processions and colourful Chinese operas. There are flag bearers and decorated floats. At the climax of the celebrations images of the nine Gods are paraded in a decorative sedan chair. Hundreds of worshippers join in the procession.

Pilgrimage to Kusu Island
September-October

There is a tale of two fishermen, one Chinese and one Malay, whose boat sank. The two were apparently carried to the safety of Kusu on the back of a giant turtle.

The Chinese Taoists make their pilgrimage in brightly decorated boats to Tua Pekong Temple to pray for prosperity, good luck and fertility. Joss-sticks, flowers, fruit, candles, red-shelled eggs and chicken are offered at the shrine.

The island is served by a regular ferry which leaves from the Singapore Cruise Centre at the World Trade Centre.

Navarathiri Festival
October

The nine nights of Navarathiri — 'Nava' meaning nine and 'Rathiri' meaning night — are devoted to intensive prayers dedicated to the goddesses Dhurga, Lakshmi and Saraswathi, the consorts of the gods of the Hindu Trinity.

Through their prayers and meditation, devotees seek help in overcoming personal weaknesses, and ask for knowledge and spiritual perfection.

Set in three cycles, the festival honours each goddess individually, and culminates in a procession at the Tank Road temple in which a bronze statue of the Lord Murugan is carried by devotees.

The festival, with its nightly classical performances, is always an excellent opportunity to experience Indian music at its best. The festival is most easily accessible to visitors at the Sri Thandaynthapani Temple in Tank Road and the Sri Maruanman Temple in South Bridge Road. Prayers and performances begin around 7.30pm each evening and visitors are welcome.

Thimithi Festival
October

Thimithi is an annual fire-walking ceremony held in honour of Draupadi who has been deified by the south Indians as the Draupadi Amman. Draupadi is the heroine of the epic poem "Mahabharata".

Every year crowds pack the Sri Mariamman Temple in South Bridge Road to watch incredulously as barefoot Hindu devotees walk across a pit of red hot embers without the slightest flinch of pain.

The festival celebrations begin at 2am and the fire-walking takes place around 2pm. It is worth visiting the temple early to obtain a good vantage point.

Deepavali
October

Deepavali, or the Festival of Lights, is a joyous Hindu celebration which marks the victory of light over darkness, of good over evil.

Housewives prepare a wide variety of delicacies for this special festival. Before dawn on Deepavali, an oil bath is taken, after which special prayers are offered at home as well as in the temples.

At night Hindu temples such as the Sri Veerama Kaliamman, the Sri Vadapathira Kaliamman and the Sri Perumal, all along Serangoon Road, as well as streets in Little India, are festooned with lights and garlands. A special light-up, which includes colourful arches over Serangoon Road, is organised to mark the occasion.

Christmas Light-up
Mid November-year's end

The length of Orchard Road is lit with bulbs as hotels and shopping centres compete with one another to produce the most innovative exterior and interior decorations.

The light-up begins in November, signifying the start of celebrations which include carol singing in the streets and special charity activities.

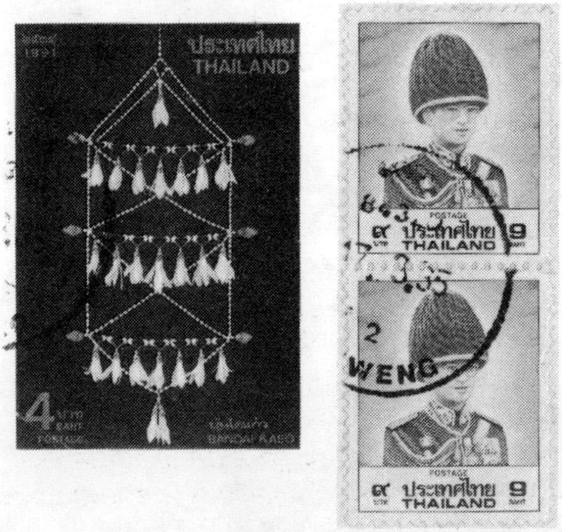

PLEASE HELP US UPDATE

This guide will be regularly updated. We would be delighted to include your comments, anecdotes and information on aspects of railway travel in Thailand, Malaysia and Singapore.

Please write to Bradt Publications, 41 Nortoft Road, Chalfont St Peter, Bucks SL9 0LA.

Tourist impact on the environment

There are an enormous number of visitors to this region. With all the benefits that this brings to the host countries there are also negative aspects. Some destinations, eg Pattaya in Thailand, simply do not have the infrastructure (sewerage, water supply, etc.) to meet the demand. A small minority of National Parks in Thailand have suffered as a result of an excessive number of visitors. The occasional beach, such as the Beach of Passionate Love in northeastern Malaysia, is despoiled by litter, some of it caused by visitors: plastic water bottles and soft drink cans are the main offenders. But it doesn't have to be much: a single cigarette packet dropped at the foot of a waterfall will destroy the experience for many.

How you can help

1. If a waiter throws servlettes etc. out of the train window stop him (the property he is disposing of is yours).

2. Try to view national parks in Thailand mid week. There are many Thais there on weekends and holidays.

3. Pick up any small amount of litter even though dropped by others. (One plastic bottle dropped or washed up on a beach will lead inevitably to more.)

4. If staying for a while at a beach and there are signs of litter do the boy scout or girl guide thing: with the assistance of local children — paying them a small fee — pick up the litter and dispose of it properly.

Many aware locals — and there are a large number — will appreciate these activities — and you may have saved an area from despoliation.

If all this sounds a bit gloomy take heart that only a very few areas are affected — so far.

See also page 97 for cultural do's and don'ts.

Chapter 5

Planning the Trip

THE CURSE OF TIME

Three weeks? Six weeks? Six months? Whatever time you have available it will not be enough. You will need more time in Thailand than Malaysia. If using a rail pass (see chapter 6) your length of stay will be influenced by the time allowed.

WHEN TO GO

If you are concerned about heat and humidity and temperatures in the 30°C region then avoid the hot season — February, March and April. However there is an absence of rain at this time and the sky is consistently bright which might outweigh the disadvantages of the heat. In the south of Thailand the main monsoon month (on the eastern side) is November. In the north it's September and October when flooding can occur. This includes Bangkok. In fact June to October is classified as the wet season in the north but except as stated above one could be forgiven for not noticing it. There are short sporadic heavy showers and then the sun comes out again. And all is well. However it is pointless going to any beach area during the actual monsoon.

West Malaysia's wet season is almost non existent but if you're on the east coast from October to February expect to be regularly soaked. Travel becomes difficult here at this time.

The wet season in Singapore is from November to January.

There have been some changes in the weather pattern over the last few years attributed to all sorts of strange phenomena, and monsoons can be early, late or right on time.

BUDGET TRAVEL

Everyone's got his or her own view on how to save on expenses; but this must be one of the world's least costly regions. Whereas say in certain parts of South America or Indonesia, prices may be marginally lower the quality of food and accommodation for what you pay here is considerably higher. It is true to say that some accommodation in Malaysia may be sub standard in that the odd cockroach or a legion of bugs put in appearances. It is also true that a bed for the night in Singapore is prohibitively expensive unless staying in a 'crash pad' (hence few budget travellers remain for long). But for value for money Thailand wins hands down.

A few hints for keeping costs down

- Travel third class on the train. If necessary sleep sitting up. Seats are not uncomfortable and you will notice that the locals are capable of hours of uninterrupted vertical slumber.
- If a student with a card — a youth hostel card will suffice — take advantage of the reductions available (third class travel) under the Eurotrain Explorer Pass (see page 111, 116) scheme operating in the three countries.
- Buy food from hawkers before getting on the train. Food, even from the itinerant vendors, is often marginally more expensive once you're moving.
- Carry a bottle of water. This symbolic representation of spartan attitudes is seen everywhere and will stop you paying for soft drinks or worse still beer (which is expensive).
- You can generally find cheap guest houses in large centres within walking distance of the station (excluding capital cities). Transport from the station at Bangkok in a 'tuk-tuk' is more costly than in other parts of the city. Bargain hard.
- Avoid alcohol and don't give a thought to 'night life'. Leave this to more decrepit but affluent people who may not be such authentic travellers.
- Head out of Singapore before you are tempted to buy a Rolex watch.
- Casual work in this region is unavailable, except perhaps teaching English which only provides a subsistence income.
- Try not to tire of rice and noodles.
- Cherish the sense of moral superiority which no doubt you will feel

because you know that you will experience the reality of the region rather than the tourist surface.

THE LONG HAUL

The best news in the region is the introduction of faster trains and continued work on 'double tracking'.

If you want to stay on board for days on end then the enjoyment can be seriously diminished by the rushing miles resulting in the complaint known as 'travellers' trance'. It is thus advisable to break the journey. A sleeper on a long haul is obviously a good idea but now that 'Sprinter' trains in Thailand are coming into service it is possible there to get from one large centre to another during the day and hence not miss the views. As mentioned before there are no sleepers on the east coast Malaysian.

ALONE OR NOT ALONE?

Of course if you are with a companion or a group then the pleasure and security may outweigh the negative aspects such as a disagreement as to destinations or time spent in one place. Your companion or companions should have the same objectives.

For a more intense and in a way more 'adventurous' journey you should travel alone. You will have plenty of people to talk to, particularly on the train and observations of the countryside will not be subject to distraction. You can be as selfish as you wish and do *exactly* what you want to do.

The vast number of travellers here go in pairs. They must like it that way or they wouldn't do it. It's also cheaper with a companion. Single rooms are sometimes hard to come by but of course a double room will cost the same if there are one or two occupants. There are also two people to keep their eyes on the belongings — an important consideration.

One of the real disadvantages of solo travel is what to do with valuables when you take off your clothes and go for a swim. If you can't leave them at the hotel in a safe deposit box then the second best thing is to put them in a bag on the sand, walk backwards towards the sea and then spend your time swimming towards the shore. Remember that if money, travellers cheques and passport all go at once you will be left in a state of particular anguish.

WOMEN TRAVELLERS

Thai and Malaysian trains day or night are safe for women. Women in out of the way places should take care. In both countries there have been reports of the rape of tourists. There are some incidents of harassment that one hears about but generally this is far less of a problem than in other regions.

Bathing naked or topless is prohibited in Malaysia and considered insulting in Thailand. But there are plenty of remote places to get a full sun-tan — but you would not be wise to be there alone.

SINGLE MALE TRAVELLERS

Particularly in Thailand — Bangkok is the worst — some 'tuk-tuk' and taxi drivers and some hotel staff will harass you. In Malaysia, particularly in Penang, trishaw drivers often suffer a sudden lack of direction and take you to a brothel. If asked if you want a 'lady' there is no point in saying you are gay, married, a monk, a lawyer, HIV positive or heavily in debt. Such a response inevitably leads to a flurry of further offers. In my experience the best response is none at all except for an expression which clearly indicates that such an encounter would lead to cataclysmic despair for all the parties concerned. AIDS is spreading fast in Thailand (see page 91) and this should be taken into account in these circumstances.

CHILDREN

Thais and Malays spoil children and no one can account for the fact that they are so well behaved. (It's because their parents are.) They will play with foreign children despite not being able to communicate. Children are of course better off in trains than buses because of the space and their own ability to stare out of windows for long periods at nothing at all. You should of course arrange adjoining sleepers.

In Thailand children are entitled to half fare only if under twelve *and* less than 150cm in height. So if you have a particularly tall youngster now is the time to start teaching him how to stoop. There is no height provision in Malaysia.

DISABLED TRAVELLERS

The region's trains have high steps and there are difficulties with entering and exiting. But plenty of cheerful help is at hand and can be easily arranged if you arrive at the station early. The same applies to boats to the islands. These inconveniences are minor and should not deter you even if travelling alone.

GETTING THERE

Bangkok, Kuala Lumpur and Singapore have a host of direct flights from Europe and Australia. If one is doing it on the cheap then fares at half the price are available from 'bucket shops'.

In London **Bridge The World** at 1-3 Ferdinand St, NW1 8ES, tel. 071-911 0900 provide a first class service as do **STA**, 86 Old Brompton Road, SW7 (tel. 071-937 9962). **Trailfinders** at 42-50 Earls Court Road, W8 (tel. 071-938 3366) have a long experience in this field as well as providing useful extras such as vaccinations.

From Australia the same applies but to a lesser extent and bucket shops are advertised in local papers. Fares should be approximately A$1000.

Cheap tickets are available in Bangkok, Penang, Kuala Lumpur and Singapore but do not go to a small agency. Some are unreliable and if they go off with the money then you've lost it and the ticket as well.

TOURIST INFORMATION — THAILAND

There is an office at Bangkok Airport. They will book you into one of a number of expensive hotels. The Tourist Office of Thailand, known as TAT, is situated at 4 Rajdamnern Nok Avenue (near the boxing stadium), Bangkok 10100, tel. 282-1143/7. The Tourist Assistance Centre will help you find a hotel, a dentist or a cup of tea, tel. 281-5051, or 281-0372 day or night. There are branches of TAT in all major centres.

Tourist information counters

Bangkok International Airport: Arrival Hall. Tel: 5238972-3

TAT Duty Free Shop: 888/60-62 Mahathun Plaza Building, Phloenchit Road. Tel: 2536451-9, 2546840-53, ext.101

Bangkok Railway Station: Hualamphong, Rama IV Road.

Local Offices

Central

Kanchanaburi: Saeng Chuto Road, Amphoe Muang, Kanchanaburi 71000. Tel/fax: (034) 511200

Pattaya: 382/1 Chaihat Road, South Pattaya 20260. Tel: (038) 428750, 429113

Rayong**: Fax: (038) 429113

North

Chiang Mai: 105/1 Chiang Mai-Lamphun Road, Amphoe Muang, Chiang Mai 50000

Chang Rai**: Tel: (053) 248604, 248607. Fax: (053) 248605

Phitsanulok: 209/7-8 Surasi Trade Center, Boromtrailokanat Road, Amphoe Muang, Phitsanulok 65000. Tel: (055) 252743. Fax: (055) 252742

Northeast

Nakhon Ratchasima: 2102-2104 Mittraphap Road, Tambon Nai Muang, Amphoe Muang, Nakhon Ratchasima 30000. Tel: (044) 243751. Fax: (044) 243427

Ubon Ratchathani: 264/1 Khaunthani Road, Amphoe Muang, Ubon Ratchathani 34000. Tel: (045) 255200, 255592. Fax: (045) 243771

Khon Kaen**: C/o Sala Prachakom (Community Center), Klang Muang Road, Khon Kaen 40000. Tel: (043) 244498, 244499. Fax: (043) 244497

South

Cha-am: 500/51 Phetkasem Road, Tambon Cha-am, Amphoe Cha-am, Phetchburi 76000

Phuket: 73-75 Phuket Road, Amphoe Muang, Phuket 83000. Tel: (076) 212213, 211036. Fax: (076) 213582

Hat Yai: 1/1 Soi 2 Niphat Uthit 3 Road, Amphoe Hat Yai, Songkhla 90110. Tel: (074) 243747, 245986. Fax: (74) 245986

Surat Thani: 5 Talat Mai Road, Ban Don, Amphoe Muang, Surat Thani 84000. Tel: (077) 282828, 281828. Fax: (077) 282828

Nakhon Si Thammarat**: 1180 Bavorn Bazar, Ratchadamnoen Road, Amphoe Muang, Nakhon Si Thammarat 80000. Tel: (075) 356356

Note: ** Temporary office.

Overseas Offices

United Kingdom

Tourism Authority of Thailand, 49 Albemarle Street, London W1X 3FE, England. Tel: (071) 499 7679 Cable: THAITOUR LONDON. Telex: 24136 TATLON G. Fax: 44-71-629-5519. Area of responsibility: United Kingdom, Northern Ireland, Iceland, Finland and Scandinavia.

Australia

Tourism Authority of Thailand, 7th Floor, Royal Exchange Bldg, 56 Pitt Street, Sydney 2000, Australia. Tel: (02) 247-7549, 247-7540. Cable: THAITOUR SYDNEY. Fax: 61 2 251-2465. Area of responsibility: Australia, New Zealand and South Pacific.

USA

Tourism Authority of Thailand, 3440 Wilshire Blvd., Suite 1100, Los Angeles, CA 90010, USA. Tel: (213) 382-2353-55. Cable: THAITOUR LOS ANGELES. Fax: (213) 3897544. Area of responsibility: Western USA, Latin America, Western Canada.

USA

Tourism Authority of Thailand, 303 East Wacker Drive, Suite 400, Chicago, Il. 60601. Tel: (312) 819-3990-6. Area of responsibility: The Americas.

USA

Tourism Authority of Thailand, 5 World Trade Center, Suite No 3443, New York, NY 10048, USA. Tel: (212) 432-0433-35. Cable: THAITOUR NEW YORK. Fax: 1 212 912 0920. Area of responsibility: Eastern USA and Eastern Canada.

Malaysia

Tourism Authority of Thailand, c/o Royal Thai Embassy, 200 Jalan Ampang, Kuala Lumpur, Malaysia. Tel: 248-0958, 248-6529. Fax: (093) 241-3002. Area of responsibility: Malaysia and Brunei.

Singapore

Tourism Authority of Thailand, c/o Royal Thai Embassy, 370 Orchard Rd., Singapore 0923. Tel: 235-7694, 235-7901, 733-6723. Cable: THAITOUR SINGAPORE. Telex: 39428 TATSIN RS. Fax: 65 733-5653. Area of responsibility: Singapore and Indonesia.

TOURIST INFORMATION — MALAYSIA

The Malay Tourist Development Corporation (TDC) has a well deserved reputation for courtesy and efficiency. There are useful guides to every state in the country.

Head office: 24-27th Floor, Menara Dato' Onn, Putra World Trade Centre, 45 Jalan Tun Ismail, 50480 Kuala Lumpur. Tel: 03-02935188. Telex: MTDCKL, MA 30093. Telefax: 03-2935884.

Malaysian Tourist Information Complex: 109 Jalan Ampang, 50450 Kuala Lumpur. Tel: 03-2434929.

Regional Offices

East Coast Region: 2243 Ground Floor, Wisma MCIAS, Jalan Sultan Sainal Abidin, 20000 Kuala Terengganu. Tel: 09-621893/621433. Telex: 51429 TDC WPT. Telefax: 09-621791.

Northern Region: 10 Jalan Tun Syed Sheh Barakbah, 10200 Penang. Tel: 04-620066/619067. Telex: 41094 TDC PEN. Telefax: 04-623688.

Southern Region: No 1 4th Floor, Kompleks Tun Razak, Jalan Wong Ah Fook, 80000 Johor Bahru, Johor. Tel: 07-223590/223591. Telex: MA 60037 TDC JHB. Telefax: 07-235502.

Overseas Offices

United Kingdom: 57 Trafalgar Square, London WC2N 5DS, England. Tel: 071-930 7932. Telex: (51) 299659 MTDC LOG. Telefax: 071-930 9015.

Australia: 65 York Street, Sydney NSWS 2000, Australia. Tel: 672-294441/1. Telex: 24675 MTDC AA. Telefax: 672-2622026.

TDC Perth Office: Malaysia Tourist Information Centre, 56 William Street, Perth, WA 6000, Australia. Tel: (09) 481 0400. Telex: MTIC 97033. Telefax: 09-3211421.

USA: 818 Suite 804, West Seventh Street, Los Angeles, CA 90017, USA. Tel: 213-689-9702. Telex: 6714719 MTIC UW. Telefax: 213-6891530.

Singapore: 10 Collyer Quay, #01-03, Ocean Building, Singapore 0104. Tel: 02-5326321/5326351. Telex: 29201 RSTDC MAL. Telefax: 02-5356650.

Thailand: Ground Floor, 315, South East Insurance Building, Silom Road, Bangkok 10500, Thailand. Tel: 236-

7606/236-2832. Telex: 22412 TDCMALBK TH. Telefax: 236-2832.

TOURIST INFORMATION — SINGAPORE

The Tourist Information Centre, 01-19 Raffles Tower (Tel: 330-0431) is helpful and efficient. There are many handy brochures and good maps; there is also a lot of advertising for consumer goods. Much information is available at the counter at Changi Airport where you can make hotel bookings but the hotels on offer can be expensive. There is no tourist office at the railway station.

Overseas offices

United Kingdom: Carrington House, 126-130 Regent Street, London W1Y 7TB. Tel: 071-437 0033.

Australia: Suite 1604 Level 16, Westpac Plaza, 60 Margaret St, Sydney 2000. Tel: 02-241-3771.
8th Floor St George's Court, 16 St George's Terrace, Perth 6000, Western Australia. Tel: 06-221-3864.

USA: NBR 12th Floor, 590 Frith St, New York 10036. Tel: 212-302-4861.
Suite 510, 8484 Wilshire Blvd, Beverley Hills, California 90211. Tel: 213-852-1901.

There are no Singapore tourist offices in either Thailand or Malaysia. Singapore Airlines in Bangkok and Kuala Lumpur will, however, offer some brochures and limited advice. The addresses are:

Kuala Lumpur: 2/4 Jalan Dang Wangi 50100. Tel: (03) 298-7033.

Bangkok: No 2, 12th Floor, Silom Centre Building, Silom Rd. 10500. Tel: 236-0303.

SOME FOREIGN EMBASSIES

Thailand

Australia: 37 Sathon Tai Road. Tel: 287-2680

Malaysia: 35 Sathon Tai Road. Tel: 286-1390/2

Singapore: 129 Sathon Tai Road. Tel: 286-2111, 286-1434.

United Kingdom: 1031 Phloenchit Rd/Wireless Rd. Tel: 253-0191/9.

USA: 95 Witthayu (Wireless) Road. Tel: 252-5040/9, 252-5171/9.

Malaysia

Australia: 6 Jalan Yap Kwan Seng. Tel: 242-3122.
Singapore: 209 Jalan Tun Razak. Tel: 261-6277.
Thailand: 206 Jalan Ampang. Tel: 248-8222.
United Kingdom: 13th floor, Wisma Damansara, Jalan Semantan. Tel: 248-7122.
United States: 376 Jalan Tun Rzak. Tel: 248-9011.

Singapore

Australia: 25 Napier Road. Tel: 737-9311.
Malaysia: 301 Jervois Road. Tel: 235-0111.
Thailand: 370 Orchard Road. Tel: 737-2644.
United Kingdom: Tanglin Road. Tel: 473-9333.
USA: 30 Hill Street. Tel: 338-0251.

SOME AIRLINES

Bangkok

Aeroflot Soviet Airlines (SU): 183 Mezzanine Floor, Regent House, Rajadamri Road, Bangkok 10330. Tel: 251-0617/8, 251-1223/5. Fax: 255-3138. Airport: 523-6921.

Air India (AI): 16th Floor Amarin Plaza, 500 Ploenchit Road, Bangkok 10330. Tel: 256-9614/8, 256-9620, 256-9144. Airport: 535-2121/2.

Bangkok Airways (PG): 144 Sukhumvit 4-6 Road, Bangkok 10110. Tel: 253-8942/8, 253-4014/6. Fax: 253-8400. Airport: 535-2497/8.

British Airways (BA): 2nd Floor, Charn Issara Tower, 942/81 Rama IV Road, Bangkok 10500. Tel: 236-0038, 236-1531. Fax: 236-6735. Airport: 535-2143/6.

Cathay Pacific Airways (CX): 5th Floor Charn Issara Tower, 942/136 Rama IV Road, Bangkok 10500. Tel: 233-6105, 235-4330. Airport: 535-2155/6. Fax: 237 1647.

China Airlines (CI): 4th Floor, Peninsula Plaza, 153 Rajadamri Road, Bangkok 10330. Tel: 253-4241/4, 253-4437/8, 253-5733/7. Fax: 253-4791. Airport: 535-2160, 535-2366.

Garuda Indonesia (GA): 27th Floor, Lumpini Tower, Rama IV Road, Bangkok 1168. Tel: 2865 6470-3. Airport: 523-8865, 535-2170.

Gulf Air (GF): 15th Floor, 518/5 Maneeya Centre Building, Ploenchit

Road, Bangkok 10330. Tel: 254-7931/4, 254-7935/8. Fax: 254-8390. Airport: 535-2313/4, 523-7369.

Royal Brunei Airlines (BI): 20th Floor, Charn Issara Tower, 942/52 Rama IV Road, Bangkok 10500. Tel: 233-0056, 233 0293. Fax: 233-0288. Airport: 535-2626/7.

Royal Jordanian (RJ): 56 Yada Building, Silom Road, Bangkok 10500. Tel: 236-8609/17, 236-0030. Fax: 236-6796. Airport: 535-2152/3. Fax: 532-1798.

Singapore Airlines (SQ): 12th Floor Silom Center Building, 2 Silom Road, Bangkok 10500. Tel: 236-0440, 236-0303, 236-0222. Fax: 234-6742. Airport: 523-7299, 535-2175.

Thai Airways International (TG): 89 Vibhavadi Rangsit Road, Bangkok 10900. Tel: 513-0121-9.
485 Silom Road, Bangkok 10500. Tel: 233-3810. Airport Ofc: 523-6121, 535-2863.
Domestic: 6 Larnluang Road, Bangkok 10200. Tel: 280-0070, 280-0080, 280-0090/100.
Airport Ofc: 535-2081-2.

Kuala Lumpur

Aeroflot: Wisma-Tong Ah, 1 Jalan Perak. Tel: 03-261-3331.

Air Lanka: Perangsang Segumal Building, Jalan Kampung Atlap. Tel: 03-274-0893.

British Airways: Hotel Merlin, Jalan Sultan Ismail. Tel: 03-242-6177.

Cathay Pacific: UBN Tower, 10 Jalan P Ramlee. Tel: 03-238-3377.

China Airlines: Amoda Building, 22 Jalan Imbi. Tel: 03-242-7344.

Garuda: 1st Floor, Angkasa Raya Building, Jalan Ampang. Tel: 03-248-3542.

KLM: Regent of KL Hotel, Jalan Sultan Ismail. Tel: 03-242-7011.

MAS: UMBC Building, Jalan Sulaiman. Tel: 03-230-8844. MAS Building, Jalan Sultan Ismail. Tel: 03-261-0555. 24 hour reservation: Tel: 03-774-7000.

Philippine Airlines: Wisma Stephens, Jalan Raja Chulan. Tel: 03-242-9040.

Qantas: UBN Tower, 10 Jalan P Ramlee. Tel: 03-238-9133

Royal Brunei: Blue Moon Travel, Merlin Hotel, Jalan Sultan Ismail. Tel: 03-242-6550.

Singapore Airlines: Wisma SIA, Jalan Dang Wangi. Tel: 03-298-7033

Thai International: Kuwasa Building, 5 Jalan Raja Laut. Tel: 03-293-7100.

Singapore

Aeroflot Soviet Airlines: 15 Queen Street, -#01-02/-02-00 Tan Chong Tower. Tel: 336-1757.

British Airways: 290 Orchard Road, #02-16, The Paragon. Tel: 253-8444/253-5922.

Cathay Pacific Airways: 10 Collyer Quay, #16-01, Ocean Building. Tel: 533-1333.

China Airlines: 400 Orchard Road, #01-29C, Orchard Towers. Tel: 737-2211.

Garuda Indonesia: 101 Thomson Road, #01-68, United Square. Tel: 250-2888.

KLM Royal Dutch Airlines: 333 Orchard Road, #01-02, Mandarin Hotel Arcade. Tel: 737-7622.

Lufthansa German Airlines: 390 Orchard Road, #05-07, Palais Renaissance. Tel: 737-9222.

Malaysian Airline System (MAS): 190 Clemenceau Avenue, #02-09, Singapore Shopping Centre. Tel: 336-6777.

Qantas Airways: 300 Orchard Road, #04-02,The Promenade. Tel: 737-3744.

Royal Brunei Airlines: 25 Scotts Road, #01-4A/4B/5, Royal Holiday Inn Crowne Plaza. Tel: 235-4672.

Royal Jordanian: 15 Beach Road, #03-11, Beach Centre. Tel: 338-8188.

Singapore Airlines (SQ): 77 Robinson Road. Tel: 223-8888.
Mandarin Hotel, Orchard Road. Tel: 229-7293/4.
North Bridge Road, Raffles City Shopping Centre. Tel: 229-7274.

ARRIVAL/ DEPARTURE BY AIR AND BY RAIL

Thailand — arrival by air

If you're fortunate enough to be carrying more than US$10,000 then this must be declared. Customs inspection at the airport is usually brief. An immigration form has to be completed and is attached to your passport. Don Muang is an efficient airport. The authorities have promised to remove unlicensed touts who regularly approach tourists. Taxis, limousines and mini buses — all official, get a ticket first — will take you to your hotel inexpensively.

You can take the regular public bus on the main highway but it is nearly always crowded and placing a bag or rucksack in the corridor will not earn the approbation of fellow passengers.

In 1992 a special 'Air-City Link' express train service was introduced. It runs from the airport to Hualamphong station

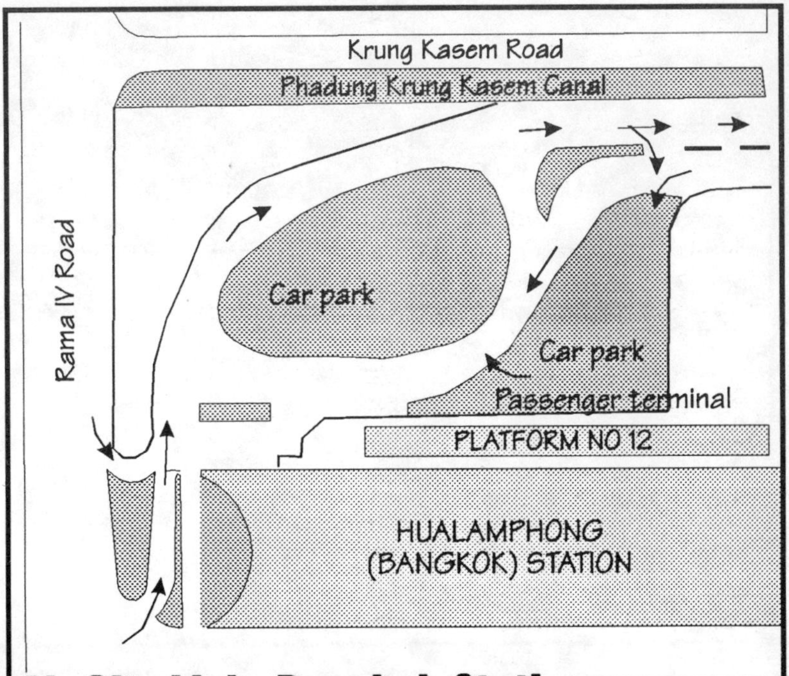

Air City Link, Bangkok Station

(Bangkok) with one stop at Sam Sen. It takes 35 minutes and costs 100 baht for air conditioned coach and 80 baht for non air-conditioned coach. This includes the shuttle bus service to the airport station (Don Muang). Tickets are sold in the arrival hall at Don Muang station and at Hualamphong (Bangkok) station on platform 12.

At the airport you can see the station and the train waiting. It is just across the main road (see diagram). But you would have to carry your luggage over the narrow footbridge owned by the Airport Hotel. For most passengers it is thus a frustration to get to the station — the shuttle bus can take half an hour in exceptionally heavy traffic. This is a pity and maybe some time in the future the position will be corrected. At present it is probably preferable to get the train if your hotel is reasonably near Hualamphong station but if, for example, you were heading for the Sukhumvit Road area then this method is not recommended, as you would need to take another long ride in a taxi from Hualamphong. (This system has proved so unpopular that unless SRT can provide a more frequent service and easier access the operation may well be suspended.)

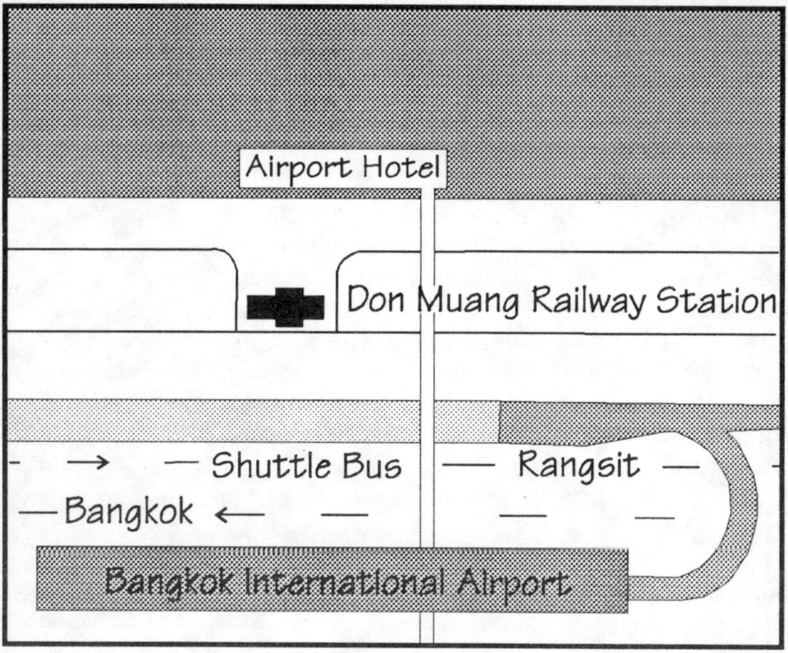

Airport Express Timetable

Bangkok — Sam Sen — Don Muang (Airport)

Outbound	Time	Time	Time	Time	Time	Time
Dep Bangkok	07.35	10.35	13.35	15.45	17.55	20.45
Dep Sam Sen	07.46	10.46	13.46	15.56	18.06	20.56
Arr Don Muang (Airport)	08.10	11.10	14.10	16.20	18.32	21.20

Don Muang (Airport) — Sam Sen — Bangkok

Inbound	Time	Time	Time	Time	Time	Time
Dep Don Muang (Airport)						
Arr Sam Sen	08.55	12.10	14.35	16.55	19.20	21.40
Arr Bangkok	09.19	12.34	14.59	17.19	19.45	22.04
	09.30	12.45	15.10	17.30	19.55	22.15

Arrival by rail

Arriving from Malaysia on the west coast you will strike customs and immigration at Padang Besar, a somewhat dismal arrival point where the formalities take place on the narrow station. The east coast frontier is determined by a river and one has to walk across the bridge to Sungai Kolak for the Thai or Malaysian train. In both places the border is open from 5.00am to 6.00pm (4.00am to 5.00pm Malaysian time). Thus you would not be able to cross into Malaysia if it's after 5.00pm Thai time.

Malaysia and Singapore

Arrival and departure procedures are similar here. There is a small departure tax. Both Subang and Changi are efficient airports. It is a particularly pleasant ride into the city from Changi (Singapore).

The procedure involving arrival and departure by train in Malaysia is outlined above. Singapore is joined to Malaysia by a causeway. When you get to Johore Baru most customs and immigration formalities will take place on the train. If coming up from Singapore then these take place on Singapore station so you must arrive at least half an hour before the train leaves. The platform is sealed off then.

Note: the penalties for carrying drugs are severe. In Malaysia and Singapore this involves the death sentence.

MAPS

There are numerous maps of the region available. In England the famous **Stanfords** (12 Long Acre, London WC2E 9LP) is the best. There are no specific rail maps. For this you need the excellent Thomas Cook Overseas Timetable. At stationers, travel agencies and some hotels maps are available and in Malaysia at petrol stations. You can hardly avoid the excellent maps in Singapore but the tone here is lowered by the advertising they contain.

If you're like me and have spent half a lifetime trying to fold maps correctly then Bartholomew's Handy Maps are the ones for you. They are concertinaed and open to a manageable size. You will not poke your neighbour in the eye and they are almost wear resistant.

WHAT TO TAKE AND WHAT NOT TO TAKE

Remember that it's hot and informal so limit your luggage. Suitcases should be left at home. There are many largish bags that can be carried with a shoulder strap and also convertible rucksacks: a few zips and the sack can be changed into a bag.

Considering that the majority of tourists in the region are young travellers then the ordinary rucksack is the most common, though not with a frame sticking out or rattling cups and plimsolls attached. (A writer in the *Bangkok Post* has suggested that people carrying huge rucksacks must have hundreds of T-shirts and shorts inside for this is all you need.)

A sheet sleeping bag is of occasional use, a small alarm clock, a torch, Swiss army knife, camera and films, toilet items best carried in a transparent map case or cosmetic bag, ear plugs, eye mask, playing cards and perhaps (for more remote areas) pictures from home (but one passenger found that his treasured postcard of Accrington, England failed to arouse even a modicum of interest), a small folded bag for use when you, with relief, leave some of your things at the left luggage or hotel. You can thus carry camera etc. on short excursions.

If you're going into the national parks then the following *additional* items are suggested: tent, compass, water container, insect repellant, first aid kit, trainers or boots, plastic raincoat, cooking utensils, small rucksack.

Clothing should be exceptionally light weight and cotton underwear is a must. All this can be obtained here at a fraction of the cost at home. Many women visitors successfully wear sarongs but not, it seems, men.

Rohan trousers, by far the best find I've come across in many years, are available for men and women. With these you can dispense with a cotton money belt which can cause "money belt tum" or a rash. The Rohans have exceptionally deep, well-zipped pockets, oodles of them. Your passport etc. will be kept safe from pickpockets. One builds up a sense of confidence with valuables. These trousers are perfect for tropical conditions, dry in an hour in the sun or in five hours in a room with fan, look good, don't need ironing and seem to last forever. Naturally enough they're a bit expensive and are obtainable in England at the Rohan shops throughout the country or from Rohan Designs PLC, 30 Maryland Road, Longwell, Milton Keynes, MK15 8HN, tel: 0908 216655.

Don't forget flip-flops or sandals which of course can be bought here for next to nothing. And something to amuse you on the train. A book (other than Proust or Joyce) will make the hours slip by on a long haul. Books in English are available at main centres but not elsewhere. In Thailand where tourists congregate there are a number of second-hand and swap shops for paperbacks. Here the quality vastly improves.

HEALTH

There are no vaccination requirements for the region, but two months before leaving home, check health recommendations at one of the excellent British Airways clinics throughout the country. The address in London is 156 Regent St, W1, tel: 071-439 9584. There is no malaria in Malaysia nor in the south of Thailand but if going north of Bangkok then the appropriate prophylactic tablets should be taken. The tiniest abrasion should be covered with an antiseptic such as iodine. Infection in the tropics is fast. With diarrhoea some prefer to 'sit it out' only drinking fluids but if travelling Lomotil seems to be recommended. (Locals will give you good advice on this malady.)

Apart from India, Thailand has the largest growing AIDS problem in Asia. There have been all sorts of surveys showing its rapid spread. Men on their own who can't resist the horizontal pleasures should always use a condom. Malaysia and Singapore are relatively better off but it still exists there.

Never drink tap water in Thailand. Fresh bottled water is readily available. Standards of hygiene in the region, excluding shanty towns, are remarkably high.

In Thailand hairdressers and others offer to 'clean your ears'. This service is best avoided as swimming thereafter can give rise to infection.

Rabies is a problem in Thailand though I've never heard of anyone being bitten by any of the gentle dogs there. This is because they sublimate their desires by spending their leisure hours taking large pieces out of other dogs.

Medical services are first rate and remarkably inexpensive but of course it's better to have insurance.

SAFETY AND SECURITY

I personally feel safer in this part of the world than anywhere else, though surprisingly Thailand has a remarkably high crime rate. Happily the inhabitants reserve their enmity for each other and mostly leave the tourist alone. But there *are* thieves, particularly in urban areas and there are cases reported of foreign tourists being raped. There are also rip-off merchants who offer valueless gems at reasonable prices. One must never accept food, drink or sweets from fellow passengers. The dear old lady may have put a sleeping potion in it and will get off at the next stop with all your belongings while you quietly doze. In order not to insult the huge majority of valid donors refuse politely perhaps indicating that you have just joined weight watchers.

Many travellers find it more sensible to carry one wallet for valuables and another, or a purse, for immediate purchases. In any event always keep your passport on your person even when sleeping in the train. In fact all valuables when travelling should be slept with. A little lock will act as a deterrent and a light chain may be useful in securing your bag to a luggage rack. Make sure that you have the key available or the combination number at the tip of your fingers before the train pulls into your destination. There's no point in tearing your bag to pieces in a frenzy.

Singapore, for a host of reasons, is freer of crime than elsewhere.

WHAT ABOUT THE COST?

There are two quite distinct levels of cost. If you are looking for first class hotels and restaurants it will certainly be cheaper than the west — and better — but prices here have risen over the last few years very steeply. However the standard hotel (see Chapter 8) still represents excellent value particularly in Thailand where a good clean room with shower and fan in a 'modern' or an 'interesting' hotel will cost 300-400 baht for two; whereas a basic room in a guest house would cost 100 baht. Malaysian accommodation is two to three times this amount and Singapore doesn't bear thinking about. Well it does as one has to but because of the elimination of the older Chinese hotels only new establishments at the medium level are available costing as much as S$150 for a double room. (Illegal 'crash pads' however are available.)

Transport in the whole region is the real bargain. Even long distance taxis are cheap in Malaysia and all conveyances in Singapore are inexpensive.

Thailand is the best country for shopping bargains though hasn't the variety of the usually more costly goods in Singapore. Food prices, whether in restaurants or stalls, are so splendidly low that one can easily overeat.

Except in department stores you must haggle hard and long. It's expected. Though you must keep calm.

It is impossible to make an approximation of individual daily costs as it depends much on the priorities of the traveller; but a rock bottom budget traveller (excluding travel costs) should be able to live on £6 per day in Thailand and £9 per day in Malaysia. A medium to high budget traveller would expect to pay two to three times this amount.

VISAS

Thailand

A visitor from most western countries can obtain a 15 day **non-extendable** visa on arrival. Tourist visas of 60 days must be obtained from any country which has a Thai Embassy. You can very readily obtain a 30 day extension on these visas for 600 baht and some travel agencies will do it for you, saving considerable time. To obtain a non-immigrant visa (becoming more difficult in the west) then evidence of financial ability, guarantees etc. must be obtained. If the visa, whatever type it is, is about to expire it is necessary to leave the country and obtain a new visa elsewhere. The favourite place is Penang, Malaysia where non-immigrant 90 day visas are easy to get and many agencies will arrange this. On the eastern side of Malaysia (Kota Bharu) only 60 day tourist visas are obtainable but of course can be extended in Thailand.

The requirement for a tax clearance certificate before leaving the country has now been abandoned.

When obtaining a visa in Malaysia or elsewhere in the east have in mind the public holidays when the embassy or consulate will be closed.

Malaysia

It is not necessary to obtain a visa if you are a commonwealth citizen (except Indian), Irish, Swiss, Dutch, German, Italian, Scandinavian, North American, Belgian, Tunisian, Icelandic or Japanese. You will be entitled to a three months' stay but initially a one month visit pass which is extendable without fee unless you specifically ask for three months which is normally given.

Singapore

The position is the same for Singapore but the time of stay is limited to two weeks. For the average traveller, unless preoccupied with shopping malls, this should be more than enough. There is a probability of extending it with sufficient financial guarantees.

MONEY

Thailand

There is an excellent system of foreign exchange in Thailand. In the vast majority of areas you visit there are exchanges open from 8.30am to 8.00pm.

Banks are open from 8.30am to 3.30pm except weekends and public holidays. Travellers cheques in dollars are the easiest to negotiate. Many of the banks — Thai Farmers Bank being one of the leading ones — will advance money on credit cards. In both cases a passport will have to be presented. Take some spare dollars in cash particularly if crossing the Malaysian border in the east.

Thai currency is the baht (฿) divided into 100 satangs (which are rarely used). There are 1 and 5 baht pieces — confusing since both come in two sizes and a new 10 baht piece. Bills come in 10, 20, 50, 100, 500 and 1000 baht denominations. Always keep small change available to pay 'tuk-tuk' and taxi drivers.

In May 1993 the exchange rate was:

UK £1 = 36.00 ฿
US $1 = 24.50 ฿
A$ 1 = 19.20 ฿

Malaysia

The Malaysians use the ringgit or Malaysian dollar which is divided into 100 cents. In the more Islamic states in the north banks are closed on Friday all day as well as Thursday afternoon but are open Saturday and Sunday. Elsewhere banks operate from 10.00am to 3.00pm Mondays to Fridays and Saturdays from 9.30am to 11.30am. Although there are not the proliferation of exchange bureaux that you find in Thailand there are many ATM (cash card) machines. In the more remote areas particularly in the northeast it is difficult to exchange travellers cheques outside banking hours even at hotels where you are offered nothing but sympathy. American dollars in travellers cheques are the most widely used and some spare dollars in cash are useful for emergencies.

In May 1993 the exchange rate was:

UK £1 = M$3.96
US $1 = M$2.57
A$ 1 = M$2.15

Singapore

Money changers, usually Indian, are common here and you get a better rate for cash than at the bank. They are open day and night. Credit cards are accepted nearly everywhere and of course advances can be obtained at the banks which have the same hours as those in Malaysia. There are an enormous number of ATM machines.

The Singapore dollar has floated upwards over the last few years which means that the Malaysian dollar is not accepted. So if for instance you are buying a through train ticket from Singapore then

Singapore dollars will have to be used and this makes it more expensive.

In May 1993 the exchange rate was:

UK £1 = S$2.53
US $1 = S$1.62
A$ 1 = S$1.30

BUSINESS HOURS

Thailand

Businesses generally open between 8.30am to 5.00pm Mondays to Fridays and the same applies to government offices except for 12 noon to 1.00pm lunch break. Department stores open 10.00am to 7.00pm (some until 10.00pm) Mondays to Saturdays. Smaller shops and street stalls never seem to close.

Malaysia

Shops open from 9.00am to 7.00pm and supermarkets and department stores are open 10.00am to 10.00pm. Government offices are open 8.00am to 4.15pm weekdays and 12.45pm on the sixth day. A Thursday and Friday weekend is observed in the states of Serengganu, Kelantan, Kedah and Perlis.

If applying for a visa in Kota Bharu to enter Thailand it is important to remember this. It normally takes two days to issue a visa.

Singapore

This is more or less the same as Malaysia. Singapore city has been described as 'one big department store' and most department stores are open seven days a week, night and day. The small shops and stalls — those that remain — keep these extensive hours.

> Thai food is not eaten with chop sticks. People normally eat with a spoon and fork. Some Thai dishes are given strange names such as 'elephant penis soup' which — perhaps fortunately — is not widely available.

FOOD AND DRINK

Thailand

One of the pleasures of travelling on the train is the food which is the equivalent of that obtainable at a reasonable restaurant. Ingredients are fresh and there is a fair variety. The caterers are privately contracted so that the menu will vary on each line. Some western dishes are available but may be restricted to bacon and eggs. There is waiter service to the seat (1st and 2nd class) or alternatively a dining car (sometimes fully occupied).

One could expect to see on a menu: omelette Thai style, chicken, pork, prawns, beef and rice or noodles, American fried rice and sweet and sour dishes. Cold Singha or Kloster beer — both quite superb — are pressed upon you.

In restaurants, although the price of sea food has risen in recent times, it is the world's best. Street markets and hawkers sell simple food cheaply. It is safe. Fresh tropical fruit juices go down well.

Tipping, though not expected, is a growing practice; the wages of workers in the service sector are just above subsistence level and the standard of such service on Thai Rail is exceedingly high. A tip is appreciated.

There is no smoking on Thai trains but local third class passengers don't know about this regulation.

Malaysia

Rice and noodles lead the way and sea food and fruit and fresh vegetables are plentiful. *Mee goreng* is a favourite and satay and equivalents are sold at street stalls. Indian restaurants are to be found though surprisingly not with the variety of dishes available say in Europe. Again hawkers' food and markets present excellent value but coffee should be avoided at these stalls. It looks, tastes and possibly *is* mud.

Train food is tremendously variable. Sometimes it is excellent and on some lines, eg the east coast, it is found wanting. There are restaurant cars in 1st and 2nd class trains and in third class there are plenty of hawkers. The train meals are rice dishes, sometimes served in polystyrene containers.

Alcohol is not available, this being an Islamic country, but for those with a huge thirst leaving or arriving in Kuala Lumpur the Travellers Rest bar provides a friendly send off or welcome. Elsewhere in the country alcohol is sold but not much in the traditional Malay states. Tiger and Anchor beer are first rate.

The same tipping rules apply as those in Thailand.

Singapore

The cheap food which had a good reputation is disappearing with the decrepit places from which it was sold. It is said that the food here is the best in the east but most of the raw ingredients are imported from Thailand and Malaysia. It is the variety and presentation that are spectacular.

This being largely a Chinese country there is no restriction on alcohol and all kinds of beers and spirits are freely available. The smoker, however, may feel uncomfortable, but not half as uncomfortable as the government has told the locals they should feel if you *do* smoke in public places.

CULTURAL KNOW-HOW

Thailand

There are inbuilt constrictions and taboos relating to Thai behaviour. Many *farangs*, not knowing them, may be perplexed at certain encounters. The Thai will make allowances, huge allowances, for *farangs* but won't tell them where they've gone wrong. It would be impolite to do so.

Here are some don'ts:

(1) Don't put feet on a table.
(2) Don't point with feet.
(3) Don't touch anyone on the head including older children.
(4) Don't say 'What a beautiful baby' — referring to a newborn — this can attract bad spirits.
(5) Never *ever* lose your temper. Any anger loses you face and you're in a worse position than you were before. Be patient. Thais are.
(6) Do not discuss 'contentious' subjects such as religion, politics or the monarchy.
(7) Respond (if you want to) to the delightful custom of *waiing*. (A *wai* is clasped hands and possibly small bow.) All right for equals and friends but not right for waiters or children who will think you're taking the mickey.
(8) If a romantic man on your own don't get swept off your feet by

> Malays are not supposed to gamble whereas Thais rarely stop gambling. Much money is won and lost at buffalo fighting. Some monks will provide tips for punters.

a Thai lady. You'll end up every day in spotless clothes but the culture gap will take some bridging. If you're female, Thai men will expect you to provide the spotless clothes.

(9) Don't try and match their courtesy with your own. You will turn into a caricature. Best to remain polite and undemonstrative.

(10) Even a flustering attempt to speak a word or two of Thai is appreciated.

Malaysia

As there are three main ethnic groups the do's and don'ts are going to vary. But tolerance and understanding prevail here and you won't be held responsible for your mistakes. These are some of the don'ts.

(1) Don't express anger.
(2) Speak slowly and softly.
(3) Do not touch people.
(4) Chinese Malays particularly will not argue the point but laugh. Girls giggle. This is the opposite to what it seems — it's serious.
(5) Do not wave a finger at waiters etc.
(6) If invited to a home, step *over* the threshold.
(7) Don't raise thorny issues such as the death penalty for drugs.

Singapore

(8) Don't jay walk, smoke in a public place (unless it's obvious that you can), chew gum or forget to flush the toilet.
(9) Be understanding of the disciplined society. They themselves are patient and courteous in the extreme.

LANGUAGE — THAILAND

English is understood by many Thais, particularly the young as it's taught in schools, but in the far north and east very few will. The station signs are in English as well as Thai. However in remoter regions significant signs, eg the train has been cancelled (a rare event indeed) may be in Thai exclusively.

> Buddhism in Thailand requires every male to become a monk for a certain period of his life (but this is proving increasing unpopular). The present king, much loved by his subjects, complied with this requirement and begged for his food like every other monk.

No matter what the station there is always *someone* in the ticket office or on the platform who speaks a little English. There are dramatic regional variations in speech, particularly in the northeast where Lao prevails.

Down south there is a different softer dialect and in the very far south Malay is spoken. Most Thais will understand the Bangkok dialect but people from Bangkok may not always understand the southern dialect.

Thai, like Chinese, is a tonal language and is quite difficult to learn in that one word can have five different meanings depending on the pitch. The grammar, however, is surprisingly simple. When bargaining the use of a few Thai words can lower the price, eg *Phaeng* (expensive). A knowledge of numbers is obviously helpful. An attempt at even mispronounced Thai will be appreciated and will be an occasion for mirth. A Thai who doesn't speak English may desire your attention by using the single abrupt English pronoun 'you' or 'Hey you mister'. He is not being impolite. This is just a direct translation of the much gentler word in Thai. Similarly the question in either language, 'Where are you going?' is equivalent to the Australian expression, 'How are you going?' The questioner would be surprised if you gave him a detailed answer. Finally, Thai words are phonetically transcribed into English which can lead to a variation in spelling, for example the town of Hat Yai can be spelled Had Yai or Hadyai, etc.

Some useful Thai words and phrases

Good morning, Good evening Good afternoon, Good night Hello, Goodbye	*Sawatdee* (to be polite, a man would say *Sawatdee krap*, a woman would say *Sawatdee ka*)
Mr/Miss/Mrs	*Khun*
Yes	*Chai, krap*
No	*Mai, mai chai*
How are you?	*Sabai dee ru, krap (ka)*
Very well. Thank you	*Sabai dee, kop koon*
Thank you	*Kop koon*
I am going to ...	*Pom bai ...*
How much is this?	*Anee tao rai?*
Too expensive	*Phaeng pai*
Any discount?	*Lot ra-kha noi dai mai?*
Understand?	*Kao jai mai?*
I don't understand	*Pom mai kao jai*
Please speak slowly	*Put cha-cha noi*
Not expensive	*Mai phaeng*

No, I won't go	*Pom mai bai*
Please drive slowly	*Khap cha-cha noi*
Please be careful	*Prot ra-wung*
Turn to the right	*Lieo khwa*
Turn to the left	*Lieo sai*
Drive straight on	*Khap trong pai*
Slow down	*Cha-Cha*
Stop	*Yut*
Where is ...	*Yuu thii nai*
Excuse me, pardon me, I'm sorry	*Kaw tohd*
Very good	*Dee mak*
No good	*Mai dee*
Good luck	*Chok dee*
National park	*Utthayen haeng chat*
Foreigner (Caucasian)	*Farang*
Restaurant	*Raan ahan*
Taxi	*Taksee*
Beach	*Haad*
Room	*Hong*
Shop	*Raan*
Street	*Thanon*
Bus	*Rot*
Menu	*Menu*
Bill	*Bin*
Water	*Nam*
Beer	*Bia*
Rice	*Kow*

Time

Today	*Wun nee*
Yesterday	*Meua wanee*
Tomorrow	*Prung nee*
Before	*Jorn*
Early	*Chao*
Now	*Dee-o nee*

Numbers

1, 2	*Nung, Song*
3, 4	*Sahm, Si*
5, 6	*Ha, Hok*
7, 8	*Jek, Bpaat*
9, 10	*Jao, Sip*
11	*Sip-et*
12	*Sip-song*

13	*Sip-sahm*
14	*Sip-si*
19	*Sip-gao*
20	*Yi-sip*
21	*Yi-sip-et*
22	*Yi-sip-song*
25	*Yi-sip-ha*
30	*Sahm-sip*
40	*Si-sip*
50	*Ha-sip*
60	*Hok-sip*
70	*Jet-sip*
80	*Bpaat-sip*
90	*Gao-sip*
100	*Nung Roi*
400	*Si Roi*
600	*Hok Roi*
1000	*Nung Phan*
10000	*Nung Mun*

Days of the week

Monday	*Wan jan*
Tuesday	*Wan angkaan*
Wednesday	*Wan Phut*
Thursday	*Wan phreuhat*
Friday	*Wan suk*
Saturday	*Wan sao*
Sunday	*Wan aathit*

On the rails

Train	*Rot fai*
Railway station	*Sat-hani rot fai*
Ticket	*Dtoo-a*
Timetable	*Dtah-rahng-weh-lah*
Seat	*Thii nung*
Sleeper (and sleeper car)	*Rot nawn*
Dining car	*Rot sa-bee-ung*
Express train	*Rot fai doo-un*
Rapid train	*Rot fai reh-u*
Ordinary train	*Rot fai thamada*
An upper berth	*Tang bon*
A lower berth	*Tang lang*
Blanket	*Phaa hom*

LANGUAGE — MALAYSIA AND SINGAPORE

Malay, which is sometimes referred to as *Bahasa Malaysia*, is the official language of Malaysia. Most people speak English and all the railway staff do. Even in the more isolated states such as Kelantan much English is spoken. It is written in the Latin alphabet but the construction of the language, like Thai, is relatively simple. It is not tonal so it is easy to pronounce. Although most travellers will never have to depart from English the use of the odd phrase is pleasing to Malays. In Singapore there are four official languages — including English which is spoken by nearly everyone you'll encounter and is the recognised way of communicating in commerce. The other official languages are Malay, Tamil and Chinese (Mandarin). The latter two are somewhat difficult.

Some useful Malay words and phrases

(Pronunciation: *a* as in far, *c* pronounced ch, *sy* pronounced sh.)

Good morning	*Selamat pagi*
Good evening/night	*Selamat malam*
Excuse me	*Maafkan saya*
Mr	*Encik*
Mrs	*Puan*
Miss	*Puan, Cik*
I	*Saya*
You (friendly)	*Awak*
You (formal)	*Encik*
How are you?	*Apa khabar?* (the most common greeting)
I'm fine	*Khabar baik* (the only reply)
Never mind	*Tak apa*
Thank you	*Terima kasih*
You're welcome	*Sama sama*
Yes	*Ya*
No	*Tidak* (more commonly *tak*)
Goodbye (to person going)	*Selamat jalan*
Goodbye (to person staying)	*Selamat tinggal*
Can you help me?	*Bolehkah encik tolong saya?*
How do I get there?	*Bagaimanakah saya boleh ke sana?*
How far?	*Berapa jauh?*
How long will it take?	*Berapa lama?*
What is this/that?	*Apakah ini/itu?*
What is your name?	*Siapa nama mu?*
When	*Bila*
Where	*Di mana*

Why	*Mengapa*
Where are you going?	*Pergi ke mana?*
I am going to ...	*Saya pergi ke ...*
Turn right	*Belok ke kanan*
Turn left	*Belok ke kiri*
Go straight	*Jalan terus*
Please stop here	*Sila berhenti di sini*
How much?	*Berapa?*
Good	*Bagus*
Here	*Di sini*
There	*Di sana*
Expensive	*Mahal*
Toilet	*Tandas*
Road	*Jalan*
Shop	*Kedai*
Beach	*Pantai*
Room	*Bilik*
Restaurant	*Restoran*
Bus	*Bas*
Telephone	*Telefon*
Water	*Air*
Rice	*Nasi*
Bill	*Daftar makanan*
Beer	*Minuman bir*

Time

Today	*Hari ini*
Yesterday	*Kelmarin*
Tomorrow	*Besok*
Hour	*Jam*
Year	*Tahun*
Week	*Minggu*

Days of the week

Monday	*Hari senen*
Tuesday	*Hari selasa*
Wednesday	*Hari rabu*
Thursday	*Hari kamis*
Friday	*Hari jum'at*
Saturday	*Hari sabtu*
Sunday	*Hari minggu*

Numbers

1	*Satu*
2	*Dua*
3	*Tiga*
4	*Empat*
5	*Lima*
6	*Enam*
7	*Tujuh*
8	*Lapan*
9	*Sembilan*
10	*Sepuluh*
11	*Sebelas*
12	*Dua belas*
20	*Dua puluh*
100	*Seratus*
1000	*Seribu*

On the rails

Train	*Keretapi*
Railway station	*Stesen*
Ticket	*Tiket*
Timetable	*Jadual perjalanan*
Seat	*Tempat duduk*
Stop	*Berhenti*
Sleeping	*Tidur*
Malay Railways	*Keretapi Tanah Melayu (KTM)*
Express	*Ekspress*
People's Express	*Ekspress Rakyat*
Arrival	*Ketibaan*
Departure	*Berlepas/Bertolak*
North	*Utara*
South	*Selatan*
East	*Kiri*
West	*Kanan*
Left	*Hadapan*
Right	*Belakang*
Front	*Timur*
Back	*Barat*

Chapter 6

Just the Ticket

RAIL PASSES

Rail enthusiasts can travel to their heart's content on the excellent value rail-passes issued by both Thailand (see page 111) and Malaysia (see page 116). There is also the even better value Eurotrain Explorer Pass for young people (see pages 111, 116).

Before you leave home invest in the latest Thomas Cook Overseas Timetable.

THAILAND: THE SYSTEM

There is no need to go to the railway station in order to purchase a ticket if you are in a main centre: a number of agents have been authorised by SRT to sell tickets. Certainly in Bangkok this is the easiest way. Otherwise one must attempt to get through the traffic to Hualamphong and this might take some time. These agents are listed on the next page.

There are rarely long queues except sometimes at weekends and almost always on public holidays when passengers have complained of waiting over an hour.

The sale of tickets and reservations is carried out efficiently and with courtesy. The system is computerised. There may be the odd problem of communication in more remote areas.

There is a helpful information counter at Hualamphong station with two members of staff at least who will speak good English. They will provide up to date timetables. If you are travelling that day then the ticket office (with ultimate destination and type of train clearly indicated) is on the left. If not, under the sign 'Advance Bookings' on the right. You are given a number and when called — probably after five minutes — the ticket is issued and reservation made. (A reservation form will have been completed.) You can now appreciate that it's to your advantage to get a travel agent to issue the ticket.

You can telephone 220341 Ext 4310, 4200, 4201, 4202, 4203 or 2236970, 2233762 for booking information.

Tickets can be purchased and reservations made from Thonburi station (for trains departing from there) and also Don Muang station across from Bangkok International Airport. Booking offices are open from 8.30 to 6.00pm weekdays and 8.30 to 12 noon weekends and public holidays and tickets may be purchased up to 30 days in advance.

You can reserve from abroad by mail. The address is: Reservations, Hualamphong Station, Ramalt Road, Bangkok 10339. You'll need to send sufficient funds to cover return mail. Best to try your Thai Tourist Office and ask them to fix it up for you. Or try faxing them at (66-2) 225-6068.

If you reserve from abroad you will need to confirm at Hualamphong station before beginning your trip.

Agents authorised by SRT to sell rail tickets

Bangkok

Airland Co Ltd	866 Phloenchit Road, Bangkok 10330	Tel: 2525557, 2759495 Fax: 2537978 Telex: 72229
Boonvanit Travel Agency	420/9-10 Siam Square Soi 1, Bangkok 10330 GPO Box: 49 Bangkok 10501	Tel: 2510526/7, 2520151, 2527892 Fax: 2541158 Telex: 82747 BVTA TH
Southern Star Tour Co Ltd	1259/8 Phahonyothin Road, Bangkok 10400	Tel: 2796448, 2797874 Telex: 84638 STAR TH
Thai Overlander Co Ltd	390/17 Sukhumvit Near Soi 18 Bangkok 10110	Tel: 2589246/7, 2581928
Trade Travel Service Co Ltd	Viengtai Hotel, 42 Tani Road, Banglamphu, Bangkok 10200	Tel: 2828670/1, 2826045 Telex: TH82976 STIC BKK
World Travel Service Ltd	1053 Charoenkrung Road, Bangkok 10500	Tel: 2335900/9 Fax: 2351421 Telex: 82680 WTS BKK TH Cable: WORTRASER
Thai Overlander Co Ltd	1157 Sukhumvit Road (Sam Roeng Nua), Bangkok 10110	Tel: 384-6997/8
Trade Travel Service Co Ltd	2169/1 Ramkham Haeng Road, Bangkok 10240	Tel: 378-5158
GM Tour Co Ltd	273 Khao San Road, Banglamphu, Bangkok 10200	Tel: 280-3760/1
ATIT Tour Co Ltd	197-199 Tanav Road, Bangkok	Tel: 224-1838

SJN Co Ltd	52/18 Ladprao Road, Soi 101, Bangkapi, Bangkok 10240	Tel: 251922
Songserm Travel Center Co Ltd	121/7 Soi Calermla Phayathai Road, Bangkok 10400	Tel: 2500768, 2525190, 2529654
Siam Exclusive Tour Co Ltd	99 Wireless Road, Lumphini, Bangkok	Tel: 2556053
Air Booking Center (1983) Co Ltd	9/150 Silom Road, Bangrak, Bangkok	Tel: 2338700
Rung Srab Travel Service Co Ltd	466-8 Yaovaraj Road, Samphanthawong, Bangkok	Tel: 2240039
Cho Phatthanayut Co Ltd	2065/9 Ramkham Haeng Road, Bangkapi, Bangkok 10240	Tel: 314-0851
Saranat Corporation	163 Prapinklao Road, Bangkok Noi	Tel: 424751

Elsewhere in Thailand

Songserm Travel Center Co Ltd	64/1-2 Chonvithi Road, Koh Samui Surat Thani 84140	Tel: (077) 421228, 421316/9 Telex: 67434 SSSAMUI TH Fax: 421544
Songserm Travel Center Co Ltd	35/1 Talad Tong Sala Koh Phangan Surat Thani	Tel: (077) 281639, 282639
Songserm Travel Center Co Ltd	54/2 Rassada Shopping Center, Rassada Road, Phuket 83000	Tel: (076) 216820, 214272 Telex: 65506 STCPKT TH Fax: 214301
Songserm Travel Center Co Ltd	295/8 Opposite Talad Kaset 2, Surat Thani 84000, Songserm Express Boat Pier	Tel: (077) 272928, 281130

Songserm Travel Center Co Ltd	30/2 Moo 3 Bangkoong, Surat Thani	Tel: 285124/6 Fax: 285127
Songserm Travel Center Co Ltd	38 Kong Road, Amphoe Muang, Krabi 81000	Tel: (075) 6126656 Fax: 612318
Songserm Travel Center Co Ltd	53 Moo 8 Amphoe Muang, Krabi, 81000 (Koh Phi Phi)	
Songserm Travel Center Co Ltd	185 Kanchanavanit Road, Amphoe Sadao, Songkhla	Tel: 411160
Phantip (1970) Co Ltd	422/24-25 Talad Mai, Amphoe Muang, Surat Thani	Tel: 272230, 272906
Phantip (1970) Co Ltd	84/1 Angthong, Chonvithi Road, Koh Samui, Surat Thani 84140	Tel: 421221/2
King Hotel	57 Phosri Road, Amphoe Muang, Udon Thani	Tel: 221634
Cathay Betong Co Ltd	17-21 Chantharothai Road, Amphoe Betong Yala	Tel: 230999
Somnuk Soup	8 Praengpradit Road, Amphoe, Na-Thani, Songkhla	Tel: 311542
Mr Visit Prachak-Rattanakit	223/4 Prachak Road, Amphoe Muang, Udon Thani	Tel: 245877
Air Booking Center (1983) Co Ltd	255 Thapae Road, Amphoe Muang, Chiang Mai	Tel: 233603
ST & T Travel Center Co Ltd	193/12 Sridonchai Road, Amphoe Muang, Chiang Mai	Tel: 251922
Trang Travel Co Ltd	9 Sathani Road, Amphoe Muang, Trang	Tel: 219598
Phantip (1970) Co Ltd	Had Rin Koh Phangan, Surat Thani	

Phantip (1970) Co Ltd	41/42 Mon Road, Amphoe Muang, Phuket	Tel: 213300
Seng Phet	346 Phomrat Road, Amphoe Muang, Ubon Ratchathani	Tel: 254228
Phavana Corporation	299 Chaloenmuang Road, Amphoe Muang, Phrae	Tel: 511475
Vitthayakarn	414 Phuphaphakdee Road, Amphoe Muang, Narathiwat	Tel: 511249
Prachak Service	125 Phi Phit Road, Amphoe Muang Phattani	Tel: 349781
Tiamprasert	13-16 Chayangkur Road, Amphoe Muang, Ubon Ratchathani	Tel: 254658
Chiang Mai Charan Business	123/1 Changmoi Road, Amphoe Muang, Chiang Mai	Tel: 232428
Samui Tour & Transport Corporation	271 Petchakasem Road, Amphoe Muang, Phangnga	Tel: 411233
Ubon Phan Tour	173 Chayangku Road, Amphoe Muang, Ubon Ratchathani	Tel: 241508
Phantip (1970) Co Ltd	171-173 Uttarakit Road, Ampohe Muang, Krabi	Tel: 672738/9
Tola Business & Travel	97/38 Phichitbomrung Road, Amphoe Muang, Narathiwat	Tel: 512484
Samui Phi Phi International Travel Agency	8 Khodchasan Road, Amphoe Muang, Chiang Mai	Tel: 286083
Khlangngon-O Sot	11/12-13 Taharn Road, Amphoe Muang, Udon Thani	Tel: 221060

Rail passes

Visit Thailand rail pass

The cost of this pass has recently been considerably reduced and it now represents a real bargain. There are two types of passes:

(1) Including supplementary charges: adult 2000฿, child 1000฿.
(2) Not including supplementary charges: adult 1100฿, child 550฿.

This covers travel in second or third class (air-conditioned or not) for 20 days anywhere. The pass is available at Bangkok Station advanced booking office (Hualamphong), tel: 223-3762, 224-7788, fax: 225-6068, 226-3656, and at other main stations. It is not available for privately run trains. A break of journey is authorised. Refund on unused rail passes is 75%. There is no refund on partially used or lost rail passes. Even though you've paid for a seat or a sleeper, there is no guarantee that a seat or sleeper will be available: they should be booked in advance as with an ordinary ticket.

SRT have indicated that these passes may soon be available overseas, at Thai tourist offices and agencies. This will be helpful as if coming up from Singapore you cannot obtain a pass in Malaysia, indeed not until Hat Yai, which is inconvenient.

Eurotrain Explorer Pass

This is valid for the total network of the SRT. It is available to those under thirty holding a student or Youth Hostel card. The cost is:

	3rd class	2nd class
7 days	US$16.50	US$21.50
14 days	US$20.00	US$26.50
21 days	US$24.00	US$31.50

As can be seen, this represents superb value.

All trains can be used. Supplementary charges for air conditioning, sleeping berths and rapid and express trains are not included but can be paid for when making a reservation. These passes can be obtained in Thailand, Malaysia and Singapore and the agencies are listed on page 111, 116 under Eurotrain Explorer Pass, ie Malaysia and Thailand have the same outlets.

Hualamphong station, Bangkok

Ordinary ticket holders — things to remember

1. You can change your journey to a later or earlier train.
2. If unable to use part of a ticket then refunds are obtainable at station of issue not later than three hours after departure time of the train by which it was intended to travel. Refund fees vary from 10 to 40% of ticket value not exceeding 300 baht, or 320 baht for through ticket to Malaysia and Singapore.
3. Passengers holding tickets for distances of 200 kilometres one way and over are allowed to break their journey once at any intermediate station for a period of not more than two days reckoned from the day after the journey was broken. For a return ticket a break of journey is allowed each way. You must have the ticket endorsed by the station master at the station where you break your trip immediately the train arrives.
4. Supplementary charges are good for one unbroken journey and with one passenger ticket only. When using another passenger ticket for the same journey supplementary charges have to be paid again.
5. Return tickets are valid for one day on distances up to 100 kilometres, 3 days for 101-200 kilometres, seven days for 201-500 kilometres, 20 days for 501 kilometres or over.
6. Passengers are allowed to carry personal luggage free of charge as follows: first class 50 kilograms, second class 40 kilograms, third class 30 kilograms. Children are allowed half the weight. (Needless to say no-one checks these weights and people have been observed carrying half a house on the railways.)

The fares

It sometimes comes as a pleasant surprise to find how inexpensive rail travel, is.

The fares in baht at various distances are as follows:

KM	First Class	Second Class	Third Class
100	84	44	22
200	161	82	40
300	232	116	56
400	299	147	70
500	366	177	85
600	433	208	99
700	500	238	114
800	567	269	128
900	634	299	143

Some examples (single fares)

		Km	1st	2nd	3rd	'Sprinter'
Bangkok to	Phitsanulok	389	292	143	69	285
	Chiang Mai	751	537	255	121	395
	Nong Khai	624	450	215	103	365
	River Kwai Bridge	136	168	59	29	-
	Surat Thani	651	470	224	107	370
	Hat Yai	945	664	313	149	299
	Butterworth	1149	927	431	-	-
	Kuala Lumpur	1531	1432	659	361	-
	Singapore	1927	1965	899	512	-

Children's fares

If between three and 12 years and under 150cms they can travel for half the adult fare provided that separate seats are not required. If travelling on 'Sprinter' trains then the fare is approximately two thirds of the adult fare.

Supplementary charges

Express train	30฿
Rapid train	20฿
Special express train	50฿
Air-conditioned 2nd/3rd coach	50฿

Sleeping berth charges

Air-conditioned 1st class berth (double cabin)	250฿ (per person)

Air-conditioned 2nd class berth	
upper	200฿
lower	250฿
2nd class berth	
upper	70฿
lower	100฿
2nd class berth (only special express)	
upper	100฿
lower	150฿
2nd class air-conditioned (only special express)	
upper	200฿
lower	250฿

MALAYSIA: THE SYSTEM

An excellent computerised system enables you to buy tickets with seat or berth reservation thirty days in advance inclusive of day of travel. Third class tickets without seat or berth booking can be purchased ten days in advance. Booking offices are at all stations but nowhere else.

Kuala Lumpur station is in Jalan Sultan Hishamuddin diagonally across from the National Mosque. Information on all services can be obtained from The Director of Passenger Services Malaysian Railway, Jalan Sultan Hishamuddin 50621, Kuala Lumpur, tel: 03-274 9422, telex: KTM MA 32716, fax: 03-274 9424.

For reservations telephone:

North	03-274-7442
South	03-274-7443
General	03-274-7435
Singapore	02-225 5165

(General enquiries relating to Singapore are on 02-222-2874.)

At the station itself enquiries are on the left and bookings are on the right. This office is extremely helpful and good English is spoken. There can be queues on public holidays.

As mentioned earlier Singapore railways form part of Malaysian Railway (KTM) so bookings can be made in each country as if in effect it is one.

Singapore station in Kepple Road has the usual booking facilities with helpful information centre straight ahead as you enter and ticket office on your left. No indication is given that you must book and be on the platform half an hour before the drain departs as customs and immigration formalities are conducted here.

Malaysian dollars are not acceptable.

The Malaysian railpass

Available for international travellers (excluding Singaporeans) there are two types:

Adults: 10 day pass for US$40 (approx 110 ringgits)
Children: 10 day pass for US$20 (approx 55 ringgits)
Adults 30 day pass for US$85 (approx 240 ringgits)
Children 30 day pass for US$43 (approx 120 ringgits)

These passes allow *unlimited* travel anywhere in Malaysia and this of course includes Singapore. It is valid for all classes — so naturally one would travel first class — and validity runs from the date of the first journey.

You must make your own reservations; seat reservations are free and for sleepers it is 20 ringgits. No refunds are allowed on unused or partly used railcards.

Rail passes can be purchased at Kuala Lumpur, Singapore, Butterworth, Johor Bahru, Port Kelang, Penang, Padang Besar and Wakaf Bahru.

As there are only *two* lines available for travel it is questionable whether this presents anything like good value, eg if you come up to Butterworth from Singapore first class the cost of a ticket is the same as a rail pass and in either case there is no guarantee that you'll get a sleeper or a seat. If you come up the west coast and go down the east you're only slightly ahead, there being no first class on the eastern line. A slightly dotty rail buff who wants to keep travelling up and down the country continuously will, of course, be a winner but other passengers could easily *lose* money on this pass unless the cost is lowered (it was raised in early 1992). KTM have indicated that it won't be long before new rolling stock is acquired and the east coast line improved, providing sleepers and first class.

If coming south from Bangkok it should be noted that Malaysian railpasses can be acquired at Butterworth or Wakaf Bahru on the other side. If coming north, they are available at the start of the journey at Singapore or Kuala Lumpur.

Eurotrain explorer pass

This provides unlimited travel for seven days for young people. It costs M$29.00.

The pass is valid for second and third class travel and is available to all students below the age of 30, and youth hostel card holders.

Seat reservation charges are included but not sleeper reservations. This represents superb value.

Kuala Lumpur railway station

Interior of Kuala Lumpur station with railbus

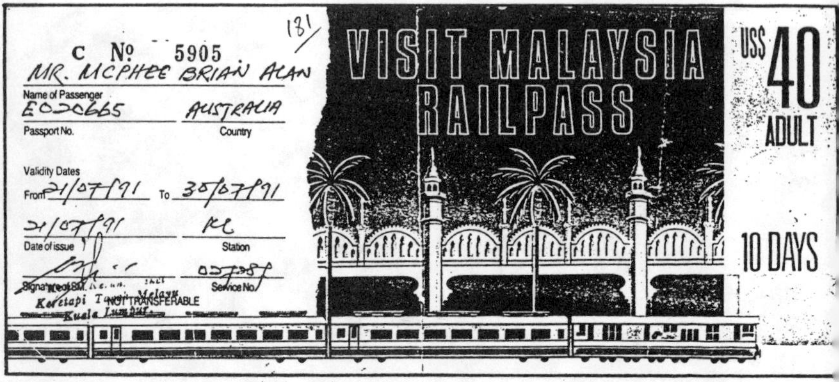

Passes are available at:

Kuala Lumpur: MSL Travel Sdn Bhd, 1st Floor, Asia Hotel, 69 Jen Hj Hussin. Tel. 03-2989722

Petaling Jaya: MSL Travel Sdn Bhd, Lot 2, Wisma MCIS Annexe, Jen Barat. Tel 03-7553191

Penang: MSL Travel Sdn Bhd, Lobby Ming Court Inn, Macalister Road. Tel: 04-372655.
340, Chulia Street. Tel: 04-616154/112

Singapore: German Asian Travels, 126, Telok Ayer Street. Tel: 2215539
MAS Travel Centre, #06-01 Tanglin Shopping Centre, Tanglin Road. Tel: 2354411
STA Travel, #02-17 Orchard Parade Hotel, Tanglin Road. Tel: 7345681
Singapore Polytechnic, 500 Dover Road. Tel: 7742270
#01-05, North Bridge Centre, 420 North Bridge Road. Tel: 3383455

Bangkok: Educational Travel Center, Room 318, Royal Hotel, 2 Rajdamnoen Avenue. Tel: 2240043, 2244800
180, Khao San Road, Banglamphu. Tel: 2827823, 2827021
5/3 Soi Ngamduplee, off Rama 4 Street. Tel: 2871477, 2869424
62 Pra Atit Road, opposite FAO/UNICEF. Tel: 2824658, 2827647

Copex Associated Travel Service/CATS, 6th Floor, Akaranupornpong Building, 130/2 Krung Kasem Road, Thewet. Tel: 2828131, 2817721
STA Travel, Thai Hotel, 78 Prachatipatai Road. Tel: 2815314, 2817031
Wall Street Tower Bldg, 14th Floor, Room 1405, Suriwong Road. Tel: 2332582, 2332626.

Phuket: On-Time Southern, 7/42 Chao-Fa Road. Tel: 211005
Hat Yai: Universal On-Time, 147 Nipat Uthit 1. Tel: 231394
Koh Samui: A.A Enterprise & Travel, 88/6 Thaweeratpakdee Road (Market Street), Moo 3, T. Angthong, Nathon. Tel: 421126, 421551.

The fares

Like Thailand rail travel here is exceptionally good value. Anyone used to travelling distances by train in USA or Europe (particularly UK) will be stomping with delight.

Examples of fares in ringgits between Kuala Lumpur and some main stations are as follows:

	Single Journey			Express		
To station	**1**	**2**	**3**	**AFC**	**ASC**	**TC**
Butterworth	54.50	22.40	13.80	63.00	31.00	18.00
Tapah Road	21.70	18.90	5.50	42.00	22.00	13.00
Singapore	55.90	23.00	14.20	64.00	31.00	19.00
Padang Besar	75.40	31.00	19.30	-	-	-
Bangkok (TH)	142.70	62.20	-	-	-	-
Kuala Lipis	57.30	23.60	14.30	-	-	-

AFC = 1st class AC
ASC = 2nd class AC
TC = 3rd class

Children's fares: Under four it is free and between four and 12 it is half the adult fare.

Supplementary charges

International special express charges (in ringgits)

1st class AC	22.60
2nd class lower	13.60
2nd class upper	9.10
2nd class lower AC	22.60
2nd class upper AC	18.10
Express charges	4.60

Sleeping berth charges

1st class AC	25.00
1st class ordinary	12.50
2nd class lower	10.00
2nd class upper	7.50

Note: 1st class cabin accommodates *two* persons.

Concession fares

Many are available and some examples are:

Category	**Reduction**
Group travel of 10 or more persons	25%
Students (only 3rd class ordinary)	50%
Handicapped persons	50%
Deaf, mute, blind persons	50%

The Railway Hotel, Ipoh

Ordinary ticket holders — odds and sods again

1. Tickets are valid for travel on day of purchase or as otherwise endorsed.
2. On all trains but express trains you can change the date of journey by seven days.
3. First, second and third class tickets with seat or berth reservations may be purchased thirty days in advance. Third class tickets for other trains can be purchased 10 days in advance.
4. There is no refund on lost or destroyed tickets. However, immediate refunds for tickets are available when the train service has been cancelled, the train is two hours late or — somewhat of a privilege — if the passenger is a foreigner. There are minor cancellation fees payable.
5. Passengers holding tickets for distances over 200km are allowed to break the journey at any intermediate station for one day for every 200km or part thereof travelled. Tickets *must* be endorsed by the station master on arrival.
6. 60kg baggage allowed for 1st class, 35kg for 2nd class, 25kg for 3rd class but this is never enforced.

FINAL HINTS AND REMINDERS FOR EASY RAIL TRAVEL

1. Plan carefully in advance. It will make things much easier.
2. Take minimum of clothing.
3. Make photocopies of passport, visa and airline tickets and keep separately.
4. Choose trains that arrive at a time suitable to you.
5. Avoid tight connections.
6. Make sure you have a current timetable.
7. Reserve in advance for busy lines particularly on weekends and holidays.
8. Make sure you've taken into account the one hour time difference between Malaysia and Thailand.
9. Note times when frontiers are shut.
10. Be aware of the different weekend in northern Malay states.
11. Keep calm and smile a lot. Nearly everyone else does.

DO NOT OPEN THE WINDOW WHILE ASLEEP

Chapter 7

Stations and Trains

STATIONS

At main stations in the region all facilities that you would normally expect are available. Details are given under individual stations. You will find that there are left luggage facilities, restaurants, toilets — normally Asian and usually clean, bookshops, rest rooms — mainly in Malaysia, and an exchange office (in the stations of the capitals). Train arrivals and departures are intelligibly displayed in English but of course one should check the ultimate train destination so as to identify the platform. Station staff everywhere are usually very helpful if not too busy.

Transport to and from the station

There seems to be an oversupply of transport and rarely are difficulties incurred. Depending on where you are there are taxis, pick-up trucks (*songthaews*), three wheeled vehicles (*samlors* or '*tuk-tuks*'), motor bikes and bicycle rickshaws. Remember to establish the fare first (except in Singapore where taxis are metered).

TRAINS — THAILAND

These are the normal diesel trains usually pulling a considerable number of carriages. Some of the rolling stock is old and carries exterior dust. Don't be put off. The interiors, though plain and unadorned, are clean and comfortable.

The type of carriage may vary from journey to journey and is usually governed by the kind of train you are on. There are four kinds: ordinary, rapid, express and 'Sprinter'. There are three classes: first, second and third.

The third class seating is of two immovable rows facing each other, ie there are four passengers to a unit so to speak, or as many as can be squeezed in — travel third class is informal and sometimes hilarious. Rapid trains do not have a first class. The seats are padded and much more comfortable than they look. On ordinary trains you will have to sit upright on wooden slatted seats causing what the Thais somewhat unsubtly refer to as 'third class bum'. There are no third class carriages on express trains. If you're travelling by local train in Bangkok you will find plastic seats just like so many other rapid transit systems. All travel here is third class.

Examine timetables to note the time advantage which on many trips is of little significance.

In second class adjustable seats face the front of the train accommodating two people. The special second class sleeper carriages have double padded seats facing each other with a barrier protecting each four seats from the adjoining pair and a table in between which can be removed. The seats are converted into upper and lower bunks at night.

First class cabins are not unlike tiny but dated hotel rooms. There are usually two bunks but (rarely) one bunk cabins are available. They are private, secure and of course expensive. There is excellent porter service, clean towel, wash basin, fan, air-conditioning, mirror. There is a small table. Drinking water is provided. In here you'll feel really snug.

There are also rail cars for some shorter trips.

A new generation of diesel engines and new carriages, all manufactured in Japan, is to come into operation in 1993.

The 'Sprinters'

These new and good to look at railbus type diesel trains have proved to be immensely popular with the travelling public. Introduced in June 1991, manufactured by Brel Ltd in Britain, they operate on all main lines. It is intended to use them for long distances only and many more will come into operation at a later date. At present the destinations are Chiang Mai, Nong Khai, Ubon Ratchathani and Surat Thani.

The trains are capable of speeds of 120kph on the flat. Generally comfortable, a few passengers complain of feeling dizzy because of the high speeds. The trains are intended for day time travel and have cut three to four hours off most journeys. They were not however *designed* for long distances and therefore facilities are

Sprinter train, Thailand

Sprinter train, interior

limited. There are no sleeping berths. Each driving car has 72 seats while the intermediate cars have 80 seats. The seats are reclining but tall people may have some difficulties. There is air-conditioning and toilets but the designers compromised here between Asian and western with the result that unless you leap away a gush of water will hit you.

Coffee and snacks are served by hostesses who have been instructed to smile all the time but would at any rate.

To bed or not to bed?

Sitting up all night is no great discomfort but on long trips berthing it is an extremely attractive proposition at little extra cost. There are air-conditioned and non air-conditioned carriages. I personally prefer the latter although it can get a little hot. Sometimes the air-conditioning is turned up too high.

Should one go for the top or bottom bunk deserves a Delphic reply. It really depends on you. If you're an octogenarian I wouldn't try the top bunk, nor if with your evening meal you intend to consume a disproportionate quantity of beer or even water. Next to the lower berth there is a window which makes things noisier if a train is going past. Your privacy is guaranteed by adequate curtains. (A passenger of six foot three informed me that he found both upper and lower berths — lower is longer — suitable in length but there were he admitted other reasons for him sleeping so well.) The linen is freshly laundered and a woollen 'rug' comes in a sealed plastic container. If you're in the top berth then you can have it made up early. Generally berths are made up at about 10pm. You can read all night as a reading lamp is provided. Ear plugs and eye mask come in handy here.

Other facilities

Windows are big and can be opened. On long trips in third class every window is usually open. There are toilet facilities (western style) with a wash basin at each end of the carriage. Usually they function satisfactorily and are normally clean.

The pleasures of food

The menu will vary from line to line as the catering is private. Whatever trip you are on you find that eating on the rails is a considerable pleasure. Of course, all sorts of food is available from hawkers and most of it is good. But a formal menu is provided by the steward (see page 95 for food generally). Third class trains don't have dining cars but the others do. Service, whether to the seat or in the dining car, is quite spectacular. European breakfasts are served and so is coffee. The steward will take your order for next morning if you are arriving early. On some lines an alternative menu for *farangs* is available: three courses for 100 baht. This is not nearly as good value as the traditional menu. Ask for *menu thamada*.

MALAYSIA – TRAINS

Trains here provide a high standard of comfort. Drawn by modern diesels on a single track the seats in first and second class are aircraft type adjustables with folding trays on the back. Most carriages are carpeted and clean — even some third class carriages.

Sleeping berths are in special carriages with small porthole windows. You can obtain the odd seat here in the corners. Lights are on all night.

There are also modern rail buses that are fast with fixed seats and a bit bumpy.

The eastern line does not (in my experience) provide the comforts of the western side. There are at the moment no first class or berths available. There is air-conditioning in first and second class. First class cabins are the equivalent of those in Thailand (see page 124)

Malaysia — The pleasures of food

As mentioned before, it is variable. Meals on the international express are first rate and the dining cars are of high standard. There is usually a choice of five items. No alcohol is served. There is waiter service in first class so a passenger here can either eat in the cabin or in the buffet car which is always next door. Meals served on the eastern side may be limited to one rice dish. Hawkers' food is delicious and very inexpensive. Railway meals are provided by private contractors.

Kings Rest House, Hua Hin station

Chapter 8

Where to Stay

THAILAND

There are no station retiring rooms and only one railway hotel (at Hat Yai — but not particularly recommended). But this shouldn't cause alarm. World weary travellers will immediately inform you that Thailand provides the best value for money of anywhere. Furthermore all sorts of accommodation is available and rarely — I will even say never — will you be unable to put your head down even during festivals. But on these occasions you may have to do a bit of searching. Most stations are situated in or on the edge of town and transport to a hotel is as easy as pie.

Accommodation in Bangkok is naturally more expensive than elsewhere. In remote areas prices are very low indeed.

All the accommodation here has been personally experienced or recommended. But change can be rapid. My own favourite hotel in Thailand — for good value — the Nora of Hat Yai, is, despite its youth, being pulled down and rebuilt. It may or may not provide the excellent friendly service that it once did.

Luxury hotels are not listed. But the enormously expensive Oriental Hotel in Bangkok on the river — considered by many connoisseurs to be the best in the world — is worth visiting. Any irate egalitarian incensed at the plushness will be soothed by the atmosphere and historical background. You can keep your Raffles. For a splurge this would be the place.

The following list is meant to serve as a mere indication of what is available. TAT issue a directory of hotels and some detailed guide books give helpful advice.

Station or Destination	Middle Range	Budget
Aranyaprathet (Arany)	Inter Hotel 108 Moo Ban Aran Tel: 231291 (There are good value bungalows near border)	Kasemsuk 39 Chitsuwan Rd Tel: 231138
Ayutthaya	U Thong Inn Rotchana Rd Tel: 242618	Pai Thong G.H. (4) (across from railway station) Tel: 241830
Bangkok	Ail Inn (R) 25 Soi Kasen San 1 Tel: 215-3029	Lee GH, 123 & 4 (4 is best) Near Soi Si Bamphen
Chiang Mai	Northlands Lodge (R) 2 Moon Muang Rd Soi 7 Tel: 6653 211889	Je T'Aime GH 247 Charoen Rat Rd Tel: 234-912
Hat Yai	Nora Hotel (if rebuilt) Thamoonvithi Rd Tel: 244944	King's Hotel Niphat Unit 1 Rd
Hua Hin	Supphamit RA 19 Amnuaisin Rd Tel: 511208	The Travellers Rest GH 12 Chomsin Rd (R) Tel: 032-511-346 (Bangkok tel: 258-3743)
Kanchanaburi	VL Guest House Saengchuto Rd	U.T. Guest House 25 Mae Nam Khwae Rd
Korat (Nakhon Ratchasima)	Sri Pattana Suranari Rd Tel: 242944	Siri Hotel 167 Phoklang Rd
Koh Samui	First Bungalow 8 Moo 3 Chaweng Tel: 077-421444 (Many bungalow complexes let out at top and bottom of range)	Hundreds at Chaweng. Best to look. All fairly similar.
Lopburi	Lopburi Inn 28 Narai Maharat Road Tel: 412300	Asia Lopburi Sorasak Road Tel: 411892

Station or Destination	Middle Range	Budget
Nakhon Pathom	Sunya 101 Moo 1 Phetkasem Rd Tel: 242938	Mittaowan (Next to Chedi on left)
Nakhon Phanom	Nakhon Phanom Hotel 403 Aphiban-Banch Rd Tel: 511074	The River Inn (R) 137 Sunthon Wichit Rd Tel: 511305
Nakhon Ratchasima (see Korat)	Mandarin 44 Moo 4 Phanon Yothin Rd Tel: 412949	Muang Thong 1-5-7 Prang Sam Yod Rd Tel: 411036
Nakhon Si Thammarat	Thai Hotel 1369-1375 Rajadamnoen Rd Tel: 356-451	Muang Thong Ho Jaemroenwithi Rd
Nong Khai	Phantawi 1241 Haisoke Rd Tel: 411568	Sukhaphan Banthoengjit Rd
Pattaya	Pattaya Visas House Soi 18 Tel: 427-676	Diana Inn Pattaya 2 Rd Tel: 429675
Phitsanulok	The Rajapruk 99 Praongdum Rd Tel: 2514621 (R)	Unachak Phayalithai Rd
Phuket Town	The Pearl Hotel Montree Road Tel: 211-044	Onion Hotel Phang-Ngard Tel: 211-154
Prachuap Khiri Khan	Mirror Mountain Bungalows Chai Thale Road	Same (all categories)
Songkhla	Saen Sabai 1 Phetkhiri Rd Tel: 311090	Narai 14 Chai Khao Rd Tel: 311078
Sukhothai	Ratchathani (R) 229 Chodwithithong Rd Tel: 611031	Sukhothai S/S Singhawat Rd Tel: 611133

Station or Destination	Middle Range	Budget
Surat Thani	Sian Thara 1/144 Donnok Rd Amphoe Muang Tel: (02) 271-0924-5	Ban Don Na Muang Rd
Trang	Queen Hotel Visetkul Rd 218522	Phet Ratchadamoen Rd 218002
Ubon Ratchathani	Pathumrat 173 Chayangkun Rd Tel: 241501	Racha 149 Chay Angkun Rd
Udon Thani	The Charoen 549 Pho Si Rd Tel: 221913	Suk Sumjai 226 Pho Si Rd

MALAYSIA AND SINGAPORE

The cost of accommodation has risen quite a bit over the last few years. This is particularly the case in Singapore where redevelopment has meant that budget and middle range hotels have been replaced by high quality accommodation with the prices that go with them. Illegal 'crash pads' are available but difficult to find. Whereas in Singapore it will cost S$100, similar but not so luxurious will cost M$30 in Malaysia. There is plenty of reasonable accommodation in Malaysia at fair prices but you don't get the bargains you will get in Thailand.

Raffles Hotel in Singapore has been badly redeveloped and is once more open for business. It is, of course, luxury class but a visit here is probably just worth it. The atmosphere is still somewhat colonial and there are interesting reminders of a past age. One has got to ignore the huge number of tourists who have the same idea as you. The splendid facade remains the same.

There are railway hotels at Ipoh and Singapore, both worthwhile but lapsing into dereliction.

The TDC issue lists of accommodation and some detailed guide books give helpful comments. The following is only meant as an indication of what is available.

Station or Destination	Middle Range	Budget
Brinchang	Kowloon Hotel 34 Brinchang Tel: 05-941366 (R)	Wong Villa Brinchang
Butterworth	Take the ferry to PENANG	
Ipoh	Station Hotel at Railway Station Tel: 512588	Embassy 37 Jalan Chamberlain
Jerantut	Sri Damak (Hotel)	
Kota Bharu	Hotel Tokyo Barhu Jalan Tok Hakim Tel: 09-749488	Rebana Hostel Jalan Sultana 15050
Kuala Lumpur	City Hotel 366 Jalan Raja Laut Tel: 4414466	Kowloon 142 Jalan Tuanku
Langkawi	Sandy Beach Motel (Pantai Cenang) (R)	Beach View Motel Budget Travel Lodge (Opposite Sandy Beach, Pantai Cenang)
Pasir Mas	Some poor hotels. Take bus to Kota Bharu	
Penang	Prince Hotel 456 Chulia	Swiss Hotel Lebuh Chulia
Perhentian Besar	Perhentian Island Resort Tel: 01-333910 (at KL 248-0811)	Many basic bungalows at beach
Taiping	Rumah Rehat Baru (Govt Rest House) Taman Tasik 3400 Tel: (04) 822044	The Double Lion Hotel 74 Jalan Kangsar
Tanah Rata	St Garden Hotel Tanah Rata	Seah Meng 39 Tanah Rata
Tembeling	No accommodation. Go on to Jerantut.	
Singapore City	Station Hotel Singapore Station Tel: 2221551	DAS Travellers Inn 87 Beach Road Tel: 338-7460

Chapter 9

The Real Journey Begins

Most rail journeys start from the capitals: Bangkok, Kuala Lumpur and Singapore. When arriving in any of these cities it is best to spend a day or two getting your bearings, perhaps making a visit to the railway station to check on timetables etc.

BANGKOK

This city presents itself to the visitor as a large scale manufacturer of misunderstandings. It can be a dauntingly difficult place in which to get around. Sometimes one has to give up entirely.

Take as an example Sukhumvit Road. In the evening it is an avenue of near despair but not to the smiling Thais. The traffic is locked into a solid block. An overworked, sweating policeman does what little he can. The lights change to green. Suddenly there is a surge of motorbikes and *tuk-tuks* (small three wheeled vehicles with an engine sound like their name). Thick, acrid smoke is discharged into the atmosphere. Vehicles dodge and weave to gain position. The policeman wipes his brow. This scene could be repeated many times.

Forty years ago water buffaloes ploughed their way along Sukhumvit Road and on either side stretched green and glistening paddy fields. Bangkok has become somewhat of a westernised muddle since then when industrialisation and a rage to build were and are the order of the day. There was and is little attempt at planning.

And over the belly of the metropolis lies a cloud of pollution that

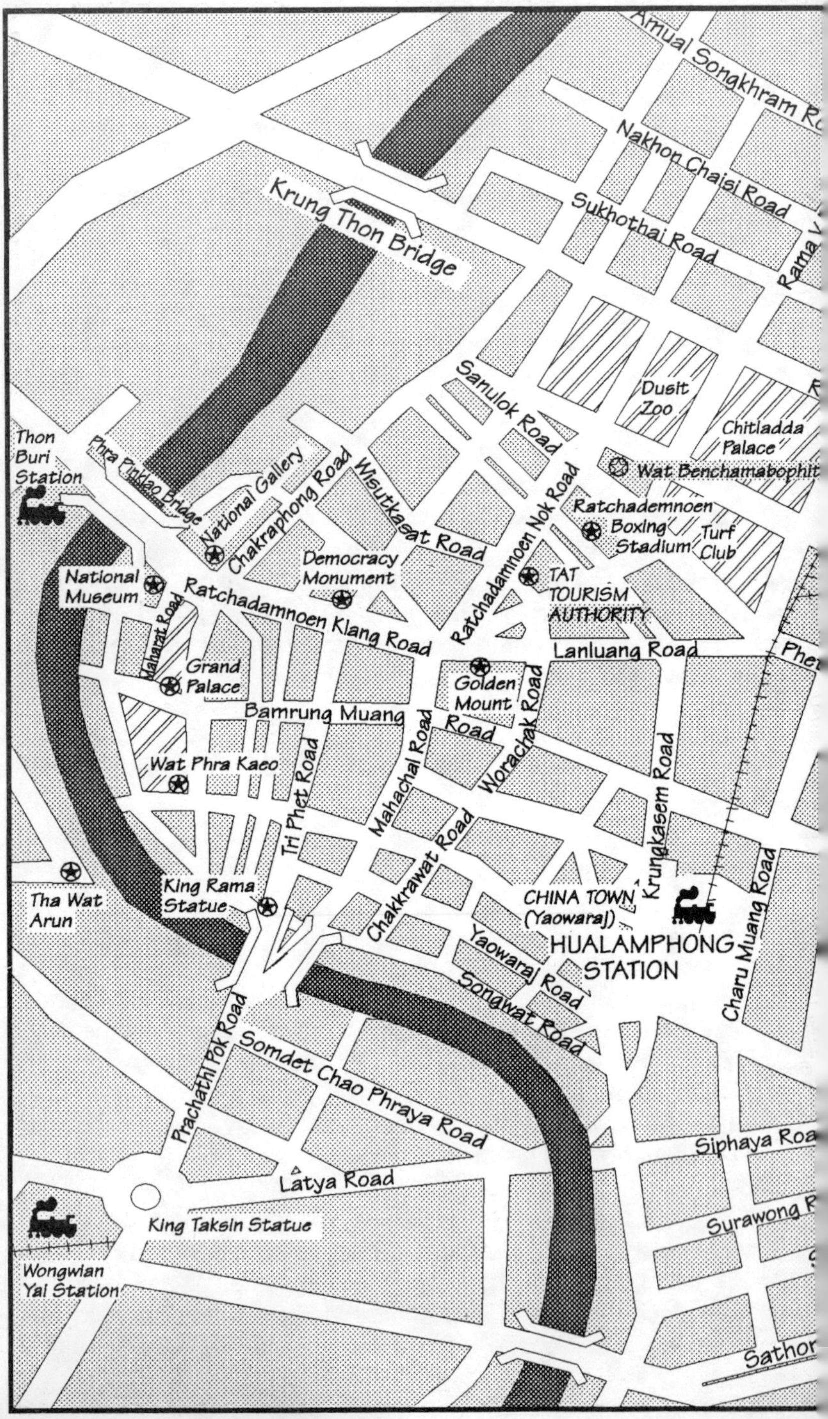

Amual Songkhram Ro
Nakhon Chaisi Road
Sukhothai Road
Krung Thon Bridge
Rama V
Sanulok Road
Dusit Zoo
Chitladda Palace
Wat Benchamabophit
Thon Buri Station
Phra Pinklao Bridge
National Gallery
Chakraphong Road
Wisutkasat Road
Ratchadamnoen Nok Road
Ratchademnoen Boxing Stadium
Turf Club
Democracy Monument
TAT TOURISM AUTHORITY
National Museum
Ratchadamnoen Klang Road
Maharat Road
Lanluang Road
Grand Palace
Golden Mount
Bamrung Muang Road
Worachak Road
Mahachai Road
Krungkasem Road
Wat Phra Kaeo
Tri Phet Road
Chakkrawat Road
Tha Wat Arun
King Rama Statue
CHINA TOWN (Yaowaraj)
HUALAMPHONG STATION
Charu Muang Road
Yaowaraj Road
Songwat Road
Prachathi Pok Road
Somdet Chao Phraya Road
Siphaya Roa
Latya Road
King Taksin Statue
Surawong R
Wongwian Yai Station
Sathor

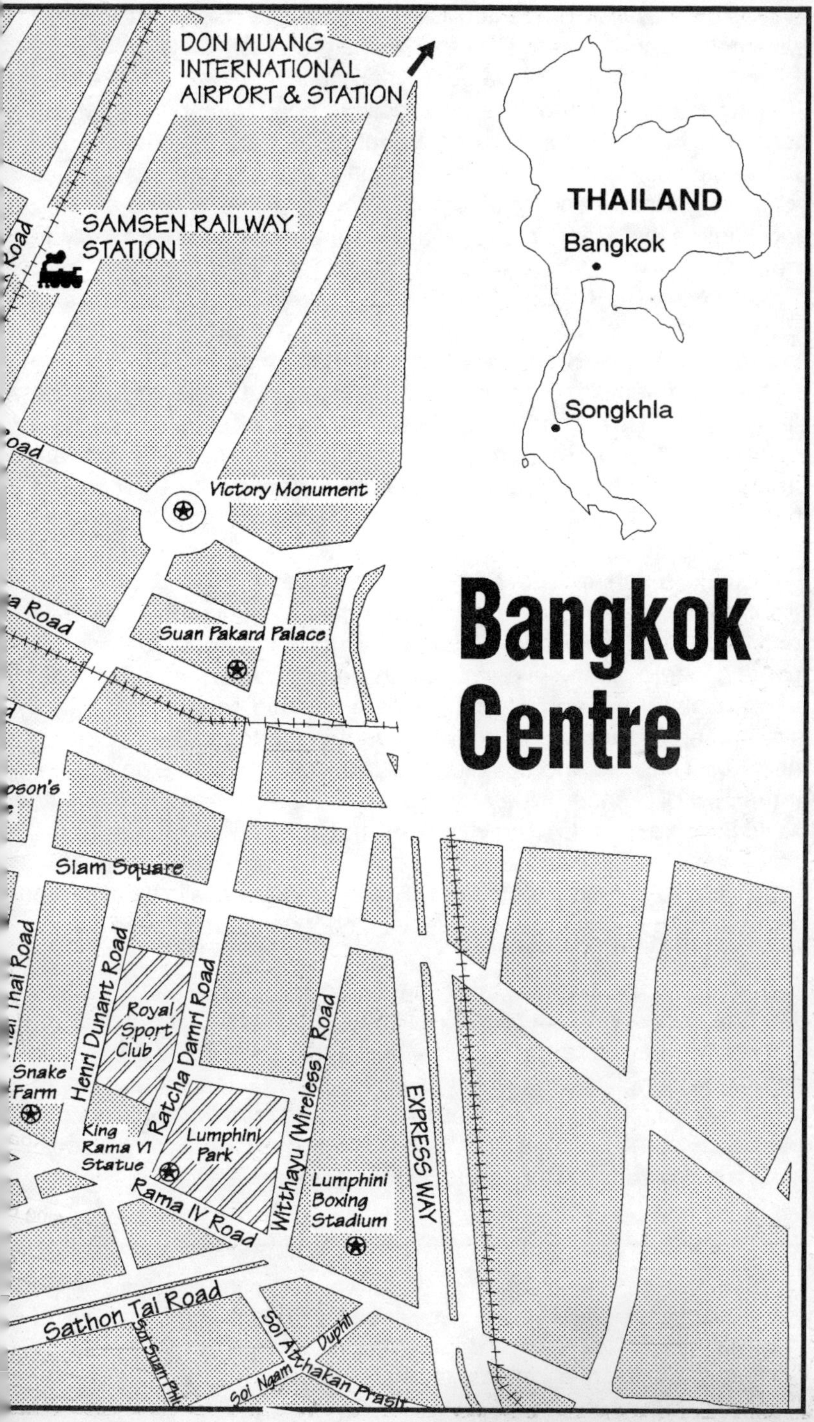
DON MUANG INTERNATIONAL AIRPORT & STATION
THAILAND
Bangkok
Songkhla
SAMSEN RAILWAY STATION
Road
oad
Victory Monument
a Road
Suan Pakard Palace
oson's
Siam Square
Henri Dunant Road
Royal Sport Club
Ratcha Damri Road
Witthayu (Wireless) Road
EXPRESS WAY
Snake Farm
King Rama VI Statue
Lumphini Park
Lumphini Boxing Stadium
Rama IV Road
Sathon Tai Road
Soi Suan Phlu
Soi Atthakan Prasit
Soi Ngam Duphli

Bangkok Centre

is said to rival that of Mexico City. You wander along the broken pavements and the heat sticks to you like a crust.

Bangkok is a place you've got to learn to love. It doesn't take long — maybe a day or two. The less resilient head immediately for the north or the beautiful relaxing beaches. A pity, for behind the unprepossessing face of this chaotic modern metropolis lies something fundamentally different, something that is both exciting and stimulating. Bangkok, for many, is the most fascinating city in the east.

It straddles the Chao Phrya River and is known to the locals at *Krung Thep* — the City of Angels. It was built to replace the splendid Ayutthaya after the Burmese destroyed that capital in 1782. It arose higgledy piggledy from a small river trading post. Once known as the Venice of the East because of the abundance of canals (*klongs*) it now possesses few of them — most were filled in to accommodate the burgeoning traffic; but there are still waterways to explore and the Chao Phrya River provides a highway in itself replete with fast ferry transport.

There is much to see and to experience: the great gold and glittering temple structures (*wats*) with their sweeping multi-layered roofs, the huge gold and bejewelled Buddha statues, the superb markets where nearly everything can be purchased at economical prices, Chinatown, and even, bless it, a relaxing central park with a lake and an assortment of heavily perspiring joggers. If you look for them you'll find old and dignified teak houses sometimes on a canal at the end of a shady side street (*soi*).

Old Bangkok hands will give you explicit instructions on how to get the best out of this city: never hurry; never travel in the rush hour — if you have to, get on a motorbike. There are many available at street corners. Take rest in the shade. Have a cool drink. *Don't have a fixed time schedule*.

Apart from the temples and the smiling populace what makes Bangkok such a popular tourist destination? The reason is, I believe, that like nowhere else the place is thoroughly *alive*. Thais live on the streets, working, talking, walking and eating at the thousands of impromptu stalls; and whatever they're doing, whether operating a sewing machine, cutting hair, selling barbecued chicken pieces, fixing a motorbike, selling shirts, working on a building site, there is

> One in ten Thais live in Bangkok. The Thai name for 'the city of angels' is the longest of any in the world, but is shortened to 'Krung Thep'. The capital claims another first: Patpong contains, for its length, the world's greatest number of entertainment establishments.

a display of ease, of relaxation, of disarming grace. This is most observable after dark when most Thais practice *sanuk* or having a good time. Jaded westerners find this a particularly cheering experience. Bangkok is packed with restaurants and the food is delicious. Nightclubs, coffee shops and bars abound. Even in the 'notorious' areas there is no undertone of villainy as there is in probably every other city in the world. These places seem to have evaded even the intrusion of seediness. This is not to say, however, that the inhabitants are immune to the gentle hush of money. This is an honest place but like everywhere else you should be careful.

One of the advantages of Bangkok is the presence of a huge number of travel agencies who will assist in planning the trip, obtaining tickets and reservations. **Expatriate Travel**, 2nd Floor, Hare & Hound 4/33-34 Soi 21 (Soi Cowboy), Sukhumvit Rd, 10110, Tel/fax: 258-3743, is run by two Englishmen, Mike Jarvis and Tom Bishop. They have an extensive knowledge of railways and have contributed to this book. It must be one of the few agencies in the world where you can buy a beer on entering and on leaving.

Those agencies authorised by SRT to sell rail tickets (but not rail passes) are listed on page 107. This is not to say that other agents can't get you a ticket. They will employ a 'runner' and the additional costs should not be more than 50 baht. It is better, however, to go to the authorised agencies.

There are two stations serving the city. The main station where nearly all trains arrive and depart is Hualamphong on Rama IV Road. The other is Thonburi Station that serves the western Kanchanaburi line to Nam Tok. You must take a ferry across the river to get there or go the more circuitous route across the bridge.

Hualamphong station is a landmark in the city, an airy half cylindrical structure of glass, concrete and corrugated fibre; it surprisingly does not possess an acceptable restaurant but has nearly everything else: a money exchange that closes at 6.30pm, left luggage — open 4.30am to 10.30pm, a large news agency, shops selling fruits and snacks. The information counter is in front of you as you enter. There is a tourist office. The ticket office is on the left (for same day bookings and reservations) and the main booking office is on the right. You are given a number on entering and a booking form to complete and your number will be called at the appropriate desk in the next room. Service is fairly quick except on holidays and is always courteous, although some passengers have complained of extensive delays.

You will use this station for virtually every destination.

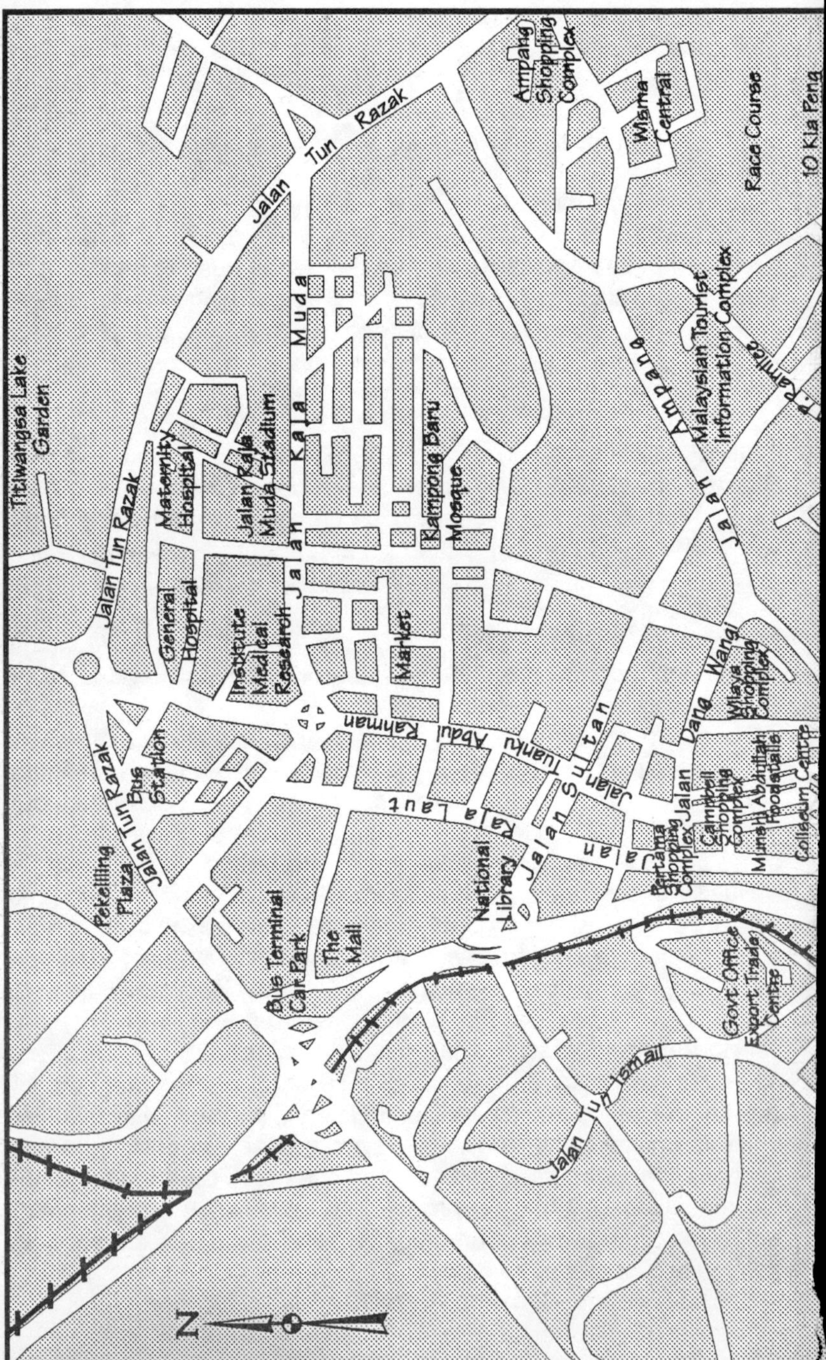
Jalan Tun Razak
Ampang Shopping Complex
Wisma Central
Race Course
10 Kia Peng
Titiwangsa Lake Garden
Jalan Raja Muda Stadium
Jalan Kaja Muda
Kampong Baru Mosque
Maternity Hospital
General Hospital
Institute Medical Research
Market
Malaysian Tourist Information Complex
Jalan Ampang
Jalan Dang Wangi
Wilaya Shopping Complex
Jalan Tuanku Abdul Rahman
Jalan Raja Laut
Jalan Sultan
Bus Station
Pekeliling Plaza
National Library
Pertama Shopping Complex
Campbell Shopping Complex
Munshi Abdullah Foodstalls
Coliseum Centre
Bus Terminal Car Park
The Mall
Govt Office
Export Trade Centre
Jalan Tun Ismail
Jalan Sultan Salahuddin
N

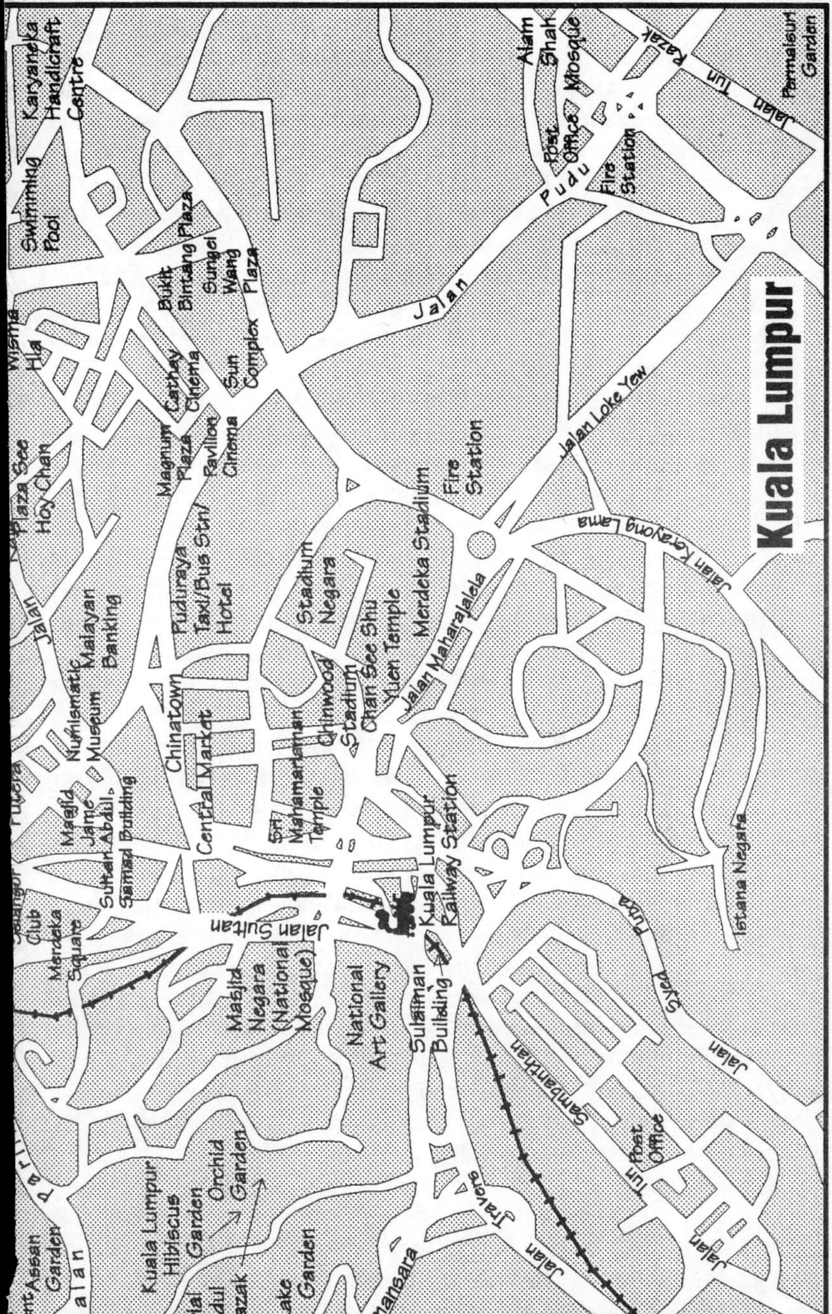
Kuala Lumpur
Karyaneka Handicraft Centre
Swimming Pool
Bukit Bintang Plaza
Sungei Wang Plaza
Wisma Hla
Cathay Cinema
Sun Complex
Magnum Plaza
Pavilion Cinema
Plaza See Hoy Chan
Jalan Pudu
Post Office
Alam Shah Mosque
Fire Station
Jalan Tun Razak
Permaisuri Garden
Jalan Loke Yew
Fire Station
Merdeka Stadium
Jalan Kerayong Lama
Malayan Banking
Puduraya Taxi/Bus Stn/ Hotel
Stadium Negara
Numismatic Museum
Chinatown
Central Market
Jalan Maharajalela
Chinwood Stadium
Chan See Shu Yuen Temple
Masjid Jame
Sultan Abdul Samad Building
Sri Mahamariaman Temple
Kuala Lumpur Railway Station
Istana Negara
Selangor Club
Merdeka Square
Jalan Sultan
Masjid Negara (National Mosque)
National Art Gallery
Sulaiman Building
Jalan Syed Putra
Jalan Sambanthan
Post Office
Jalan Tun
Jalan Travers
Jalan Bangsar
Monument Assan Garden
Jalan Parliament
Kuala Lumpur Hibiscus Garden
Orchid Garden
Memorial Tun Abdul Razak
Lake Garden
Jalan Damansara

KUALA LUMPUR

It is surprising that the inhabitants of Kuala Lumpur are exceedingly law abiding. It wasn't always so. A hundred years ago the Chinese population all but eliminated itself in murderous wars between the various secret societies or died of the fevers. Tin was king and the capital owes its existence to it. (It owes its name to the configuration of two muddy rivers — that is what Kuala Lumpur means.) Later the shanty town that stood there was gradually disembowelled. The population swelled. The millionaires built their mansions and sat back with pride. And then in 1896, ten years after the Port Klang railway was constructed, it became the capital of the Federated Malay States; and it still is a sparkling new capital.

It is perhaps not surprising that this forbidding history remains buried. The brown rivers are there, of course, and the faded Chinese shop houses give a warm impression of age. Some of the pavements are disconcertingly worn but otherwise much of the city is glistening with modernity. It is this feature, I think, that surprises the visitor: a clean bright ordered metropolis of our age. This is not to make comparisons with other contemporary cities. No comparisons are tenable. Kuala Lumpur is not European, it is not in one sense Asiatic. It is Islamic through and through from the mosques and minarets to the traditional dress of many of its inhabitants. Even the sky scrapers reflect this influence in their shape and embellishments. There is not the fussy adornment of yesteryear. The buildings are actually elegant and stand tall and independent as if in admonishment of their western cousins.

Kuala Lumpur has not made the mistake of Singapore: there has not been the wholesale slaughter of old and interesting locations. Chinatown remains with its bizarre air of calamity, its venerable shop houses, its pungent odours and its busy, busy people. Every trade imaginable is practised here and much exotica is sold. There are fortune tellers, pet shops, funeral parlours, food stalls, slatternly grease filled garages, jewellers, leather workers and much, much more. In another area there are Indian traders, their wives and daughters in colourful saris; and then there is elsewhere the dominance of Muslim traditional raiment and all this combined with western dress presents a pleasing contrast.

It is the *blend* that wins the day for this city. A tiny Hindu temple cheekily settles itself against a glistening high rise, a British colonial building is fronted by a *padang* (park) which is a cricket green. Minarets break the skyline and, of course, there are slums.

Kuala Lumpur is quite small. Not long ago one could walk around and see all the sights but nowadays it is best to use four wheels. Flyovers and new highways may obstruct. There is not here the confusion or pollution of Bangkok but traffic jams do occur during peak hours. Nor is there the allure and excitement that exists there. The city doesn't pulsate. It is a relatively ordered place without suffering the constrictions of Singapore. Transport is good and inexpensive.

Best of all, the city lies in the jungle. You can see it on a good day. It's not far away.

The city's gem for the railway traveller is the folly central railway station, just across from the National Mosque. It is indeed an impressive sight. It looks exactly what it's not. One could be forgiven for assuming that it is a large over-adorned mosque, a reminder of the Moorish settlers who put their stamp on the whole country. Arches, domes, minarets and towers jostle for dominance. A colonial edifice, it was constructed by the British — perhaps as a traditional British compromise — in 1911. But it is not only the exterior that impresses. Inside all is coolness and calm 'Victorian' modernity. The facilities here are probably better than any station in Southeast Asia.

There is a good computerised arrival and departure display, a fast food restaurant and a simple Malay one (on number one platform). On the right and left as you enter passenger information and bookings (8.30am to 9.00pm) where the public is treated as the public thinks it ought to be, small clean toilets, left luggage (open 6.00am until 8.30pm), a government and private tourist office providing inexpensive — and if you don't object to it — excellent city tours. All in all a delight. No hassle and rarely big crowds. There's also video TV if you get bored.

What would have made this station almost perfect was the completion of the station hotel development. Unfortunately the builder went bankrupt. But all is not lost. Across the road the splendid Railway Administration building, itself an architectural triumph, will be converted into an hotel and the administration moved elsewhere. What more could one want?

You should be warned, however, not to leave left luggage at the station if you are catching the night express to Singapore as the office closes well before the train leaves — an unhappy state of affairs.

SINGAPORE CITY

Singapore is notable for its intense newness and neatness of feature. It is not the place for a traveller with a museum mentality. It is a positive delight for shoppers.

On the train you come to it much as it came to itself: with magical swiftness. Not that long ago the island was little more than a fetid

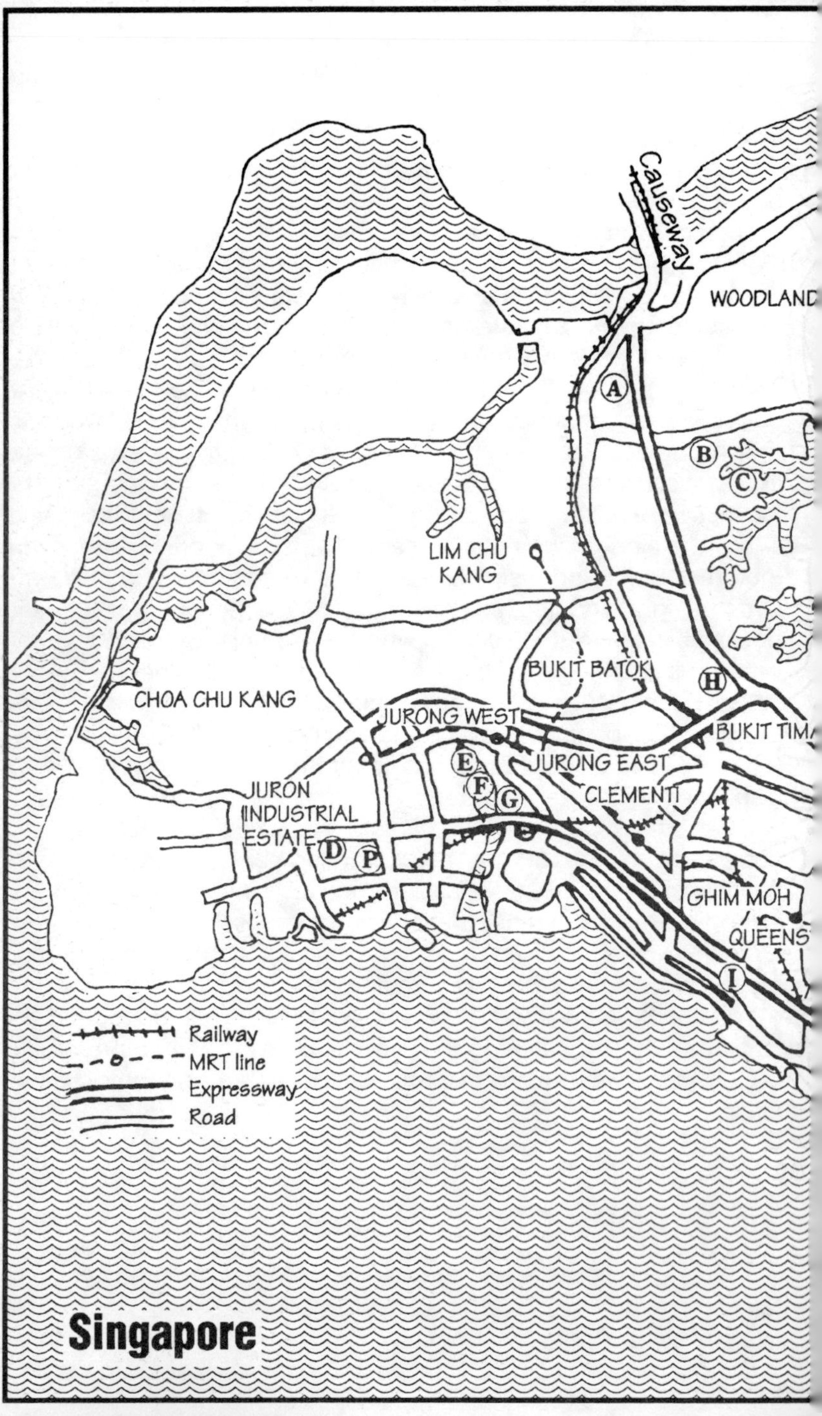
Causeway
WOODLAND
LIM CHU KANG
BUKIT BATOK
CHOA CHU KANG
JURONG WEST
BUKIT TIM
JURONG EAST
JURON INDUSTRIAL ESTATE
CLEMENTI
GHIM MOH
QUEENS
A
B
C
D
P
E
F
G
H
I
Railway
MRT line
Expressway
Road
Singapore

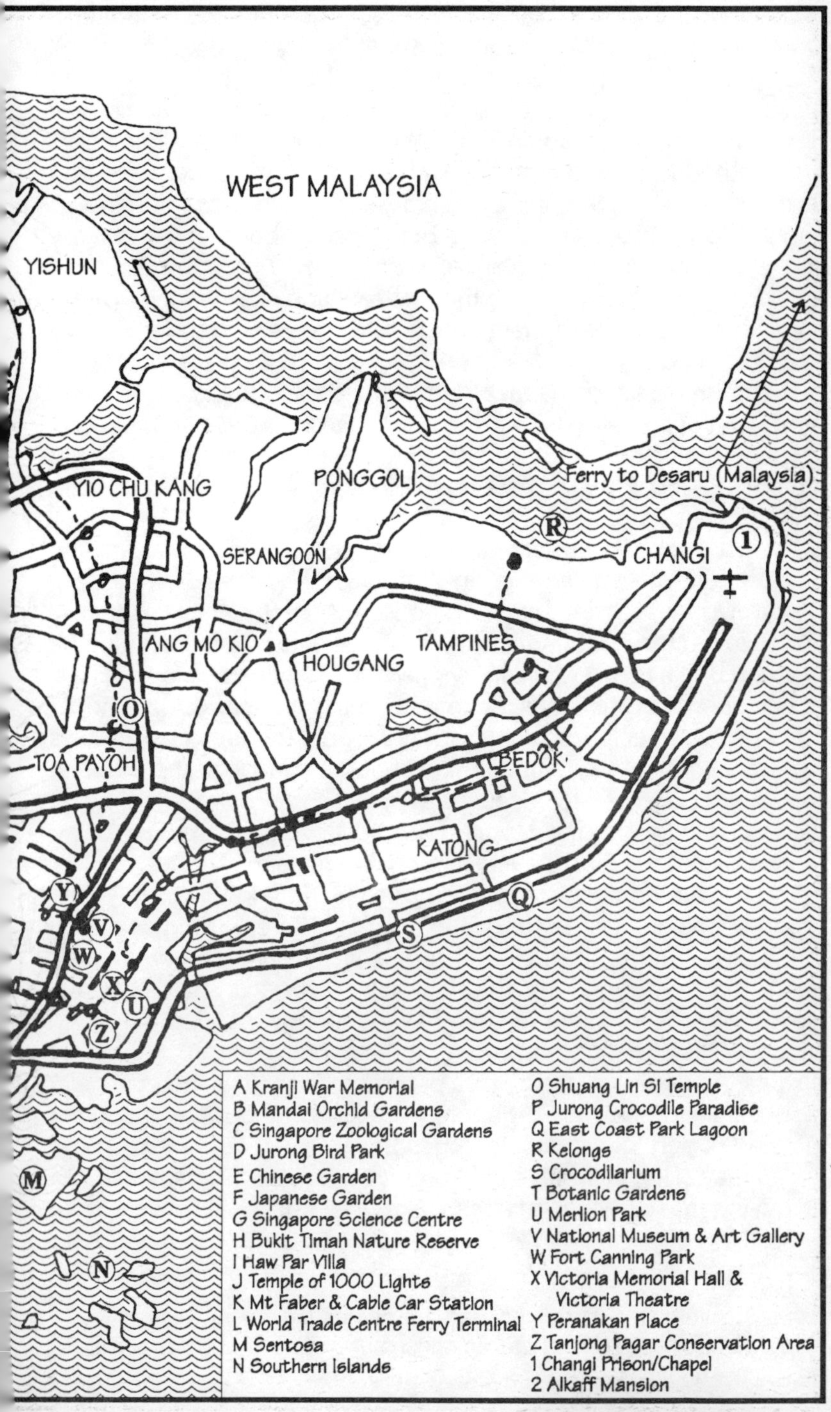
WEST MALAYSIA
YISHUN
YIO CHU KANG
PONGGOL
Ferry to Desaru (Malaysia)
SERANGOON
CHANGI
ANG MO KIO
TAMPINES
HOUGANG
TOA PAYOH
BEDOK
KATONG
A Kranji War Memorial
B Mandai Orchid Gardens
C Singapore Zoological Gardens
D Jurong Bird Park
E Chinese Garden
F Japanese Garden
G Singapore Science Centre
H Bukit Timah Nature Reserve
I Haw Par Villa
J Temple of 1000 Lights
K Mt Faber & Cable Car Station
L World Trade Centre Ferry Terminal
M Sentosa
N Southern Islands
O Shuang Lin Si Temple
P Jurong Crocodile Paradise
Q East Coast Park Lagoon
R Kelongs
S Crocodilarium
T Botanic Gardens
U Merlion Park
V National Museum & Art Gallery
W Fort Canning Park
X Victoria Memorial Hall & Victoria Theatre
Y Peranakan Place
Z Tanjong Pagar Conservation Area
1 Changi Prison/Chapel
2 Alkaff Mansion

swamp. Now it is solid and achieved and rich beyond its dreams. There is nothing facile or slipshod about its speedy development. If you remove from your vision the colonial buildings and the odd mosque — the only relics from a recent past (themselves distinguished) — you could imagine yourself in Florida. Nearly all is modern and fresh and glittering with bright brick and concrete and steel and glass. Shopping complexes and department stores abound. Contemporary high rise buildings surround you and there is a multitude of fashionable restaurants. But probably its most noteworthy achievements are the pleasant and well cared for public housing estates, not to mention the tidy streets that seem to have been polished.

The negative aspect is that Singapore learned too late that if you bulldoze your past your future will be bland. Despite the huge Chinese population (and except during the festivals, see page 67) there is not much feel of Asia here. Singapore is a modern western city and it's proud of it.

The real tourist attractions are out of town, although minute pockets of interest remain in the city: the small remnant of Chinatown with its restored shop houses, Arab Street, Little India — but this is currently under the developers' hammer — and the restored Bugis Street with its wayside stalls and dearth of customers. (It has been found impossible to restore the old atmosphere here.) The best spectacle for many is the **Juron Bird Park**, the world's largest outdoor aviary, but mention should be made of the island of **Sentosa**, now joined by a causeway. Building and re-building never ceases and even the main artery, Orchard Road, is being reconstructed for reasons that are not at all clear.

You will not be able to avoid the word 'Raffles' in this city. Raffles was responsible for the foundation of Singapore, having arranged the lease of the island in 1819 from a local Sultan. Since then — apart from the tragedy of the Japanese invasion — it has hardly looked back. The island declared its independence in 1965 and in January 1992 the chewing of gum was declared an offence — despite the departure from office of Mr Lee Kuan Yew, the man most responsible for making Singapore the second most affluent country in Asia (its port is the world's largest).

You may shop in 'Raffles City' or anywhere else. There is a frenzy of buying despite the fact that this duty free area, which once

Sir Stamford Raffles, the founder of modern Singapore — who gave his name to the famous hotel amongst other things — spent only nine months on the island.

provided real value for money, doesn't do so any more. The consumer goods are there and superbly displayed, but nowadays it is said that Bangkok provides some better bargains particularly in textiles.

For the long term visitor it is true to say that there exists a vague strain of unease here but this takes a time to present itself. The tourist passing through may hardly notice it; but a train traveller arriving from the north will be greeted at the station with a warning in large lettering that if he is found carrying fireworks he will be fined *and caned*. Woe betide the traveller who is not only carrying fireworks but is also chewing gum!

It is a pity that the budget traveller has to give Singapore short shrift, put off by the very high cost of accommodation, for there is much to be admired in this progressive metropolis and on the rest of the island.

Singapore station is part of the KTM (ie Malaysian) system and is situated in Kepple Road. An imposing but externally dull building with cars parked in the front, all the usual facilities are here with clear arrival and departure times, left luggage and very helpful information. The interior is adorned with huge high murals. This is an immigration and customs area so passengers going to Malaysia must turn up half an hour early. The rapidly disintegrating railway hotel is here and is good value (but the station is quite a way from the centre of the city). The hotel was once a notable five star establishment. Not so any more.

Transport from the station by taxi is, as elsewhere in Singapore, well ordered. Taxis are metered and are not expensive. Some trishaws are available for hire in what remains of Chinatown.

The Mass Rapid Transit system, recently completed, serves 42 stations. It is certainly worth taking a trip on this subway even for no apparent purpose. It is the last word in modernity and efficiency. The rails are enclosed at the stations by glass 'curtains' that quietly slide open when the train comes in.

THE INTERNATIONAL EXPRESS: THAILAND, MALAYSIA & SINGAPORE

Apart from the luxury Eastern and Oriental Express due to begin operation in 1993 (see page 10), there is no *single* train from Bangkok to Singapore via Kuala Lumpur or vice versa. It is necessary in both instances to change trains in Malaysia and sometimes this can be a little bit tricky. On the eastern side no train crosses the border and a short walk and 30 minute bus or taxi trip is necessary to connect the Thai and Malay systems.

Tickets for the whole journey can be obtained in the various countries but no reservations can be made except for travel in the country in which you bought the ticket. (Singapore is part of the Malaysian KTM system so the two countries for rail travel purposes are, in most instances, conveniently treated as one). If travelling south and despite what is said above, you will have to obtain a reservation on the Singapore train at Kuala Lumpur and the office will be closed when you arrive. More often than not you will have to sit up all night to Singapore. (This train is usually heavily booked, particularly at weekends.) Refunds can be obtained at Singapore station. There is one express train per day going south leaving Bangkok station at 15.15. There is one express train a day going north leaving Singapore at 22.15 and Kuala Lumpur at 7.15.

The border on the west side is crossed at Padang Besar where customs and immigration formalities take place. The station is narrow, uncomfortable and unkempt but the procedure usually is fairly quick depending on the number of passengers. The train waits an hour and watches should be put forward an hour to match Malay time. There is no need to remove luggage from the train. This situation may now have changed, and it could be necessary to change on to a Malay train. The schedules, however, remain the same. For more information on this route see page 173.

The second border crossing is at the Malay Singapore causeway at Johore Bahru. Customs and immigration are carried out on the train and at Singapore station.

The eastern border crossing is between Sungai Kolak and Rantau Panjang, requiring another form of transport, eg trishaw and a short walk across the bridge. Customs and immigration are side by side and there are informal money changers.

With luck, on this long 40 hour plus journey on the western side, you can spend two nights asleep, but as mentioned before only one night's sleep can be guaranteed. It is better then to break the journey at Butterworth so as to take the short ferry across to Penang, 'the Pearl of the Orient', and a favourite tourist destination and then carry on refreshed next day. On the eastern side the Thai Malay border — you've got to get alternative transport at any rate — is a good stop over point. You can take a bus or shared taxi for 1½ hours to Kota Bharu, an interesting town. The train can be joined next day at Pasir Mas which is closer than Kota Bharu's station at Wakaf Bharu.

Coming up from Singapore (western side) on the 22.15 the connections will be tight and one prays that there are no delays. Regrettably sometimes there are and it's quite frustrating to miss a train by a minute or two. They don't wait. It is necessary to change at Kuala Lumpur where the train to the north leaves 10 minutes later and then at Bukit Mertajam, the station *before* Butterworth where the connection is 13 minutes later. (There have been complaints about late arrivals here.)

International Express suggested timetable: western side

Bangkok		15.15	8.35		
			17.05		Dept
Hat Yai		7.05	16.47		
Padang Besar (border)		8.00	16.05	(T)	Dept
	Dept	10.00 (M)	16.15		
Butterworth		12.25			
	Dept	15.00			
Bukit Mertajam			13.53		Dept
			13.35		
Kuala Lumpur		21.50	7.15		Dept
	Dept	22.15	7.05		
Gemas					
Singapore		7.10	22.15		

Note: (1) Although the southern line timetable for Thailand was issued in November 1992 and the timetable for the whole of the Malaysian system in April 1992 they are variable at some points by up to ten minutes.

(2) Malaysian time is one hour *ahead* of Thai time, ie if you arrive at the Thai border *from the north* at 8.00 then it is 9.00 Malaysian time.

On the eastern side going south, which in Malaysia provides a more captivating scenic experience as it's nearly all jungle, you will need to change at the Thai/Malay border or Pasir Mas and Gemas, both connections allowing adequate times for delays (as they do on the northward trip). The Malay trains have only 2nd and 3rd class *and no sleepers*. So if you come this way you can only put your head down on the Thai section. If going to Kuala Lumpur then you change at Gemas and head north west on the Singapore Kuala Lumpur train.

All this sounds somewhat more complicated and testing than it is. Although some passengers find that such a long time on a train is monotonous it is invariably comfortable and there are treats: good service and delicious food is provided by both SRT and KTM, though no alcohol is served on Malaysian trains. Dipsomaniacs, however, can bring their own into the dining car.

Those of an extrovert nature will find ample opportunity to display their talents on the 'jungle express' part of the eastern Malaysian line. There are very few *farangs*. One female New Zealander traveller reports receiving a proposal of marriage within minutes of meeting a middle aged Malay gentleman. Locals sometimes refer to this train as the *chatter chatter express*.

International Express suggested timetable: eastern side

↑ Bangkok	14.00		6.55
Hat Yai	7.05		15.16
	7.20	dept	15.00
Sungai Kolak (border)	9.40	Connect by taxi/bus/walking	11.25 (T)
Pasir Mas	14.41		11.00
Gemas	24.00		
	1.15	dept Singapore	22.20 dept
	1.35	dept Kuala Lumpur	1.03
Kuala Lumpur	5.45		
Singapore	16.25		2.00

Note: (1) There is also a rapid train leaving Bangkok for Sungai Kolak at 12.35 arriving at 8.35 next morning. A second train from Sungai Kolak, also a rapid, leaves at 10.10 arriving at 6.35 next day.

(2) Thai time is one hour *behind* Malaysia so if crossing the border *from the south* at 11.00 then it will be 10.00 Thai time.

Chapter 10

On the Rails in Thailand

NORTHERN LINE: BANGKOK TO CHIANG MAI

This run to Thailand's second city is popular so should be booked early. It's usually taken in the evening with advantage of sleeping berths. As mentioned before the new 'Sprinter' trains are operating on this line. At present one a day leaves at 8.10 and arrives at 19.00 thereby reducing the travelling time by three hours and making the day trip a good option. The normal run takes fourteen hours and there are six trains a day. A good idea would be to go by 'Sprinter' and return on a night train with a sleeper. There is no possibility of going across country to join up with the next terminus, Nong Khai on the Laotian border, though if one was so inclined you could return to Phitsanulok and then use other transport.

After Phitsanulok the scenery is quite magnificent. There are the usual rice paddies but also forests of teak and bamboo, long valleys with villages sometimes tucked into the folds, ravines, waterfalls and much more.

Less than an hour and a half out of Bangkok on the ordinary train you will pass through **Ayutthaya**, the old capital and probably the most significant historical site in the country. (This is dealt with later on the basis that most travellers would want to visit it from Bangkok.)

In another hour **Lopburi** is reached. Dramatic ruins dating from Khmer times and stretching to the 17th Century are here and Wat Phra Si Ratana Mahahat and Pra Prang San Yot are smack up against the railway line. The site itself for some reason hasn't received the guide book accolades that it deserves. Of course one can get off, look around and take a subsequent train, but don't miss it if passing as it's the best historical glimpse you'll get from a train window in Thailand. It is on your right as you travel north.

Phitsanulok mustn't be missed, not for the town itself but for the ancient site of Sukhothai which is an hour and a quarter away by bus. Phitsanulok is on the Nan River and although there is not much here there are hordes of excellent food stalls and cafes. To be next to the river — you can eat on a house boat — is indeed a pleasant experience.

The station itself has reasonable facilities. An old British locomotive is on display. Accommodation is only a few minutes away. The bus station is also fairly close and regular buses serve the ancient city.

From the town of Sukhothai you can get a *tuk-tuk* to the site twenty minutes away. You can hire the vehicle for a few hours or take an official tour or hire a motorcycle or bicycle. The place is extensive, atmospheric and breathtakingly beautiful. It's not worth rushing it. It was the site of the first Thai capital and was built in the 13th Century.

Lamphung is a quiet provincial capital, older than Chiang Mai and 26km south of that city. (The temples go back to the 8th Century.) Hence tourists usually approach it by day trips from Chiang Mai. Despite its partial modernity it has a tranquil pleasantness about it.

You should reserve a seat for the continuation of the journey as these trains are often crowded.

Chiang Mai station, the terminus, is surprisingly small. Amongst the facilities are a left luggage office (closes 8.30pm) and a number of people offering accommodation as well as an informal accommodation office — with free transport. The cost of transport from the station is somewhat inflated. An ancient locomotive is on display.

On the banks of the Ping River this city retains an old world charm. It is pleasantly

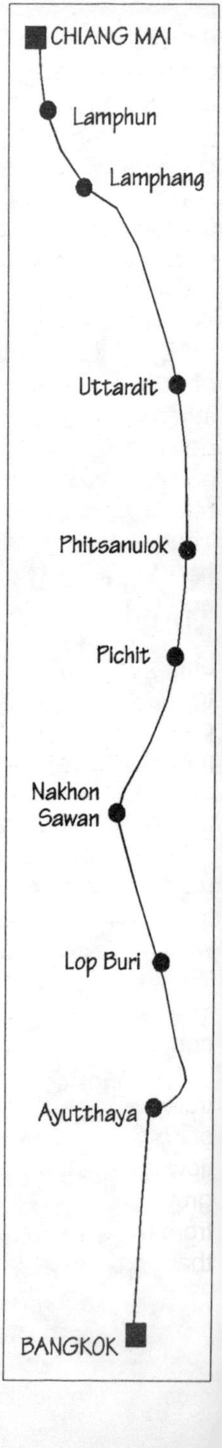

relaxed though there are a huge number of foreigners here. As in Bangkok there are travel agencies galore. This is the centre for travel to the well known sites in the north and west. Trekking in groups can be arranged with ease though the independent traveller may like to go to an outlying village and try his luck on his own or with a local guide of which there are many.

From Chiang Mai you can go north to Chang Rai, then to Mae Sai from where it is possible to cross into **Burma** for the day, with possible extensions to Kengtung, heart of the Golden Triangle.

Doi Inthanon National Park is located 58km west of Chiang Mai. You reach it via Chomtong by coach and minibus. You can go by road to the summit of Thailand's highest mountain with superb views of richly forested valleys, streams and waterfalls. **Mae Ya Waterfall** south of the park is the highest in Thailand. This is an ornithologist's delight with 383 species and bird watching is best between February and April. Most large wild animals are locally extinct. Some primates remain: the leaf monkey, the slow loris and pig-tailed macaque. There is a large variety of orchids. There is an ongoing legal battle here between the two hill tribes in the region, who slash and burn, and conservationists.

There are also agreeable day trips by coach from Chiang Mai to Lamphun (see before), the **Mae Sa Valley**, 14km north — referred to as 'the little Switzerland' with ordered landscaped views of some charm, and near at hand **Ban Sang**, 'the umbrella village'. Whether made of cloth or paper these hand-painted items are bought in great quantities by tourists who rarely if ever use them to protect themselves from the rain.

Doi Khun Tan National Park, which until 1992 could *only* be reached by train (access at Khuntan Railway Station two hours south from Chiang Mai on the main Bangkok line, see page 31), is a very worthwhile destination and on weekdays almost free of visitors. Khun Tan tunnel here, the longest in Thailand, was built over a period of 11 years from 1907-1918 by German engineers and is a marvel of construction. Unfortunately it cost over 1000 lives.

And finally, for totally dedicated railway buffs, there are two local trains per day going south and after 45km is the prize winning station of **Sala Maetha** — tiny, isolated, devoid of passengers, full of flowers and as pretty as a picture. The neatly uniformed staff will greet you warmly as perhaps you will be the only person to step from the train. (The station has the distinction of being used by less than ten people per day.)

NORTH EASTERN LINE: BANGKOK TO NONG KHAI

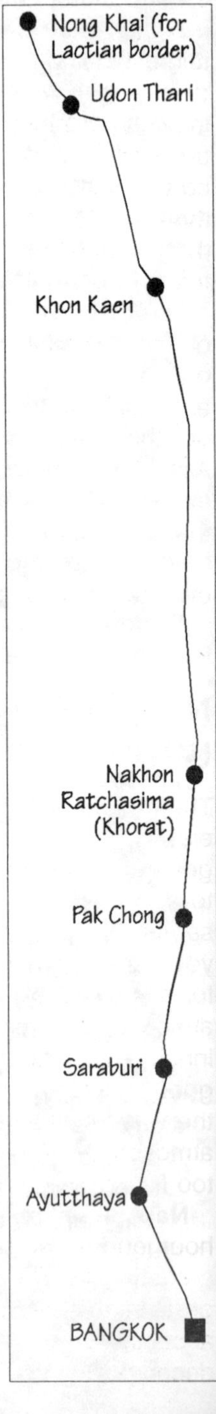

This 11 hour trip to the Laotian border takes in Udon Thani. It is referred to as the 'sticky rice express' because of the north easterners' preference for this type of food. One branch of the line goes to Ubon Ratchathani via Nakhon Ratchasima. Our train heads north via Udon Thani to the Mekong River. There are four trains a day. It is a pleasant trip without any great scenic wonders but a dramatic contrast as you reach the northern regions with the paddy fields and sugar cane plantations. This is obviously a good journey to take at night with a sleeper though a 'Sprinter' train once a day from Bangkok (6.15) will take nine hours.

Udon Thani town is rather dead. There also seems to be a shortage of good accommodation here. The station itself is like a lavatory but there is a left luggage office (8.30pm close).

There seems to be little reason to get off the train here as you are nearly at the end of the line. It is the second last stop. Nong Khai is only an hour away. But although this town has lost its 'glory' — it was a large US base during the Vietnam War — this is the stop you need if you want to visit **Ban Chiang**.

The flat one hour trip by regular bus which passes along the main road takes you to this atmospheric and wonderfully friendly town where the women of Laotian origin redden their faces. The bus driver will let you off where a sign indicates that the site exists and then it's a 10 baht motorcycle or *tuk-tuk* ride. The reason for the interest in this strange location is the discovery of the existence of an advanced bronze age culture placing the dawn of civilisation before that of the Tigris and Euphrates. There is little to look at here however. Two pits have been left open. The tiny museum on two floors with bronze, iron and pottery exhibits is superb. Many exhibits, however, are in the National Museum at Bangkok. Regrettably there is little literature in

English about this fascinating area.

Nong Khai then is the end of the line with its tiny station ten minutes out of town (left luggage 5.30am to 7.30pm). There is a very definite atmosphere prevalent here. The town has significant Lao influence. Its interest lies in the views of the Mekong, though there are better views elsewhere. Boats ply regularly across the great coffee coloured river to Laos. A view of Laos can be obtained through a telescope. The capital, Vientiane, is not far away — but the Laotians one sees look exactly like the people on your side of the river which is not surprising.

The town has gained greater significance because of the easing of the border restrictions. At the time of writing visas can be obtained in Bangkok or Nong Khan. 'Bill,' who owns a pleasant bar and cafe somewhat unoriginally called the 'Kangaroo Bar', is a mine of information. The Friendship Bridge now being constructed by the Australian government has provision for a train track so that eventually the two countries will have a rail link. There is little doubt that the opening of the bridge will also open Laos to the tourist.

If you don't want to go back the same way then you can go overland — heaven forbid — briefly described on page 156.

NORTH EASTERN LINE: BANGKOK TO UBON RATCHATHANI

There are seven trains a day and the time taken is approximately eleven hours except by 'Sprinter' which takes eight hours. The route goes through **Nakhon Ratchasima** and **Surin**. From tiny scabby towns one arrives in the rice region where, as far as the eye can see, the land is swathed in glistening green. In the dry season all you will see is dust and stubble. But once you have been travelling for some hours and you enter *Issan* country there is a change of atmosphere. The land is poor. The soil is not fertile. But the inhabitants, who are a Laotian mix, move about with the impassive good manners and smiling features of their more affluent cousins in the west. So this trip is one whereby you experience a change of atmosphere rather than any spectacular views. The countryside is too flat for that.

Nakhon Ratchasima (Korat) is 250km northeast of Bangkok, a five hour journey, and is the gateway to the northeast. As such it forms a starting point for surrounding travel rather than possessing any great interest itself. It is a big commercial centre. There is plenty of accommodation. A new railway station, rather uninspiring, adjoins a decomposing one. There is a coffee shop and left luggage office open 24 hours a day. An old locomotive is displayed.

Phimai, Thailand's answer to Angkor Wat in Cambodia, is one and a quarter hours away on the regular public bus. The trip is a bit hot and somewhat uncomfortable. (There are of course tours that will take you there.) Many consider this to be one of the most fascinating ruins in the country. The site is mainly 12th Century Khmer and can be traversed by foot but leave plenty of time. It closes at 5.00pm. Regrettably the museum here is no more.

And so on to the end of the line via **Surin**. There is no point in getting off here unless it is November and you've booked accommodation in advance. This is the time of the annual elephant round up, observed by huge crowds.

Ubon Ratchathani, the heart of *Issan*, possesses a tiny, clean, almost 'cute' station with a locomotive on display. The town is situated on the Mun River and is a long way from the Mekong which forms the border with Laos. It was an American base during the Vietnam War. It is now a largish dull place. Good basic restaurants provide spicy *Issan* food. The town closes down at night and suffers from a lack of lighting.

The Mekong can be observed sixty five kilometres to the east. In the region of Khong Chiam it joins the Mun River. This is an excursion worth taking. The very helpful TAT Office provides cheap transport to this and other interesting sites.

If at this point the traveller, instead of going back on the same line, wants to join the northeastern line by going overland, then he can take a bus firstly to Nakhon Phanom where atmospheric views of the Mekong exist, and then travel on next day by bus to meet the train at Nong Khai or Udon Thani. There is an acceptable paucity of the infamous lorry drivers on this overland route.

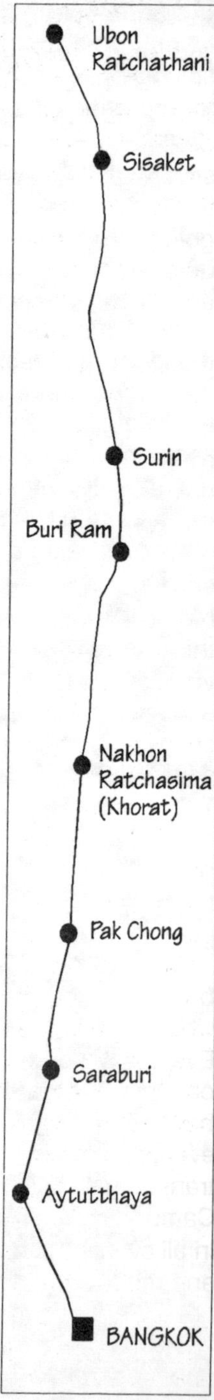

EASTERN LINE: BANGKOK TO ARANYAPRATHET (ARAN)

This line is of little scenic interest, but is detailed here because of the changing political situation in Cambodia which may admit tourists via this route, although at the time of going to press the political situation is deteriorating. The journey is by diesel rail car and takes approximately 5½ hours.

Virtually the whole of the trip is through rice paddies: it passes through the fields themselves and you can nearly stretch out and pick the stuff. The land seems endless, flat as a pancake and green (in season). There are no interesting towns on the way, and most of the stations are little more than small sheds.

From the minute station at Aranyaprathet a short distance from the town a trishaw or motorbike with huge carriage affixed to it — I think unique in Thailand — will take you to your hotel. In the weekends here accommodation is difficult. Hordes come to shop at the border markets. The town itself is small and neat with its full share of shops. There is tension here however which is not surprising considering its geographical position smack on the Cambodian border and the presence of the refugee camps. There are plenty of road blocks.

One must take public transport to the border but at present, despite the thousands of locals who do cross, foreigners are not admitted. Eventually you may be able to take the train on into Cambodia to Phnom Penh and beyond. It all depends on future political events. Already returning immigrants are transported by train the whole way, the Cambodian line having been recently repaired. In all events the hordes scrambling in the dust and mud — many being transported by crude hand cars — present an amazing spectacle. (There is now a special train leaving Bangkok daily at 6.00 and arriving at the border near Poipet, Cambodia, at 12.00.)

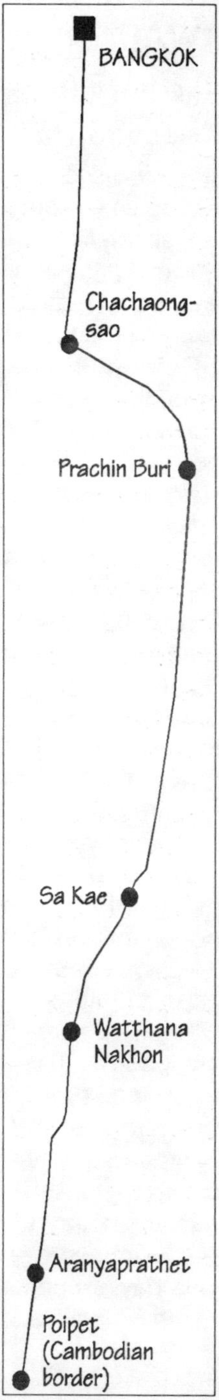

"THE BRIDGE ON THE RIVER KWAI"

Nakhon Pathom, Kanchanaburi, River Kwai and Nam Tok

by Tom Bishop

As routes radiate from the capital, this should be simply classified as the western line. However, its history makes it the most famous (infamous?) stretch of railway in Southeast Asia, the so-called 'Death Railway'.

Somewhat shorter in route length to former days, the remaining section from Taling Chan junction, through Kanchanaburi, to Nam Tok is now served by one train daily. This 130km stretch was the most integral part of the Thailand to Burma railway, commissioned under the auspices of the occupying Imperial Japanese Army in June 1942.

The bridging of the Kwai Yai river at Kanchanaburi and the subsequent traversing of the Kwai Noi river valley, en route to Burma, was a major natural obstacle to be overcome in the construction of a supply route through to Singapore. Today, the records of that construction, the Kwai bridge itself and the topography make Kanchanaburi the central attraction of any trip along the line. The whole trip is a must, although the scenery beyond Kanchanaburi is far more impressive than that before, whether coming from Bangkok or Nakhon Pathom.

From Bangkok one has to board at Thonburi station at 8.00, arriving at Nakhon Pathom an hour and a quarter later, Kanchanaburi another hour and ten minutes, River Kwai five minutes later and Nam Tok an hour and a quarter after this. One only has a fleeting five minutes before the train returns to Bangkok. A minimum two day trip is advisable although a one day excursion exists (see page 164) for those on a whistle stop tour.

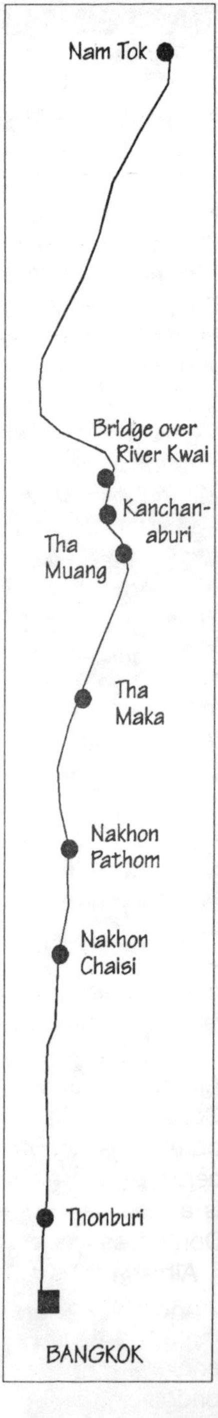

If boarding or detraining in Nakhon Pathom one will no doubt create time to visit Phra Pathom Chedi, the world's tallest Buddhist monument. It is a short walk from the railway station and overwhelming in its grandeur. Nakhon Pathom is served by frequent trains from Hualamphong.

At Kanchanaburi everyone comes to see the bridge, which is fine because it is a monument of a different kind, not 'overwhelming in its grandeur' but more important as a memorial and an innocuous reminder of both the horrors of war and the cruelty of man. The structure itself is not unattractive although Isambard Kingdom Brunel would not have approved. It is the facts behind the erection of the bridge that bring home an awareness to the casual visitor.

The nine curved spans on view are original while the two central square spans are post war-replacements. The latter spans were lost along with many Thai, allied POW and Japanese lives during allied bombing raids in 1945. Finished in 11 months, the steel bridge was constructed by manpower alone with a few pulleys and derricks. A wooden bridge was also built some 800 metres up river and this was finished in only eight months! At very low water some stumps still remain in view to this day.

At that time Japan did not recognise the Geneva Convention humanitarian code pertaining to POWs. This, coupled with malnutrition, tropical disease, cholera and general exhaustion resulted in over 18,000 POW deaths. This is a small figure when compared to the 100,000 Asiatic labourers who also lost their lives, 'recruited' by the Japanese to reinforce the allied contingent. Workers were marched along the track-bed to camps along the 415 kilometre route, finishing in Moulmein, Burma. Monsoon weather and flooding made conditions worse and many were simply buried where they fell. The lucky ones were buried in Kanchanaburi allied war cemeteries, well worth visiting if you haven't visited the JEATH museum first. Chung Kai cemetery is recommended as it takes a ferry ride and a pleasant river walk to reach there.

The **JEATH museum** (an acronym of Japan, England, Australia/America, Thailand and Holland) is a replica of a typical POW hut. Combined with the information and photographs on view this portrays a vivid impression of life 'working on the railway'. A cemetery trip after this is not high on the list of 'must do's'. Neither is a meal at the restaurant located on the former POW camp site. Don't miss the museum.

Albeit, this is a railway trip and at River Kwai Bridge station there are several locomotives, rolling stock and photographs on view depicting, once again, the 'lest we forget' theme. Most of the engines on view are war-time originals. One can walk across the bridge and contemplate all that it stands for from the quiet side of

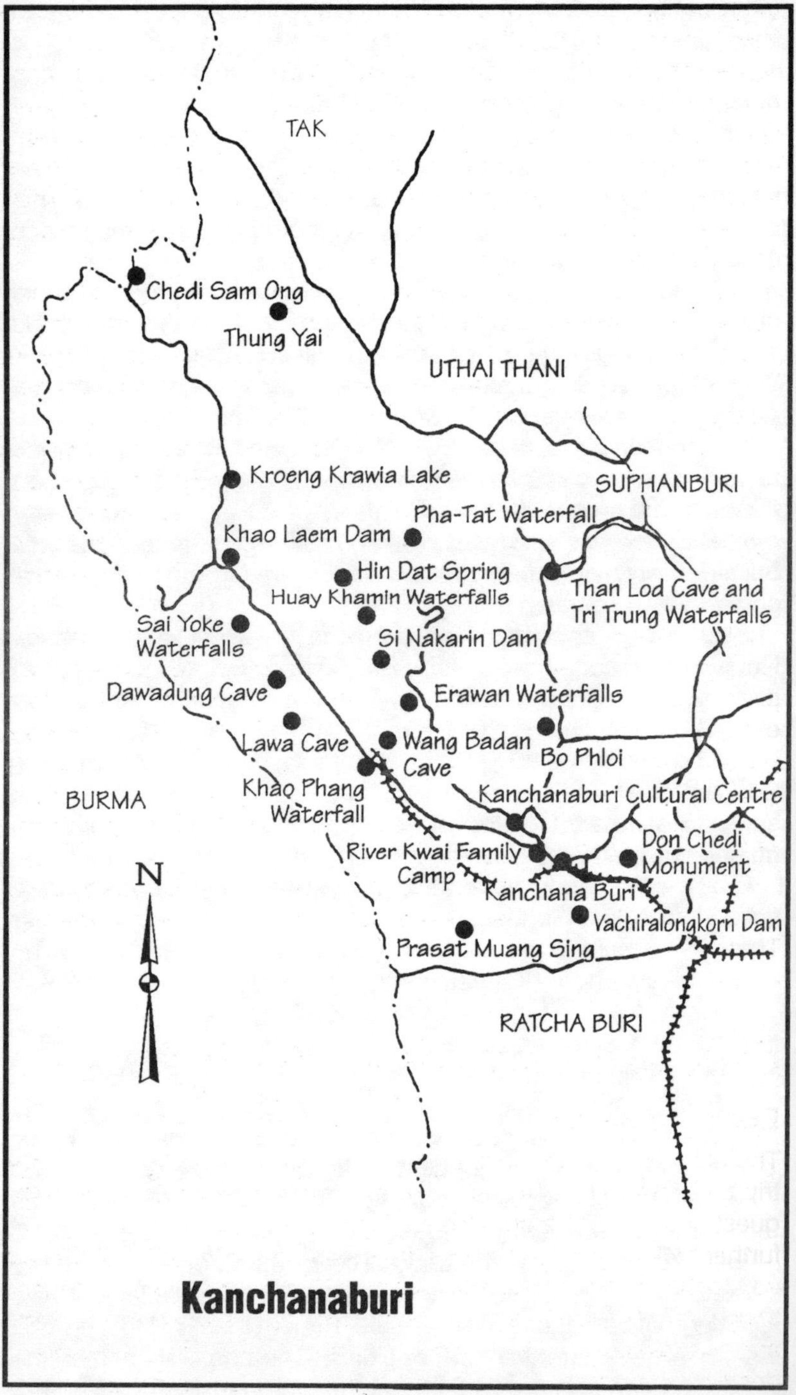
TAK
Chedi Sam Ong
Thung Yai
UTHAI THANI
SUPHANBURI
Kroeng Krawia Lake
Pha-Tat Waterfall
Khao Laem Dam
Hin Dat Spring
Than Lod Cave and
Tri Trung Waterfalls
Huay Khamin Waterfalls
Sai Yoke
Waterfalls
Si Nakarin Dam
Dawadung Cave
Erawan Waterfalls
Lawa Cave
Wang Badan
Cave
Bo Phloi
BURMA
Khao Phang
Waterfall
Kanchanaburi Cultural Centre
Don Chedi
Monument
River Kwai Family
Camp
Kanchana Buri
Vachiralongkorn Dam
Prasat Muang Sing
N
RATCHA BURI

Kanchanaburi

the river, but naturally the best way to cross is by the snail's pace train heading for Nam Tok.

After the bridge the land becomes lush and green with many cultivated properties penned between the line and the river bank. The highlight of this 75 minute scenic trip is the eerie, squeaky trundling of the train over the double wooden trestle viaduct at Wang Po, some 16km before Nam Tok. It's as scary as a slow roller coaster — it lasts too long and one questions if the carriage will stay on the tracks!

At this point one is only beginning to enter the lush jungle which claimed so many lives, for Three Pagodas Pass is still another 150km and Moulmein, the original terminus, is 350km away. Vegetation has now reclaimed the old track route and workers' camps beyond Nam Tok.

None of this should deter the potential Death Railway traveller for as morbid as it may seen the journey is highly recommended and the town of Kanchanaburi is an excellent place to spend a few days of relaxation. Raft or longtail boat trips on the river, waterfall visits and a general sense of international camaraderie are all available, some at no charge.

River Kwai Bridge Week is held annually during the last week of November and is aimed at increasing international awareness for a peaceful future. A party atmosphere prevails and amongst the many exhibits is a nightly *Son et Lumiere* show at 'The Bridge over the River Kwai' complete with fake air attacks and lots of fireworks. Special trains run from Hualamphong during this period and a special steam train usually runs on the last day. Book early for these trains, it's a popular festival.

Finally, don't expect to see the thick vegetation or the rocky waters from which Alec Guinness saw 'his' bridge destroyed in the film. That's in Sri Lanka.

OTHER SHORT TRIPS FROM BANGKOK

Erawan National Park

The rail connection here is at Kanchanaburi by regular bus and the trip takes two hours or you can rent a motor cycle from many of the guest houses. There are also special excursions by mini-bus. It is a further 1½km from the bus stop at Erawan and a motor bike will take you to the entrance. This is a very popular and 'developed' park and there is accommodation and camp sites. You can hire a tent. There are crowds at weekends and holidays. The area is covered in deciduous rain forest but the big attraction is the spectacular seven-tiered waterfall considered the most impressive in the country. The wildlife is similar in variety to that at Sai Yok National Park (see below).

Sai Yok National Park

Nam Tok, the rail connection to the park, is at the end of the line near the Burmese border. The town never intended itself to be inspiring and inspiring it is not: a small dusty settlement from which one can take a minibus 2km to the park. The more popular rail connection is at Kanchanaburi 100km away from where a bus may be taken. As in many other parks larger wildlife, such as elephant and tiger, are unusually observed, but here lives the two gram Kitt's hog-nosed bat which is probably the world's smallest mammal. There are also barking deer, white handed gibbons, wild pig, etc. Near the park headquarters is the waterfall that attracts many visitors. There are many creeks and rivers and one can take a long raft trip down to the Kwai Noi river. There are a number of quite spectacular limestone caves in the park. It is probably best to visit the park during the rainy season, broadly June to December.

Ayutthaya

The magnificent ancient city, Thailand's last capital, is on the northern Chiang Mai line. It takes one and a half hours to get there and there are eight trains a day. In order to avoid travelling both ways you can take the long river trip which leaves Tha Thien Pier at 10.00am or return by this method. Better still — and by special arrangement — the luxury river cruiser *Oriental Queen* can take you one way — but at huge expense. It leaves the Oriental Hotel Pier at 10.00am each day. (The city is on the Chao Phraya River.)

From the tiny railway station you can get a mini bus or other transport the short distance into town. Like Sukhothai this site is worth giving a lot of time to. It is very extensive. The atmosphere here is unique. But it is necessary to take it easy. There are plenty of *samlors* and *songthaews* to hire at reasonable rates. The drivers however are not guides and can rarely speak English. They will express their enthusiasm for the remarkable sites with pointing fingers and expansive grins.

Pattaya

This is not a real rail destination. There is however a train that leaves Hualamphong at 6.26 daily and arriving at Pattaya on its way to Ban Plu Ta Luang at 9.32, a slow trip. SRT intends to upgrade this line one day and run a regular service.

Pattaya itself, Thailand's well-known beach resort, has been deservedly receiving a bad press of late. The beach is quite attractive but the sea is only to be observed. It is highly polluted. There are a massive number of hotels, bars and places of entertainment. The atmosphere is not unpleasant and the bar girls who flock here — they not being interested in swimming at any rate — wear happy smiles and seem to spend all their time making beckoning signs to single middle aged male tourists — itself a spectacle, particularly if one is a middle aged male tourist.

Samut Songkhram

This short one hour trip to the Gulf of Thailand where the River Kwai enters the sea is not a tourist destination and for good reasons. It has, however, a certain appeal. Wong Wian Yai station is the starting point and this is situated on the far side of the Chao Phrya River not far from the Taksin Bridge crossing. A Herculean effort is required to find it, however, as it's surrounded by a dense market which spills over onto the platform. (All the decrepit stations on this route are similarly afflicted.) The trains are third class and are enough to cause respectable cattle to complain. They are extravagantly dirty and often crowded. It is an hourly service and all the signs are in Thai.

The line heads southwest, unfortunately skirting the salt marshes. Some of the most squalid slums in Thailand can be observed on the way. There are fetid hovels and large rats. Litter forms much of the landscape. The trip may be worth it for this reason — this is how *real* life is for many. Predictably the inhabitants maintain their dispositions. One wonders how.

The destination, a large, busy, heavily populated port, is bereft of tourists. It is a fishing and boat building region. The rough and not so rough sea food restaurants are superb but surprisingly no cheaper than Bangkok despite the sight of numerous prawn mountains. A boat trip can be taken but bargain hard. The boats can carry five passengers and should cost 150฿ for one hour.

The river mouth is thick with junks, sampans, long tail boats and other craft. Here in April and May a bar of worm shells which is quite spectacular can be observed. It's easy to get the bus back as an alternative but this arid road trip must represent the least rewarding hour that one can experience in the kingdom.

RAIL EXCURSIONS FROM BANGKOK

These organised trips are by diesel rail car. Many of the destinations can be reached by the ordinary lines but others are by train and bus and some involve a cooperation between SRT and a private operator. Unless there are sufficient passengers on certain specified excursions they don't run. The programmes also have a habit of changing with the speed of light. They are organised on weekends and public holidays. Meals are not included unless specified.

They represent excellent value. At certain times there is a heavy demand particularly for the Kanchanaburi region and SRT are developing new trips which could be interesting.

Ratchaburi, Khao Bin Cave

Includes Nakhon Pathom and floating market.
One day. Adult 140฿, child 100฿.

Hua Hin Beach

Includes Nakhon Pathom, time on beach, cloth printing factory.
One day. Adult 75฿, child 40฿.

Kusuma Resort, Jed Sao Noi Waterfalls

Also Thai Danish dairy farm.
One day. Adult 120฿, child 95฿.

Khao Pang Waterfall

Stops at Nakhon Pathom, River Kwai, Nam Tok, Kanchanaburi War Cemetery.
One day. Adult 75฿, child 40฿.

Khao Yai National Park

Includes bus. Lunch provided. This trip has been suspended due to new park rules but may be restored soon.
One day. Adult 140฿ Child 115฿.

River Kwai and Nam Tok

This one day excursion, which is a bit rushed, goes to Nakhon Pathom, River Kwai bridge, Mae Klong River, War cemetery, etc. You leave at 6.35am and get back at 7.35pm.
One day. Adult 280฿ Child 240฿.

River Kwai, Nam Tok, Krasae Cave Bridge

This two day excursion takes in Nakhon Pathom, Kwai bridge, Sai Yok Noi waterfalls, Krasae Cave bridge, and a night in a river rest house.
Two days. Adult 580฿ Child 400฿.

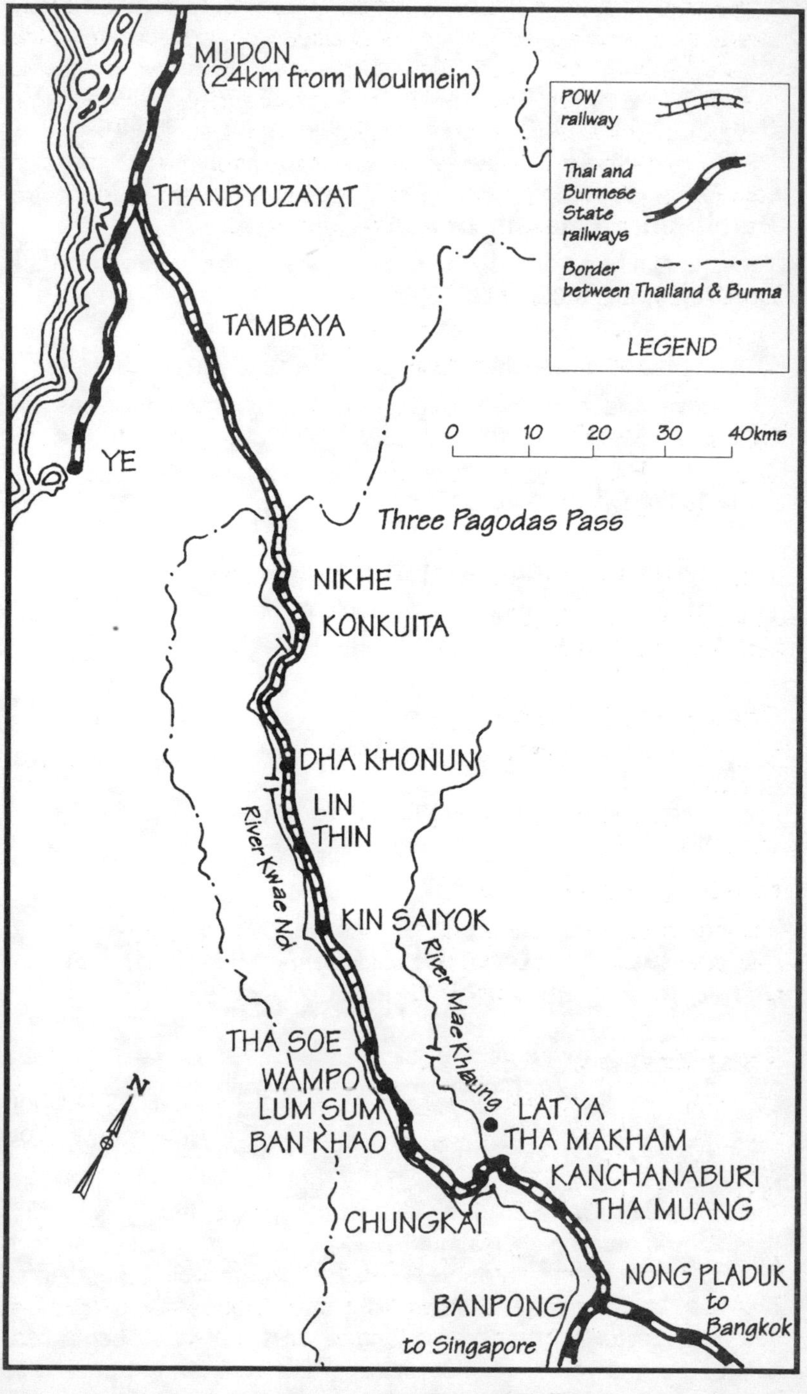
MUDON
(24km from Moulmein)
THANBYUZAYAT
TAMBAYA
YE
Three Pagodas Pass
NIKHE
KONKUITA
DHA KHONUN
LIN
THIN
River Kwae Noi
KIN SAIYOK
River Mae Khlaung
THA SOE
WAMPO
LUM SUM
BAN KHAO
LAT YA
THA MAKHAM
KANCHANABURI
THA MUANG
CHUNGKAI
NONG PLADUK
to
Bangkok
BANPONG
to Singapore
N
POW
railway
Thai and
Burmese
State
railways
Border
between Thailand & Burma
LEGEND
0 10 20 30 40kms

Sri Nakarin Dam and Erawan Waterfalls

This excursion goes to Nakhon Pathom, River Kwai bridge, bus to Sri Nakarin dam then Erawan Waterfalls then to Kanchanaburi.
One day. Adult 270฿ Child 235฿.

Petchaburi, Cha-am Beach

Takes in Nakhon Pathom. Includes bus. Beaches. Lunch provided.
One day. Adult 140฿ Child 100฿.

Chumphon, Saire Beach, Islands and caves

Two days and one night but group of six minimum necessary. Departs Fridays am. Beaches, islands, Ban Rubror, monkeys picking coconuts etc.
Adult 1300฿ Child 940฿.

Surat Thani, Samui, Ang Thong Islands

Three days and four nights. Six people minimum.
Takes in Big Buddha, Lamai Wats and museum. (This is a long way to go for a very short stay.)
Adult 2360฿ Child 1820฿.

Cambodian border

There is a special train leaving Bangkok daily at 6.00 and arriving at the border near Poipet, Cambodia at 12.00.

THE SOUTHERN LINE TO PADANG BESAR (WEST) *OR* SUNGAI KOLAK (EAST)

The panoramas that unfold on this journey are significantly different from those in the north and east. After the train crosses the Chao Phrya River and passes for some hours through some rather dreary countryside and less than interesting settlements and after the ubiquitous rice paddies we reach coconut and oil palm plantations and important towns, distant views of mountains, the eye catching limestone outcrops, Islamic areas with mosque-dominated conurbations, seemingly endless swathes of neat rubber plantations, and then you are on the border.

If you are taking the international express to Kuala Lumpur or Singapore and you are not stopping in Thailand (an unpardonable sin) then this train leaves at 15.15 hours.

Hua Hin

This, the oldest beach resort in the country, is on the western bank of the Gulf of Thailand. For railway buffs, if only for nostalgic reasons, it is a must. For others, if heading south to the more attractive Koh Samui, it is probably worth a limited stopover. Hua Hin has a rocky but extensive and agreeable beach.

There are 11 trains daily and the journey takes 3½ hours and the 'Sprinter' three hours.

The small railway station is the 'prettiest' in the country. It is painted in the old colours of cream and burgundy and it is rather like a cherished toy. The King's old waiting room in the shape of a temple is here. The town in effect was created by the railway and a small fishing village became a popular but nevertheless peaceful holiday resort. It remained that way for a long time. Regrettably the ambience has been recently impaired by a monstrous and desperately ugly high rise hotel that overlooks it.

The Sofitel Central Hua Hin Hotel however compensates for this unwarranted intrusion. It was built at the time of the railway but has been redeveloped since. It retains an elegant colonial aura. It is a luxury hotel, slightly removed from the town and is set in beautiful landscaped gardens. This was the original Railway Hotel and many of the old features have been retained, if a little artificially.

There is a dining room furnished as a railway carriage or is it the other way around? Some of the King's original dining utensils are on display. The cost of staying is very high indeed. Even if not staying you can ask to be guided around. Your guide will summon a liveried waiter who, after giving you a deep bow, will present you with a drink. Unfortunately this is only iced water but the gesture is worth a round of beers.

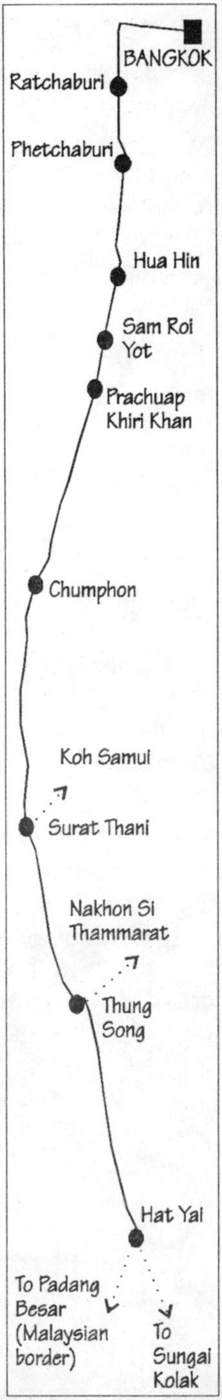

Khao Sam Roi Yot National Park

Access to this park is from Hua Hin and is a

little difficult. One suggestion is to take a tour organised by an agent. Otherwise you must take the bus to Pranburi to the park access and then hitch a ride 20km to the park entrance.

The name in Thai means 'the Mountain of Three Hundred Peaks' and there are particularly scenic views of the coastline from here. Also spectacular are the many limestone hills. Rarely seen but nevertheless sharing this habitat are the leopard cat, Javan mongoose, the slow loris, Malayan porcupine and the goat antelope. The real highlight is the spectacle of migratory birds which find sanctuary in the marshes and mud-flats, including herons, egrets, eagles, painted storks, etc.

There are some excellent walking trails and worthwhile caves to explore. Bungalows are available at park headquarters and there are two campsites. There has been, however, commercial exploitation of the area by shrimp and prawn farmers who have caused salination in the creeks.

Prachuap Khiri Khan

Approximately an hour and a half further south down the track, this provincial capital has been described with a fair measure of hyperbole as 'the Rio of Thailand'. The half cylindrical bay has its own 'Sugarloaf Mountain'. This is the narrowest point in Thailand. Burma is only 12km away. Scenic trips can be arranged up and down the coast and to Khao Sam Roi Yot National Park. Not many tourists have as yet discovered this part of the world.

Koh Samui and surrounding islands

If suffering from the malady of 'wat rejection' (too many temples in too short a time) then this might be your place. A period here will lead ineluctably to unconstrained lethargy and peace of mind. Koh Samui, not all that long ago, was populated only by fishermen and coconut palms and ... etc. The tourists, mainly young travellers, come in their thousands. Still, there are quiet beaches and the massive development is bungalow style and usually blends. The only real annoyance are the tourists themselves who roar around the island on motorbikes and with unfailing regularity fall off them. Chaweng and Lamai are the two best palm-fringed beaches and Boh Phut and Mai Nam have less attractive beaches but are much quieter and more genuine. The nearby island of Phangan is a favourite with young travellers. The less developed Koh Chao is further out and attracts divers. But even this 'getting away from it all' island has a large number of visitors getting away from it all.

Surat Thani is the jumping off station. There are nine trains a day. The journey takes about 11 hours from Bangkok except the 'Sprinter' which takes nine. This is a good trip to accomplish at night.

Surat Thani itself will not engage much attention. The nearer pier for the boat is 12km out of town. At the station are hordes of acceptably polite 'touts' selling boat tickets and bungalow accommodation.

The easiest, but not the quickest way, to the islands is by buying a train/boat ticket from an agent in the centres of Bangkok, Hua Hin or Hat Yai. Book early for the train in the busy times or weekends.

Once you get off the train there is no problem. You will be given all sorts of helpful advice and the buses are waiting. The express ferry *Songserm* leaves the Tha Thong Pier and takes two and a half hours to Koh Samui and three and a half to Phangan. The car ferry, which takes passengers, leaves Dom Sak Pier and is faster and more comfortable but perhaps less fun. The connecting buses for the car ferry sometimes don't go to the railway station but arrive and depart from the town centre which is confusing for someone arriving for the first time. All sorts of new ferry services are coming into operation.

From Surat Thani or better still Koh Samui you can visit the beautiful **Ang Thong National Marine Park** of 40 uninhabited islands. It is true there is little marine life here — the Andaman Sea off the west coast overshadows it in this respect — but the thickly forested limestone outcrops are spectacular. **Mae Hoh** possesses an eye catching luminously green lake. You can rent bungalows on Koh Wua Ja Lap but the park is normally experienced by a day trip. Most agents in Surat Thani or Koh Samui can organise this.

To Phuket

Surat Thani may seem a strange place to connect with Phuket, which is an island joining the mainland by a bridge in the Andaman Sea on the *west* coast. It is true that very few travellers from either direction use the rails for this trip but the advantage is that you can spend a comfortable night asleep on the train and then take an early morning bus from the town to Phuket — a spectacular journey through the mountains on a good road. Better still purchase a joint rail bus ticket at Bangkok or elsewhere (the carrier is Songserm Travel) and an air-conditioned coach will meet the train. Phuket itself is a very attractive island with white sand beaches and jungles; but there is a huge tourist population, much hotel development and many bars and nightclubs. The best time here weatherwise is between November and April. (The east and west coast have different monsoon seasons.) The lovely island of Phi Phi can be reached from here, as can Krabi, a quieter spot further down the coast.

Fishing boats at Koh Samui

King's Rest House, Hua Hin station

Hat Yai and Songkhla

This commercial centre is considered to be a border town despite being nowhere near the border. But it *is* a railway junction. Here the line divides to take the western and eastern branches down to Malaysia. It is 950km from Bangkok and the trip takes about 17 hours. It's probably better to get a rapid or express in the evening and reserve a sleeper. (Better still get off at Surat Thani for an island break.)

The station here is modern, spruce and a bit characterless. It has a hotel adjoining and an old locomotive on display. There is an information office and left luggage service. The centre of Hat Yai is only five minutes away and good accommodation is even closer.

The town itself is merely functional with plenty of contraband articles on sale. (When the police tried to close down these shops recently the complaints were so vociferous that they were immediately reinstated.) It is a satisfactory stop for one night unless you are a 'fun lover' when you might want to stay for ever: the place is alive with all forms of entertainment.

The train service to Songkhla has now been suspended. It is forty minutes by a fast and somewhat hair-raising taxi journey to this pleasant beach. The area is picturesque without any real grandeur, and there are few western tourists.

The water fowl sanctuary at Khu-Khut, which is an hour and a quarter further by bus, would make even a non ornithologist chirp with pleasure. The excursion on the flat bottomed boat is a memorable one and not only because of the bird life (see page 37).

Also within striking distance by bus from Hat Yai is the outstanding national park of **Thale Ban**, rarely featured in guide books. The area is covered in heavy rainforest. It doesn't suffer from 'people pollution' like many other parks. Furthermore, the bird life — there are over 200 varieties — is absorbing and ornithologists may see some rare species such as the bat hawk or peregrine falcon. You can usually observe gibbons and monkeys. Trails lead from the headquarters situated on an attractive lake. Along the way frog lovers will identify the numerous tree frogs and will not assume that the loud barking originates from ferocious dogs but in fact barking frogs. To get there you must take the Satun bus or inexpensive share-taxi and ask to be dropped at the park entrance 90km away.

Two side trips from Thum Song

Nakhon Si Thammarat

Two trains a day arrive here direct from Bangkok. You can of course pick them up anywhere along the line. It's about a 14½ hour trip to this major town. If in Hat Yai or Surat Thani then it's true that a bus is much quicker.

The smallish rather unprepossessing station is of temple design and has an ancient locomotive on display. All conveniences are provided but at night it serves as a haven for dossers who appear to have formed a convivial social club. The station is in town and accommodation is five minutes away.

Wat Phra Mahathat, the biggest in the south, is here. It is deeply impressive. The huge 14th Century chedi has been restored.

The town is also infamous as the murder and gangster centre of Thailand. Signs at some places of entertainment and restaurants ask patrons (in Thai) to leave their guns outside. Alas, on my visits here I failed to notice a single dishonourable person. All was disappointingly peaceful.

Thum Song

If stuck at this small railway junction for the night then it's probably best to pray for the morning. There is a dusty station, a lot of rolling stock, much shunting. Even the locals will tell you it's boring. The weekend market breaks the monotony. One can always walk up the main street and then walk down again. The station is ten minutes by motor bike out of town.

Trang

The other branch goes to Kan Tang which is a sea port but there's no reason for a traveller to go there. Trang is the attraction here. A neat, clean, interesting town, it is rarely visited by western tourists. There is one train a day from Bangkok arriving at 10.10.

The town is inland. Along the coast are good beaches some of which are dirty. There is a minor national park (**Hat Chao Mai**, of interest to bird-watchers) and some spectacular waterfalls. The islands off the coast are undeveloped and quite beautiful. There are many limestone outcrops.

Koh Hai (or Tai) is arguably the best island to visit. A shared taxi will take you to the pier at Pak Meng. Here everyone working for the boats on the pier is asleep but when the boat comes in they suddenly jump up and announce a stupendous sum to get there. You have to bargain. There are two or three official boats a day. The island itself has resorts. As yet accommodation is expensive.

CROSSING INTO MALAYSIA

If one is heading down to Kuala Lumpur is it best to go by the west coast (most do) or give the east coast a try? If the latter then you miss the splendid island of Penang. On the other hand you are in 'true' Malaysia, traditional, solidly Islamic and less developed. It is significantly more scenic. You pass through the jungle. The west coast has a far greater population with an ethnic mix, and a huge proportion of Chinese. For those on a budget the east coast is cheaper.

The western side: to Padang Besar and Butterworth (Malaysia)

You will have to take the international express and can pick it up anywhere along the route. It leaves Bangkok at 15.15 daily, Hat Yai at 7.20 the next morning, crosses the border an hour later and arrives in Butterworth at 12.25 Malaysian time. The customs and immigration formalities (at Padang Besar) are fairly quick. The train waits an hour. The station itself is dusty, narrow and of dismal appearance. Remember that this Thai train continues on over the Malaysian line. You will need change to a Malaysian train when you reach Butterworth. The situation has recently changed. You may change at Butterworth or at the border, so check locally. (The Kuala Lumpur train leaves at 14.25.)

Langkawi Island(s) (Malaysia)

If you want to go to the island of Langkawi (see page 178) then you can take a taxi — very cheaply — at Padang Besar. (The train doesn't stop at the nearer station of Alor Star but it does if travelling north.) From the crowded ferry terminal — soon to be redeveloped at Kuala Perlis — it's a 45 minute trip in real comfort to this fascinating destination. The island is becoming better known these days and a new bitumen road around it has things much easier. The place has a natural non touristy atmosphere mainly because of its size and its large working population involved with rice, rubber, palm oil and coconuts. **Pantai Cenang** is the popular beach destination with reasonable accommodation. You can also reach the island by ferry from Penang.

The eastern side: to Sungai Kolak and Pasir Mas (Malaysia)

There are two trains a day, one leaving Bangkok at 12.35, Hat Yai 4.32 next morning and arriving at Sungai Kolak at 8.35. The second leaves Bangkok at 14.00, arrives in Hat Yai at 5.47 next morning and reaches Sungai Kolak at 9.40. (Third class is available on these trains.)

This is rubber plantation country. You will pass through the rather uninteresting configuration of concrete (Pattani) to the clean and bright Muslim town of Yala. This may be worth a stop but there are naturally enough more interesting Muslim towns in Malaysia.

At Sungai Kolak you've reached the end of the line. There is no rail connection with Malaysia. It is necessary to walk over the bridge or get a motor cycle — there are many of them — for a ten minute trip to the frontier. Customs and immigration are side by side. The passenger service from here has been suspended. You can therefore get a taxi to Pasir Mas, the nearest rail link, and head south. But it would be a pity to miss the interesting town of Kota Bharu and it's a very cheap shared taxi ride on to there.

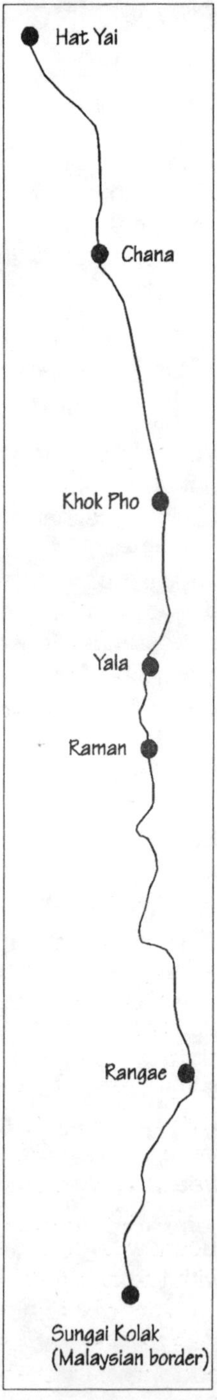

> On the island of Koh Samui in Thailand one of the major causes of unnatural death is by coconuts falling on the head, although no foreigners (*farangs*) appear to have suffered this fate.

Chapter 11

On the Rails in Malaysia

WEST COAST LINE

Butterworth (and Penang)

Butterworth station is due for redevelopment which according to KTM will happen soon. There are few facilities. A left luggage service however is available. There is a clear departure and arrival board. An ancient engine is on display. The station, which is an unprepossessing structure with corrugated fibre roof, is really an extension of the ferry terminal. You get to the pier on metal walkways. The ferries for the short trip to Georgetown, Penang's capital, operate twenty four hours a day and are very regular. One will leave every twenty minutes for a ludicrously cheap fare. The ride is free on the way back.

Georgetown, which is largely Chinese, is a happy mix of old ornate shops and houses, interesting colonial buildings and temples and high rise developments. Transport is by trishaw, usually with Tamil drivers who will even take you to places you don't want to go to. There is a very worthwhile funicular railway extension up Penang Hill for a spectacular view. It is best to avoid going to the hill on weekends and holidays as you can wait an hour or more.

The beaches of Penang are splendid but don't possess the translucent waters of the east coast. There are 'comfortable' tourist spots with luxury hotels. Batu Ferringhi is a favourite beach destination.

For onward train bookings and reservations there is no need to take the ferry across the straits to Butterworth. There is an efficient booking office at the terminal on the island (tel: 04-610290), at Weld Quay.

There are five trains a day going on to Kuala Lumpur via Ipoh. The international express leaves Butterworth at 15.00, arriving at Kuala Lumpur at 21.50. Another express leaves at 7.30 arriving at 14.40. The slow trains take nine hours or more. Make sure you leave Georgetown early so as to accommodate the ferry crossing.

For shorter distances there are one or two rail cars per day, eg between Butterworth and Arau, Ipoh and Butterworth, Ipoh and Kuala Lumpur.

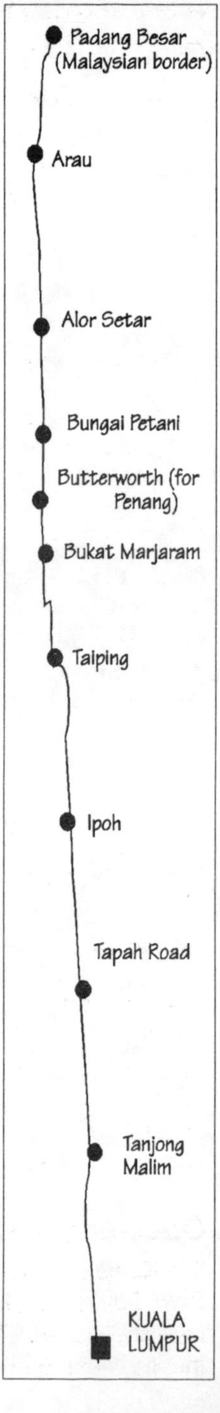

Tapah Road and the Cameron Highlands

The run down towards Kuala Lumpur passes through two old tin mining towns of Taiping and Ipoh, the capital of Perak.

Taiping has a railway past. Malaysia's first line, built to transport tin ore to the port of Port Weld, was constructed here in 1885. It has been closed (see page 6).

Not far from the town is the tiny peaceful hill station of Maxwell Hill (**Bukit Larut**), certainly worth stopping off to see if you are not going to the Cameron Highlands which are much more interesting. It is a challenge to walk up to the top along the sharply winding road. Three and a half hours should be allowed. Otherwise government transport in the shape of landrovers can be hired at the station above Taiping Lake Gardens.

Ipoh is a sprawling city and has a detectable 'rough' atmosphere. There are excellent restaurants but very little to see. Its attraction may be the large railway station (left luggage counter is open 24 hours per day). Attached to it is the amazing colonial neoclassic hotel. Not for asthmatics: dust lies everywhere. But the high ceilinged rooms are worth staying in. It is often booked as is nearly everything else in Ipoh on weekends. Once famous for its meals the enormous dining room with threadbare carpet is frequently empty. This may have something to do with the fact that the portions are so small as to be in danger of being blown off the plate by the many ceiling fans.

The city is of historical interest because of the tin mines and the Chinese settlements.

Tapah Road is five comfortable hours from Butterworth and just over two hours on the fast trains from Kuala Lumpur. Here you can take the not-to-be-missed trip up into the misty hills. The tops provide coolness and an 'ever so English' ambience and architecture (sweet cottages, etc).

The tiny railway station, three miles from the town of Tapah, has left luggage facilities. There are odd taxis waiting here for the train. You can go to the bus station in town and await the hourly bus or share a taxi to the top for M$8 which is good value considering the difficult winding ascent (itself an experience). You will end up at Ringlet, Tanah Rata or Brinchang. There are all grades of (rather tame) jungle walks, all sorts of excursions to such sites as tea plantations and butterfly farms — significantly more fascinating than they sound — and an opportunity to 'take tea' with strawberries and cream and adopt a reserved demeanour like many of the local people.

Buses and taxis will take you back. The buses sometimes arrive late so allow for this if catching the train.

SHORT TRIPS FROM KUALA LUMPUR

Port Kelang

There are four trains a day each way and all are railcars. It takes one and a half hours to get there. The ride is fast and a bit bumpy through the outer suburbs of Kuala Lumpur. Though not dramatic, this is nevertheless a pleasant journey. The station is at the port on the river. There are splendid views of steamships and fishing boats and an overcrowded craft will take you on a harbour cruise. This is certainly not a tourist location. It is a busy commercial port. The total absence of tourists provides an extra dimension of interest. The sunsets here are spectacular.

Odds and sods

If in Kuala Lumpur at the weekend it is possible to reach the famous Batu Caves 13 kilometres away by train. The railway station is quite near the caves. The departure is at 9.00am and return at 11.30, an inconvenient time.

RAIL EXCURSIONS FROM KUALA LUMPUR

Langkawi

These islands are right up off the northwest coast near the Thai border (see page 173) and are rarely visited by foreign tourists because of the attractions of nearby Penang. Their remoteness is their appeal and some of the beaches are pleasantly isolated.

Departures are every Tuesday, Thursday and Saturday organised by KTM and the tour lasts four days. The cost is M$224 with optional extras.

This region is a duty free area.

Reservations are on 03-274 9422, fax 03-274 9424.

Kenong Rimba Park

Another KTM organised tour. This one is for three days and four nights. You stop off at Kuala Lipis station and take a boat. The rest of the time is spent mainly jungle trekking.

Reservations should be made ten days in advance on 03-274 7435 where the current cost of the trip will be passed on.

Langkawi Island

FROM KUALA LUMPUR SOUTH TO SINGAPORE

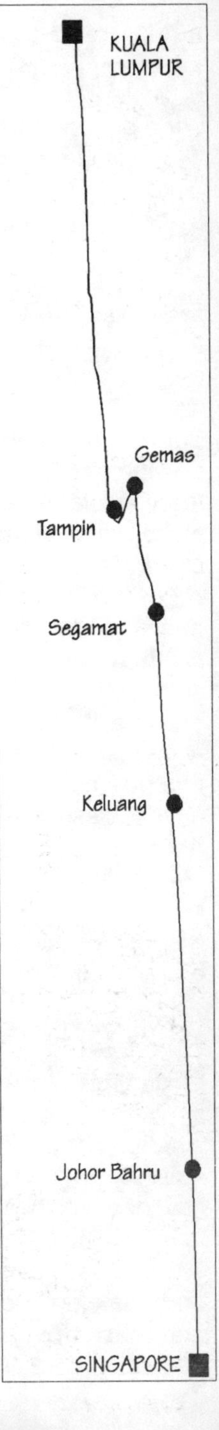

Continuing south the first significant station is Tampin, gateway to **Malacca**. This fascinating city is quite a distance from the line. It is no doubt simpler if coming from Kuala Lumpur to get the bus direct. But do not be tempted. The bus passes along a new highway through nothing but rubber plantations. Of course, on the train, you may be underwhelmed by these extensive estates but at least there are a number of *kampongs* to be seen. You will also go through Seremban, the capital of Negri Sembilan, an attractive town with housing of unique design. This town also used to be the connecting link to Port Dickson but the old and interesting line to this is not so interesting destination is not now used for passenger traffic.

There are five trains a day and it takes an hour and a quarter on the fast ones.

For many Malacca is Malaysia's most agreeable surprise. It is an hour by bus from near the station at Tampin. The attraction of course is its amazing history. Malay, Chinese, Portuguese, Dutch and British influences intermingle. Trishaw is the method of transport recommended but walking is probably better through the old town. A trip down the river, which is genuinely filthy, will give you the sight of crocodiles, huge monitor lizards, desperate shanty dwellings, half sunken hulks and mud. The smell is also worthy of comment.

The train then proceeds to Gemas the junction with the eastern route. You would have to come down this far if taking this route north. We then proceed on to Johore Bahru. Because of this town's proximity to Singapore, which is just across the causeway, it is of little interest to the international visitor. Customs and immigration procedures are carried out on the train here and at Singapore station. There's no need to get off.

THE EASTERN ROUTE GOING NORTH FROM SINGAPORE

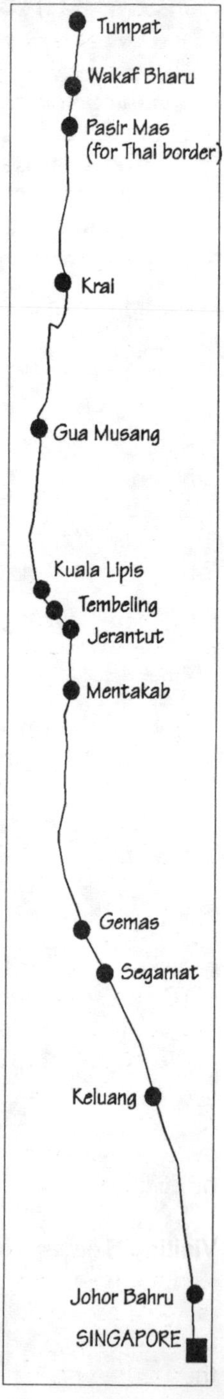

For a general description of this line see page 149. The atmosphere in the carriage is usually quite jolly. If leaving Singapore it is necessary to be at the station half an hour before for customs and immigration procedures.

There is one train a day, the 20.00 arriving at Gemas 01.51. The connection is at 2.20 and the whole trip, Singapore to Pasir Mas (the train goes on to Tumpat) is 15 hours. There are also rail buses running shorter distances. Both trains are ordinary which means there are no sleepers but there is a dining car. Usually there is plenty of room. You can, of course, make reservations. There is second and third class.

The condition of the trains and the service provided including meals is not up to the high standard of the western line. There are 34 stops to Pasir Mas.

It is a pity that the first part of this trip is accomplished at night as the jungle views — though no animals or bird life — are nevertheless absorbing for a time. The line runs virtually through the centre of the peninsula and one has to sacrifice the eastern coast with its beautiful remote beaches and islands. If you are heading for Thailand then you are fully compensated for this loss there.

Kuala Lipis and Kenong Rimba Park

Kuala Lipis is not a tourist destination, just a large sleepy pleasant town edging onto the jungle. The park, which is designed for recreation rather than as a 'wilderness park', nevertheless has some excellent short and long trail walks through the dense forests. There is also cave exploring, fishing, swimming and camping. However there's absolutely no point in stopping here if you're on your way to Taman Negara. The only reason would be to get a touch of the atmosphere of 'the green centre' of the peninsula in the shortest possible time. The jetty is not far away from the railway station at Sungai Jelai and a sampan will take you on an enjoyable 20 minute ride to Tanpung Kiara. You can reserve through the Tourist Information Centre at Kuala Lipis Station, tel: 09-313277, fax: 09-313302. Guides can be hired. The wildlife here doesn't compete with that in Taman Negara. It is more of a 'picnic area'.

Tembeling, Jerantut and Taman Negara

Taman Negara is the big attraction on this line. If you are interested in jungles you'd probably have a better short experience here than in the Brazilian rain forest.

In most wild life sanctuaries outside Africa there is a paucity of mammals — and here it's the same — the flora and bird life make up for it. There are river trips, fishing, jungle treks, camping and accessible hides and salt licks where there is a meagre possibility of seeing say a tapir or a tiger. (I know someone who swears he's seen both here.) But you need time and patience.

The park is very well organised — the adventurous would say too much so. There is provision for all grades of visitors. It is closed from mid November to mid January. You can book accommodation in Kuala Lumpur (tel. 03-2915299). If you don't book you might find that you have to stay in a tent which is no bad thing.

The station, or rather siding, for the park is Tembeling Halt but you arrive here at 5.26 when it is pitch black. Without a torch it is unwise to move from the station (you'll end up sliding). You must also tell the guard on the train to stop here. It is also possible to get to the park from Jerantut.

From Tembeling it is half an hour's walk along the main road (turn right) to the river. There are boat trips at 9.00am and 2.00pm and some more besides. It is three hours into the park.

To continue north it is necessary to leave the park the afternoon before (boats leave at 9.00 and 2.00, but 2.30 on Fridays). You take a shared taxi or bus to Jerantut. This is a pleasant friendly town with good simple accommodation. The train north departs at 5.08 requiring an early call and a dark walk to the nearby station. As everyone around at that time is conscious of this event you will have no difficulties.

Visiting Taman Negara from the north If you are heading for Kuala Lumpur then the train leaves Pasir Mas near the Thai border at 14.41 arriving at Jerantut at 20.42 where you can spend the night. In the morning a shared taxi or bus will take you to the boat, and thus to the park.

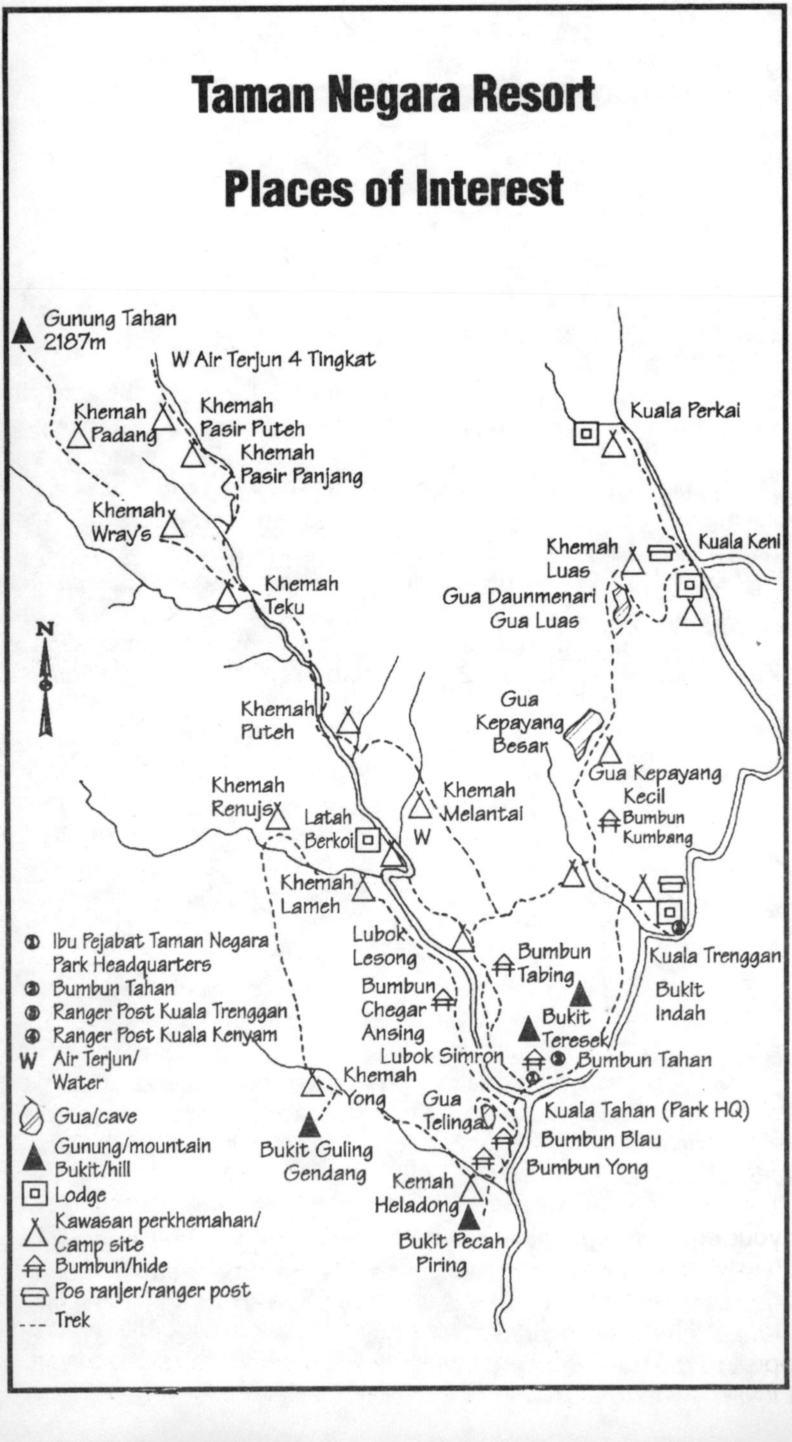
Taman Negara Resort
Places of Interest
Gunung Tahan
2187m
W Air Terjun 4 Tingkat
Khemah Padang
Khemah Pasir Puteh
Khemah Pasir Panjang
Khemah Wray's
Khemah Teku
N
Kuala Perkai
Khemah Luas
Kuala Keni
Gua Daunmenari
Gua Luas
Gua Kepayang Besar
Khemah Puteh
Gua Kepayang Kecil
Bumbun Kumbang
Khemah Renujs
Latah Berkoi
W
Khemah Melantai
Khemah Lameh
Lubok Lesong
Bumbun Tabing
Kuala Trenggan
Bukit Indah
Bumbun Chegar Ansing
Bukit Teresek
Lubok Simron
Bumbun Tahan
Khemah Yong
Gua Telinga
Kuala Tahan (Park HQ)
Bumbun Blau
Bumbun Yong
Bukit Guling Gendang
Kemah Heladong
Bukit Pecah Piring
① Ibu Pejabat Taman Negara Park Headquarters
② Bumbun Tahan
③ Ranger Post Kuala Trenggan
④ Ranger Post Kuala Kenyam
W Air Terjun/ Water
Gua/cave
Gunung/mountain Bukit/hill
Lodge
Kawasan perkhemahan/ Camp site
Bumbun/hide
Pos ranjer/ranger post
Trek

CONTINUING NORTH TO PASIR MAS, KOTA BHARU AND THAILAND

The terminus of this line is at Tumpat but the nearest station to the Thai border is Pasir Mas. The desired stop over would be Kota Bharu (the new spelling is Baru) further on which is served by the station at Wakaf Bharu which is a long way from town. It is sensible therefore to alight at Pasir Mas and take a bus or shared taxi into Kota Bharu or alternatively get the taxi or bus on to the border. (Maps indicate that the line goes on to the frontier at Rantau Panjang. This is true but because of limited use the passenger service has been suspended.)

As has been said, you are somewhat disadvantaged in one way by taking the eastern (or central) line in that the very popular island of Tioman is missed. The islands further up the east coast, eg Kapas (opposite Marang) are quieter. Kota Bharu gives access to the sea but the beach here, 'The Beach of Passionate Love', is disappointing. The town itself, the capital of Kelantan, is solidly Islamic and traditional. The state wants to change its legal system to the Islamic code which may have a negative effect on travellers. The place itself is friendly. There is much new eye catching architecture The food stalls are perhaps the best in the region.

The Thai consulate is here if you need a visa but it will be closed on certain Malay and Thai holidays. Allow 2-3 working days. From the main bus station you can take a 1½ hour journey to the border at Rantau Panjang. Customs and immigration are side by side. There are money changers but Malay money is accepted in Sungai Kolak. You will have to walk the short distance across the frontier which is formed by the Golak River.

Thai time is one hour behind Malaysian time. There are two trains per day going north to Hat Yai and Bangkok, one at 10.10 and the next at 11.25.

Perhentian Islands

From Kota Bharu it is a 1½ hour bus trip to **Kuala Beset**, a peaceful fishing village which is the jumping off point for the two Perhentian Islands. There is a regular boat service and it takes 40 minutes.

It is not quite understood why these lovely islands, where peace is your constant companion, are not on the tourist map and have escaped development but this is, of course, the great attraction: namely isolation. The white beaches and clear green waters here are amongst the best in the whole region. Paradise is for once the appropriate word. There are jungles and coconut groves and a host of idyllic views. The place is for those who don't mind 'roughing it'

— there are very few amenities although diving equipment and guidance is provided for coral reef viewing.

There is one high grade bungalow resort and the rest of the accommodation is very basic. Water comes from wells. Many might think that this is a considerably higher state of existence than that provided by creature comforts. Perhentian Kecil contains a village but the larger island of Perhentian Besar across the channel has the accommodation.

Taman Negara

If coming from the north into Malaysia then the two trains arrive in Sungai Kolak at 8.35 and 9.40 respectively, ample time to connect with the single south going Malay train, which leaves Pasir Mas at 14.41, even allowing for the difference in Malay time.

Endpieces

STEAMING ALONG: MERELY A MEMORY

Thailand

No steam locomotives are used on the tracks today except for a limited number of special trains run on certain public holidays by private arrangements and these are noted below. See page 164 for details of the special steam excursion to the River Kwai and see also page 5 for a short history of Thai railways.

Railway enthusiasts will welcome an excursion to the new **Thai Railway Hall of Fame** in Bangkok, opened as recently as September 1990. Short on exhibits but a mine of information, it is open on Saturdays and Sundays from 9.00-13.00.

Situated at the northern end of Chatachak Park, it is easy to combine with a trip to the famous **Chatachak Weekend Market** where one can buy anything and everything. Local enthusiasts gather at the museum (formerly housing the Royal Train) and are vehement in their pursuit of information from foreign visitors.

In front of the building is the museum's pride and joy, a 33 Soongnern steam locomotive, Japanese built and restored in Thailand. The locomotive saw service in Nakhon Ratchasima some 40 years ago hauling firewood trains. Appropriately this region saw the completion of the first phase of Thailand's national railway system. A detailed history of the nation's railways is found inside the museum as well as a general exhibit on the development of world railways.

The Hall of Fame is administered by the Thai Railway Fan Club, a non-profit organisation with offices in Samsen Road, Bangkok (243

2037-9). Mr Sanpsiri Viryasiri, club president, will be glad to 'talk trains' if you telephone him. Better still, see him at the museum at weekends.

Malaysia

It is a pity that there are no steam engines in use today as the age of steam in this country was a somewhat romantic one (see page 5). The locomotive buff is referred to *Locomotive Centennial* by Hafi Shamsuddin, first published in 1985 and available at some book shops and at Kuala Lumpur main station. The work gives a tremendously detailed and technical account of the railway development together with listing and photographs of locomotives used — a few of which are available for inspection at some main stations and elsewhere.

FURTHER READING

Thailand

Thailand: A Travel Survival Kit (Lonely Planet).
Everyone and his dog seems to have this book. Masses of detailed information and good local maps.

Travellers Guide to Thailand by Seen Sanuk. (Published by the *Nation Newspaper*)
A splendid guide, published at an economic price. Only available in Thailand.

Thailand: the Rough Guide by Paul Gray and Lucy Ridout (1992).
Bang up to date, concise and splendidly organised and winner of the 1993 Thomas Cook Travel Guide Award, this may be the most practical guide to the region. Published by Rough Guides and distributed by Penguin.

Thailand: Collins Illustrated Guide (Collins)
Concise. Excellent limited descriptions and good photographs but takes in only main destinations.

The Insiders Guide to Thailand (Asia Books)
Very detailed and good photographs.

Thailand: The Lotus Kingdom by Alastair Shearer (John Murray)
Travel literature at its best.

Cockatoo's Handbook: Thailand
An encyclopedic, accurate, in depth guide detailing even the obscure parts of the country missed by other guides. Heavy, prosaic and intensely useful for those who want to make a serious study of the region.

Insight Guide to Thailand (Apa Publications)
Probably the best photography of any guide with prose to match. A bit heavy to carry.

The Balancing Act: A History of Modern Thailand by Joseph J Wright Jr (Asia Books, Bangkok).
Up to date and very readable, though 'political'. Does not, of course, take in the May 1992 uprising.

Monsoon Country by Pira Sudham (Shire Books, Bangkok)
People of Esarn (Issan) by Pira Sudham (Shire Books, Bangkok)
Despite the former being a novel, a moving account of life in the northeast.

Culture Shock: Thailand by Robert & Nanthapa Cooper.
Just the right things for the train. Informative and highly amusing.

Jim Thompson: The Legendary American of Thailand by William Warren (Jim Thomson Thai Silk Company)
Overdramatised but fascinating. Good for the train.

Temples of Thailand: their form and function by Michael Freeman (Asia Books, Bangkok)
A guide in photography to this fascinating subject with simple readable descriptions.

Bound Tightly with Banana Leaves by Nicholas Greenwood (Right Now Books)
An amusing, observant account of travels through Burma, Vietnam, Laos and Thailand.

National Parks of Thailand by Denis Gray, Collin Piprell, Mark Graham. Published by Communications Resources (Thailand) Ltd.
The perfect companion for the train travelling naturalist. Published in soft back at a reasonable price, it gives a clear and smack up to date account of the parks in the region with stunning photography.

Waylaid by the Bimbos by James Eckart. Published by Post Publishing Co Ltd, Bangkok.
Despite the title, this is a highly acclaimed, wonderfully humorous (and sometimes wonderfully serious) account of *farang* life in Thailand; but reading it on the train could disturb other passengers.

Malaysia and Singapore

Malaysia, Singapore & Brunei: A Travel Survival Kit (Lonely Planet)
Competes with the Koran as the most popular book in the region.

Insight Malaysia and Insight Singapore (Apa Publications)
Big, detailed and excellent photographs.

Collins Illustrated Guide to Malaysia and *Collins Illustrated Guide to Singapore*
Concise up to date and very readable with good photographs. Only

highlights main tourist destinations.

Malaysia: The New Straits Times Annual (Benita Publishing SDN.BHD, Kuala Lumpur)
Current articles on almost everything from fashion to insect life with excellent photography.

In Malaysia by Stella Martin and Denis Walls (Bradt Publications)
An excellent guide to the way of life in Malaysia with travel information as well.

A Short History of Malaysia, Singapore and Brunei by C. Mary Turnbull (Cassel Australia)
A clear and concise account of the region's history.

Living Crafts of Malaysia by Sheppard, Mubin.
The best and easiest to absorb account of Malay crafts. Illustrated.

Malayan Animal Life by M Tweedie & J Harrison (Longman)
Longstanding and educative work for the naturalist.

The Birds of the Malay Peninsula, Singapore and Penang (Oxford University Press)
More for the ornithologist than the layman.

The Malayan Trilogy by Anthony Burgess.
Now published under the title *The Long Day Wanes* (Penguin)
A novel — or three — in which Burgess sets out to teach and entertain. And succeeds.

Culture Shock: Singapore and Malaysia by Jo Ann Craig. A readable investigation into these societies, aimed at increasing cultural awareness in the visitor.

The Singapore Grip by J G Farrell (Fontana Paperback)
Good for the train. Quality fiction by a master craftsman.

The Consul's File by Paul Theroux (Penguin)
The well known travel writer presents some clever colonial stories with humour.

In Search of Conrad by Gavin Young (Penguin)
Joint winner of the 1992 Thomas Cook award, it brilliantly evokes the past and convincingly describes the present. The region becomes alive. A gem.

TIMETABLES AND FARES: THAILAND

NORTHERN LINE: OUTGOING												
STATIONS		RAP 35	SPRIN-TER 907	SPRIN-TER 901	RAP 37	SPRIN-TER 903	EXP 7	RAP 53	EXP SP 5	RAP 57	RAP 59	SPRIN-TER 905
Bangkok	Dep	06.40	08.10	10.55	16.00	16.35	18.00	18.10	19.40	20.00	22.00	23.10
Samsen	Dep	06.52	08.21	11.05	15.12	16.46	18.12	18.20	19.50	20.10	22.10	23.21
Bangsue	Dep	07.02	08.28	11.11	15.19	16.52	18.19	18.27	19.57	20.17	22.17	23.27
Bangkhen	Dep		08.36	11.19		17.00		18.37				23.35
DONMUENG	Dep	07.23	08.47	11.31	15.42	17.13	18.43	18.53	20.20	20.40	22.43	23.46
Ayutthaya	Arr	08.02			16.19		19.22	19.34	20.59	21.20	23.22	
Lopburi	Arr	09.02	10.10		17.27		20.23	20.38		22.20	00.25	
Nakhornsawan	Arr	10.33	11.35	14.14	19.06	20.00	21.57	22.10	23.27	23.57	01.59	02.57
Taphanhin	Arr	11.35	12.25	15.15	20.10	20.57	22.57	23.15		01.25	03.15	03.58
Phichit	Arr	11.58		15.37	20.36	21.20	23.19	23.52		01.50	03.40	04.35
PHITSANULOK	Arr	12.33	13.13	16.10	21.15	22.00	00.06	00.35		02.29	04.27	05.15
Uttaraditr	Arr	13.54	14.20	*****	23.04	*****	01.32	02.11		03.55	05.59	*****
Sila At	Arr	13.59			23.11		01.38	02.20	03.01	04.00	06.06	
Denchai	Arr	14.56	15.12		00.29		02.56	*****	04.04	04.55	07.14	
Lampang	Arr	17.34	17.07		03.00		05.15		06.06		09.37	
CHIANGMAI	Arr	19.45	19.00		05.15		07.25		08.05		11.55	

NORTHERN LINE: INCOMING

STATIONS		RAP 58	SPRIN-TER 906	RAP 38	EX 8	SPRIN-TER 908	SP EX 6	RAP 60	SPRIN-TER 902	RAP 51	RAP 36	SPRIN-TER 904
CHIANGMAI	Dep			15.30	16.40	19.50	21.05	20.40			06.35	
Lampang	Dep			17.50	18.59	21.29	23.10	22.49			08.50	
Denchai	Dep	19.00		20.11	21.18	23.28	01.23	00.59			10.55	
Sila At	Dep	20.03		21.17	22.25		02.25	02.09		07.10	11.58	
Uttaraditr	Dep	20.10		21.25	22.33	00.19		02.15		07.16	12.04	
PHITSANULOK	Dep	21.42	22.45	22.55	23.49	01.22		04.12	08.50	09.05	13.50	16.55
Phichit	Dep	22.24	23.21	23.37	00.24	01.53		04.53	09.23	09.41	14.26	17.28
Taphanhin	Dep	22.50	23.42	00.02				05.18	09.44	10.04	14.50	17.49
Nakhornsawar	Dep	00.16	00.50	01.18	02.01	03.01	05.44	06.23	10.46	11.16	15.54	18.46
Lopburi	Dep	02.02		03.05	03.36			07.57		13.06	17.29	20.18
Ayutthaya	Dep	03.02		04.09	04.37		08.17	09.06		14.02	18.43	
DONMUENG	Arr	03.41	04.04	04.48	05.16	05.43	08.56	09.43	13.40	14.39	19.23	21.49
Bangkhen	Arr		04.18			05.55			13.51	14.52		22.00
Bangsue	Arr	04.03	04.27	05.11	05.41	06.06	09.20	10.06	13.59	15.02	19.47	22.08
Samsen	Arr	04.13	04.33	05.18	05.48	06.13	09.27	10.13	14.05	15.08	19.54	22.14
BANGKOK	Arr	04.25	04.45	05.30	06.00	06.25	09.40	10.25	14.15	15.20	20.05	22.25

Northeastern Line: Bangkok-Ubon Ratchathani/Nong Khai										
Stations		RAP 31	ORD 63	RAP 39	EXP 1 SL	RAP 51	ORD 65	RAP 33	RAP 29	EXP 3
		2-3	2-3	2-3	1-2-3	2-3	2-3	2-3	2-3	2-3
Bangkok	d	06.50	15.25	18.45	21.00	22.45	23.25	06.15	19.00	20.30
Don Muang	d	07.35	16.12	19.26	21.42	23.26	00.09	16.55	19.42	21.12
Ayutthaya	d	08.14	16.59	20.07	22.24	00.08	00.56	07.32	20.23	21.54
Ban Phachi	d	08.35	17.24	20.29	‖	‖	01.19	07.52	‖	‖
Saraburi	d	08.57	17.58	20.52	23.06	00.48	01.54	08.14	21.01	22.36
Kaeng Khoi Jn	d	09.10	18.19	21.05	23.25	01.03	02.21	08.27	21.15	22.53
Muak Lek	d	09.44	19.02	‖	‖	01.45	03.31			
Pak Chong	d	10.17	19.40	22.24	00.38	02.36	04.08			
Nakhon Ratchasima	d	11.36	21.28	23.56	01.58	04.02	05.35			
Thanon Chira Jn	d	11.44	21.35	00.08	‖	04.09	05.41			
Lam Plai Mat	d	12.53	23.41	01.15	‖	05.23	07.18			
Buri Ram	a	13.17	00.12	01.46	03.35	05.52	07.55			
Surin	a	14.05	01.07	02.36	04.20	06.42	08.55			
Sikhoraphum	a	14.36	02.00	03.11	04.57	07.16	09.46			
Si Sa Ket	a	15.40	03.13	04.16	05.57	08.26	11.03			
Ubon Ratchathani	a	16.45	04.20	05.20	07.05	09.35	12.20			
Bua Yai Jn	a							12.19	01.21	02.59
Ban Phai Jn	a							13.29	02.35	04.06
Kkon Kaen	a							14.06	03.16	04.47
Udon Thani	a							15.56	05.15	06.33
Nong Khai	a							16.50	06.15	07.30

Northeastern Line: Bangkok-Ubon Ratchathani/Nong Khai

Stations		ORD 64	RAP 52	RAP 40	EXP 2 SL	RAP 32	ORD 62	RAP 30	EXP 4 SL	RAP 34
		2-3	2-3	2-3	1-2-3	2-3	2-3	2-3	1-2-3	2-3
Nong Khai	d							17.40	19.00	07.40
Udon Thani	d							18.41	19.55	08.34
Khon Kaen	d							20.40	21.45	10.32
Ban Phai	d							21.22	22.28	11.08
Bua Yai Jn	d							22.36	23.39	12.22
Ubon Ratchathani	d	13.45	16.50	17.45	19.00	06.40	07.10			
Si Sa Ket	d	14.53	17.49	18.55	20.07	07.55	08.29			
Sikhoraphum	d	16.19	18.53	20.04	21.10	09.09	09.49			
Surin	d	17.02	19.27	20.47	21.46	09.41	10.29			
Buri Ram	d	18.04	20.14	21.38	22.31	10.30	11.22			
Lam Plai Mat	d	18.37	20.43	22.06	|	11.00	11.55			
Thanon Chira Jn	d	20.10	21.59	23.19	|	12.23	13.34			
Nakhon Ratchasima	d	20.26	22.10	23.30	00.15	12.35	13.50			
Pak Chong	d	22.25	23.47	01.06	01.49	13.57	15.34			
Muak Lek	d	23.04	|	01.46	|	14.26	16.09			
Kaeng Kho Jn	d	23.55	01.05	02.19	02.56	14.59	16.52	02.38	03.43	16.15
Saraburi	a	00.10	01.19	02.30	03.09	15.13	17.05	02.52	03.56	16.29
Ban Phachi	a	00.51	|	02.54	|	15.38	17.42	03.17	|	16.54
Ayutthaya	a	01.18	02.04	03.15	03.56	15.59	18.04	03.39	04.40	17.16
Don Muang	a	02.11	02.46	03.55	04.38	16.39	18.53	04.20	05.20	17.55
Bangkok	a	03.00	03.30	04.35	05.20	17.25	19.40	05.00	06.00	18.40

Eastern Line: Bangkok-Aranyaprathet									
STATIONS		DRC 109	DRC 151	DRC 203	DRC 183	MIX 251	DRC 187	DRC 185	DRC 181
		3	3	3	3	3	3	3	3
Bangkok	d	06.00	07.00	08.05	09.40	11.25	13.10	15.10	17.25
Makkasan	d	06.12	07.19	08.17	09.53	11.46	13.21	15.21	17.37
Hua Mak	d	06.26	07.39	08.34	10.12	12.03	13.35	15.35	17.51
Hua Takhe	d	06.59	08.04	08.59	10.36	12.28	13.58	15.59	18.20
Chachoengsao	a	07.04	08.40	09.31	11.12	13.25	14.32	16.35	18.57
Prachin Buri	a	08.55		10.41	12.15	15.30	15.56	17.59	20.00
Prachantakham	a	09.15		10.00		15.58	16.17	18.16	
Kabin Buri	a	09.45		11.30		16.35	16.45	18.45	
Aranyaprathet	a	11.30					18.20		

STATIONS		DRC 182	MIX 252	DRC 186	DRC 188	DRC 154	DRC 204	DRC 184	DRC 110
		3	3	3	3	3	3	3	3
Aranyaprathet	d				06.40				13.05
Kabin Buri	d		05.05	07.05	08.13		12.35		14.47
Prachantakham	d		05.41	07.33	08.37		13.04		15.17
Prachin Buri	d	05.10	06.08	07.50	08.58		13.22	14.15	15.38
Chachoengsao	d	06.21	07.53	09.10	10.17	12.35	14.34	15.21	17.00
Hua Takhe	d	06.58	09.01	09.50	10.57	13.11	15.08	16.01	17.37
Hua Mak	d	07.24	09.32	10.11	11.25	13.36	15.36	16.26	18.10
Makkasan	a	07.40	09.49	10.24	11.38	13.49	15.49	16.38	18.23
Bangkok	a	07.55	10.10	10.35	11.50	14.00	16.00	16.50	18.35

ALL TRAINS RUN DAILY	SP = Special Express EXP = Express train RAP = Rapid train ORD = Ordinary train DRC = Diesel Railcar	EXP DRC = Express Diesel Railcar SPC DRC = Special Diesel Railcar SL = Sleeping car accommodation	AC = Air-conditioned second class coach ↳ Train from main line 1.2.3 = Classes ‖ No stop

Southern Line (including western branch)											
Bangkok... Hat Yai-Sungai Kolak & Butterworth Thonburi ... River Kwai Bridge-Nam Tok											
Stations	DRC 233	RAP 45	DRC 117	SP EX 19	SP EX 11	RAP 43	EX 13	RAP 41	EX 15	RAP 47	SPR 981
Bangkok	09.25	10.20	13.40	14.00	15.15	15.50	17.05	18.30	19.20	19.45	22.35
Nakhon Pathom	10.57	11.43	15.08	15.18	16.27	17.05	18.20	19.54	20.36	21.01	23.39
Ratchaburi	11.58	12.33	16.29	16.09	17.18	18.07		20.44	21.26	21.52	
Petchaburi	12.40	13.16	17.33	16.53	18.09	18.55		21.26	22.09	22.34	
Hua Hin	13.40	14.12	18.38	17.49	19.01	19.50	20.50	22.20	23.03	23.26	01.35
Prachuap Khiri Khan	*****	15.39	20.00	19.10		21.13		23.40	00.32	01.05	02.51
Chumphon		18.13	*****	21.42	22.51	00.29	00.53	02.40	03.16	04.15	05.10
Chaiya		20.56				02.54		05.03	05.27	06.31	06.56
Surat Thani		21.35		00.51	02.02	03.33	04.09	05.45	06.07	07.10	07.30
Thung Song Jn		00.03		03.00	04.09	05.51	06.23	08.28	08.51	09.53	*****
Trang		|		|	|	|	08.00	10.10	|	|	
Kantang		|		|	|	|	*****	10.45	|	|	
Nakhon Si Thammarat		|		|	|	|		*****	10.05	11.20	
Hat Yai Jn		03.01		05.57	07.05	08.58			*****	*****	
Yala		04.58		07.49	|	11.10					
Sungai Kolak		06.45		09.40	|	*****					
Padang Besar		*****		*****	08.00						
					10.00						
Butterworth (for Penang)					12.25						

The International Express trains (Nos 11/12) will operate between Bangkok-Padang Besar and Padang Besar-Bangkok (instead of Bangkok-Butterworth-Bangkok) and the Malaysian Railway will provide trains service for the connecting section between Padang Besar-Butterworth-Padang Besar at the same schedules as before.

Southern Line (including western branch)											
Butterworth — Thonburi ... River Kwai Bridge — Nam Tok											
Stations	**RAP 46**	**RAP 48**	**RAP 42**	**EX 16**	**EX 14**	**SP EX 12**	**RAP 44**	**SP EX 20**	**DRC 118**	**DRC 234**	**SPR 982**
Butterworth (for Penang) dep						13.40					
Padang Besar arr						15.27					
dep						17.00					
Sungai Kolak	07.55					|		15.00			
Yala	09.45					|	14.30	16.45			
Hat Yai Jn	11.45					18.10	16.55	18.40			
Nakhon Si Thammarat	|	13.40		15.35		|	|	|			
Katang	|	|	13.05	|		|	|	|			
Trang	|	|	13.39	|	18.10	|	|	|			
Thung Song Jn	14.47	15.00	15.18	16.42	19.50	21.15	20.10	21.48			
Surat Thani	16.55	17.32	17.50	19.05	22.01	23.22	22.20	23.58			11.05
Chaiya	17.32	18.08	18.30	19.43							11.37
Chumphon	19.55	20.22	20.50	21.59	01.05	02.20	01.42	02.58			13.20
Prachuap Khiri Khan	23.11	23.42	00.04	00.35			04.29		05.00		15.22
Hua Hin	00.51	01.12	01.40	01.57	05.25	05.59	06.21	06.47	06.27	14.30	16.28
Petchaburi	01.55	02.20	02.38	02.53			07.04		07.29	15.28	
Ratchaburi	02.41	03.07	03.25	03.39		07.39	07.52	08.23	08.26	16.11	
Nakhon Pathom	03.29	03.54	04.16	04.29	07.50	08.30	08.46	09.45	09.29	17.22	18.38
Bangkok	04.50	05.10	05.35	05.50	09.10	09.50	10.05	10.35	11.00	19.10	19.45

Note: There are two trains daily running to Kanchanaburi from Thonburi at 8.00 and 1.50, the former going to Nam Tok, but times are to be altered and should be checked.

RAILCAR SPECIAL

Bangkok-Phitsanulok

SPC 901 DRC	SPC 903 DRC	SPC 905 DRC	STATIONS		SPC 906 DRC	SPC 902 DRC	SPC 904 DRC
10.55	16.35	23.10	d Bangkok	a	04.45	14.15	22.25
11.05	16.46	23.21	d Sam Sen	a	04.33	14.05	22.14
11.30	17.12	23.46	d Don Muang	a	04.04	13.40	21.49
14.14	20.01	03.10	a Nakhon Sawan	d	00.50	10.49	18.46
15.37	21.20	04.35	a Phichit	d	23.21	09.23	17.28
16.10	22.00	05.15	a Phitsanulok	d	22.45	08.50	16.55

Bangkok-Udon Thani

SPC 945 DRC	SPC 947 DRC	STATIONS		SPC 946 DRC	SPC 948 DRC
08.02	22.25	d Bangkok	a	16.30	05.40
08.31	22.36	d Sam Sen	a	16.19	05.29
08.58	23.02	d Don Muang	a	15.54	05.02
12.22	02.56	a Nakhon Ratchasima	d	12.24	01.07
15.25	05.57	a Khon Kaen	d	09.33	22.16
17.05	07.35	a Udon Thani	d	07.55	20.35

Bangkok-Surin

SPC 931 DRC	SPC 933 DRC	STATIONS		SPC 934 DRC	SPC 932 DRC
11.05	21.50	d Bangkok	a	04.00	15.00
11.15	22.00	d Sam Sen	a	03.49	14.48
11.40	22.29	d Don Muang	a	03.20	14.18
15.12	02.31	a Nakhon Ratchasima	d	22.57	10.30
16.54	04.17	a Buri Ram	d	21.06	08.44
17.35	05.00	a Surin	d	20.25	08.05

ALL TRAINS RUN DAILY	SP = Special Express EXP = Express train RAP = Rapid train ORD = Ordinary train DRC = Diesel Railcar	EXP DRC = Express Diesel Railcar SPC DRC = Special Diesel Railcar SL = Sleeping car accommodation	AC = Air-conditioned second class coach ↓ Train from main line 1.2.3 = Classes ‖ No stop

FARES (Single)				
Northern Line				
From Bangkok to				
Stations	**Kms**	**1st**	**2nd**	**3rd**
Don Muang	22	18	10	5
Bang Pai-in	58	49	26	12
Ayutthaya	71	60	31	15
Lop Buri	133	111	57	28
Ban Takhli	193	157	80	39
Nakhon Sawan	246	197	99	48
Taphan Hin	319	245	122	58
Phichit	347	266	131	63
Phitsanulok	389	293	143	69
Uttaradit	485	356	172	82
Sila At	488	359	174	83
Den Chai	534	389	188	90
Mae Mo	609	440	211	100
Nakhon Lampang	642	463	221	106
Khun Tan	683	490	233	111
Lamphun	729	520	247	118
Chiang Mai	751	537	255	121
Northeastern Line				
From Bangkok to				
Stations	**Kms**	**1st**	**2nd**	**3rd**
Muak Lek	152	126	65	31
Pak Chong	180	146	74	346
Nakhon Ratchasima	264	207	104	40
Surin	420	312	153	73
Si Sa Ket	515	376	182	87
Ubon Ratchathani	575	416	200	95
Bua Yai	346	266	131	63
Ban Phai	408	306	150	71
Khon Kaen	450	333	162	77
Udon Thani	569	413	198	95
Nong Khai	624	450	215	103
Eastern Line				
From Bangkok to				
Stations	**Kms**	**1st**	**2nd**	**3rd**
Hua Takhe	31	-	-	7
Chachoengsao	61	-	-	13
Prachin Buri	122	-	-	26
Kabin Buri	161	-	-	33
Aranyaprathet	255	-	-	48

Supplementary charges		
		Baht per person
Express train charge		30.00
Rapid train charge		20.00
Special express train charge		50.00
Air-conditioned 2nd, 3rd coach charge		50.00
Sleeping berth charges Air-conditioned 1st class berth	double cabin	250.00
Air-conditioned 2nd class berth for Rapid	upper	200.00
	lower	250.00
2nd class berth for Rapid	upper	70.00
	lower	100.00
2nd class berth (for special express)	upper	100.00
	lower	150.00
2nd class berth air-conditioned (only special express)	upper	200.00
	lower	250.00

Sample Fares	
Express Diesel Railcar Including food, snack, tea & coffee	
Northern Line	
Samsen	154
Bangsue	154
Bangkhen	156
Don Muang	160
Nakhorn Sawan	249
Taphan Hin	272
Phitsanulok	285
Uttaradit	315
Den Chai	330
Lampang	365
Chiang Mai	395

FARES (Single)				
Southern Line (with western branch)				
From Bangkok to				Single
Stations	Kms	1st	2nd	3rd
Nakhon Pathom	64	54	28	14
Kanchanaburi	133	111	57	28
River Kwai Bridge	136	115	59	29
Nam Tok	210	168	85	41
Ratchaburi	117	99	52	25
Phetchaburi	167	138	71	34
Hua Hin	229	182	92	44
Prachuap Khiri Khan	318	245	122	58
Chumphon	485	356	172	82
Surat Thani	651	470	224	107
Thung Song Jn	773	550	261	124
Trang	845	597	282	135
Kantang	866	614	290	138
Nakhon Si Thammarat	832	590	279	133
Phatthalung	862	611	288	137
Hat Yai	945	664	313	149
Yala	1055	738	346	165
Sungai Kolak	1159	808	378	180
Padang Besar	990	694	326	156
Butterworth	1149	1015	457	

Supplementary charges		
		Baht per person
Express train charge		30.00
Rapid train charge		20.00
Special express train charge		50.00
Air-conditioned 2nd, 3rd coach charge		50.00
Sleeping berth charges	double	250.00
Air-conditioned 1st class berth	cabin	
Air-conditioned 2nd class berth for Rapid	upper	200.00
	lower	250.00
2nd class berth for Rapid	upper	70.00
	lower	100.00
2nd class berth (for special express)	upper	100.00
	lower	150.00
2nd class berth air-conditioned (only special express)	upper	200.00
	lower	250.00
Additional supplementary charges		
From Padang Besar to Butterworth		
Express train charge		45.00
Air-conditioned 1st, 2nd class		45.00

Fares	
Express Diesel Railcar Including food, snack, tea & coffee	
Southern Line	
Samsen	154
Bangsue	154
Nakhon Pathom	156
Hua Hin	170
Prachuap Khiri Khan	235
Chumphon	265
Lang Suan	315
Chaiya	335
Surat Thani	355
Thung Song Jn	370
Phatthalung	405
Hat Yai Jn	430
	455

Fares				
Southern Line				
Station	**Kms**	**1 $ C**	**2 $ C**	**3 $ C**
Ipoh	1331	29.00	17.00	10.00
Kuala Lumpur	1531	54.00	28.00	17.00
Gemas	1692	76.00	38.00	23.00
Singapore	1927	102.00	50.00	30.00

Supplementary charges	$
Express train charge	4
Air-conditioned 1st class berth	25
1st class Berth (non air-conditioned)	12.50
2nd Berth Lower	10
Upper	7.50

TIMETABLES AND FARES: MALAYSIA

Butterworth/Kuala Lumpur/Singapore

Stations		ER 1 A AC	ER 1 A AC	M 51	B 59	XSP 3 A AC	SM 61	B 53	SM 55	XSP 5 A AC	M 57
		1-2-3	1-2-3	2-3	2-3	1-2	1-2	2-3	1-2	1-2	2-3
Butterworth	d	07.40		08.30		14.15		20.15	22.30		
Bt Mertajam	a	07.54		08.50		14.29		20.35	22.50		
Ipoh	a	10.37		13.16		17.04		00.38	02.26		
Taplah Road	a	11.30		14.36		17.58		02.41	03.52		
Kuala Lumpur	a	**14.00**		**18.15**		**20.25**		**06.00**	**07.00**		
	d		14.20		20.20		22.00			07.30	08.30
Seremban	a		16.13		22.33		22.54			09.23	10.28
Segamat	a		18.34		01.38		03.01			11.15	13.48
Johor Bahru	a		21.02		05.15		06.06			13.29	17.32
Singapore	a		**22.00**		**06.15**		**07.00**			**14.20**	**18.30**

Singapore/Kuala Lumpur/Butterworth

Stations		ER 2 A AC	ER 2 A AC	XSP 6 A AC	M 58	B 54	SM 56	B 60	SM 62	XSP 4 A AC	M 52
		1-2-3	1-2-3	1-2	2-3	2-3	1-2	2-3	1-2	1-2	2-3
Singapore	d	07.30		15.00	08.30			20.00	22.15		
Johor Bahru	a	07.58		15.27	09.50			20.35	22.50		
Segamat	a	10.21		17.42	12.42			00.23	01.58		
Seremban	a	12.33		19.56	15.46			03.35	04.55		
Kuala Lumpur	a	**14.30**		**21.40**	**18.30**			05.45	07.00		
	d		15.00			20.30	22.15			07.15	08.30
Tapah Road	a		17.30			23.36	01.18			09.40	11.59
Ipoh	a		18.18			00.51	02.45			10.23	13.09
Bt Mertajam	a		21.05			05.10	06.37			13.16	17.20
Butterworth	a		**21.30**			**05.55**	**07.10**			**13.35**	**18.00**

North bound train schedule: Kuala Lumpur-Ipoh-Butterworth-Arau-Kuala Lumpur

Type/train no	XSP/4	M/52	EL*8	ER/2	B/54	SM/56		ER/1	M/51	EL/7	XSP/3	B/53	SM/55
KUALA LUMPUR	07.15	08.30	07.15	14.45	20.30	22.00		14.40	18.45	05.20	21.50	06.20	07.00
Sungei Buloh	-	08.58	-	-	20.57	-		-	18.05	-	-	05.42	-
Rawang	-	09.19	-	-	21.35	22.44		-	17.47	-	-	05.23	06.00
Kuala Kubi Road	-	09.59	-	-	22.29	23.37		-	16.50	-	-	04.34	05.14
Tanjong Malim	-	10.23	-	-	22.52	24.00		-	15.55	-	-	04.11	04.52
Behrang	-	10.36	-	-	23.05	-		-	15.43	-	-	03.58	-
Slim River	-	10.48	-	-	23.17	-		-	15.30	-	-	03.45	-
Tralak	-	10.59	-	-	-	-		-	15.20	-	-	-	-
Sungkai	-	11.15	-	-	23.43	-		-	15.04	-	-	03.20	-
Bidor	-	11.28	-	-	23.55	-		-	14.51	-	-	-	-
TAPAH ROAD	10.03	12.00	10.03	17.38	00.08	01.09		11.30	14.34	02.25	18.50	02.48	03.38
Kampar	-	12.27	-	17.53	00.32	01.32		11.16	14.12	-	-	01.53	03.18
Malim Nawar	-	12.37	-	-	00.41	01.41		-	14.04	-	-	01.45	-
Kota Bharu	-	-	-	-	-	-		-	13.55	-	-	-	-
Batu Gajah	-	12.59	-	18.14	01.00	02.28		10.55	13.44	-	-	01.25	02.54
IPOH	10.54	13.20	10.54	18.30	01.29	02.59		10.25	12.52	01.12	17.50	00.44	01.57
Tanjong Rambutan	-	13.58	-	-	02.08	-		-	12.33	-	-	00.25	-
Chemor	-	14.07	-	-	02.18	-		-	12.25	-	-	00.16	-
Sungei Siput	-	14.21	-	-	02.32	-		-	12.11	-	-	00.02	-
KUALA KANGSAR	11.24	14.46	11.24	19.25	02.56	04.17		09.33	11.20	-	17.00	23.39	01.05
Padang Rengas	-	15.00	-	-	03.09	-		-	11.07	-	-	23.28	-
TAIPING	12.20	15.33	12.20	20.00	03.39	04.58		08.58	10.32	23.45	16.26	22.56	00.24
Kamunting	-	-	-	-	-	-		-	10.23	-	-	-	-
Pondok Tanjong	-	15.58	-	-	-	-		-	10.10	-	-	-	-
Bukit Merah	-	16.27	-	-	-	-		-	09.57	-	-	-	-
Bagan Serai	-	16.42	-	-	04.30	05.44		-	09.41	-	-	22.09	23.39
Parit Buntar	-	16.57	-	20.50	04.44	05.58		08.09	09.26	-	-	21.55	23.25
Nibong Tebal	-	17.06	-	-	04.52	06.07		-	09.19	-	-	21.47	23.17
Simpang Ampat	-	17.20	-	-	-	-		-	09.05	-	-	-	-
BUKIT MERTAJAM	13.35	17.31	13.35	21.15	05.16	06.30		07.43	08.45	22.20	15.12	20.45	22.45
BUTTERWORTH	14.25	18.20	-	21.40	06.05	07.10		07.30	08.30	-	15.00	20.30	22.30
Sungei Petani	-	-	14.39	-	-	-		-	-	21.45	-	-	-
Alor Star	-	-	15.29	-	-	-		-	-	20.55	-	-	-
ARAU	-	-	16.05	-	-	-		-	-	20.30	-	-	-

South-bound train schedule:
Kuala Lumpur-Gemas-Singapore-Kuala Lumpur

Type/Train No		SXP/5	M/57	ER/1	B/59*	SM/61		ER/2	M/5B	XSP/6	B/60*	SM/62
KUALA LUMPUR	D	07.30	08.30	15.00	20.15	22.15	A	14.15	18.05	21.30	05.45	07.05
Kajang	E		09.10		21.10		R		17.05		04.45	
SEREMBAN	P	09.00	10.12	16.30	22.11	23.55	R	12.22	15.36	19.48	03.36	05.00
Rembau	A		10.48		22.45		I		15.10		03.10	
TAMPIN	R	09.40	11.14	17.10	23.11	00.55	V	11.40	14.31	19.09	02.33	03.58
Tebong	T		12.00		23.35		E		14.15			
Batang Melaka			12.13		23.48				14.02		02.02	
A K South			12.25		00.01				13.50		01.50	
GEMAS			12.47	17.59	00.27	02.14		10.54	13.08		01.03	02.38
Batu Anam					01.22				12.55		00.50	
SEGAMAT		10.59	13.43	18.30	01.38	03.10		10.29	12.32	17.59	00.27	02.01
Tenang			14.08		02.23				12.13			
Labis			14.21		02.36				12.00		23.54	
Bekok			14.40		02.55				11.34		23.34	
Jagoh			14.47						11.27			
Beradin									11.21			
Paloh			15.00	19.22	03.12				11.14		23.16	
B Ridin									11.08			
Chamek			15.18		03.24				11.02		23.04	
Niyor			15.22						10.52		22.54	
KLUANG		12.10	15.32	19.43	03.44	04.43		09.13	10.37	16.43	22.39	00.23
Mengkibol			15.54						10.29			
Rengam			16.12		04.10				10.16		22.17	
Layang-Layang	A		16.42		04.23		D		10.03		22.04	
Sedenak	R		16.57				E		09.49		21.50	
Kulai	R		17.09		04.47		P		09.37		21.38	
Kempas Bahru	I						A		09.18			
JOHOR BHARU	V	13.25	17.42	21.00	05.21	06.10	R	07.55	08.58	15.25	20.27	22.42
SINGAPORE	E	14.20	18.55	22.00	06.25	07.10	T	07.30	08.30	15.00	20.00	22.15

* Will convey passenger to/from east coast stations

East Coast Train Schedule: Kuala Lumpur/Singapore-Tumpat-Kuala Lumpur/Singapore									
		B/59		B/60			No 12		No 11
KUALA LUMPUR	dep	20.15	arr	05.45	GEMAS	dep	02.20	arr	24.00
Kajang		21.10		04.45	Bahau		02.52		23.07
SEREMBAN		22.11		03.36	Kemayan		03.28		23.31
Rembau		22.45		03.10	Triang		03.43		22.12
TAMPIN		23.11		02.33	MENTAKAB		04.18		21.35
Tebong		23.34			KUALA KRAU		04.43		21.09
Batang Melaka		23.48		02.02	Jerantut		05.08		20.42
A K South		00.01		01.50	Tembeling		05.26		
Arrive GEMAS	arr	00.27	dep	01.35	Mela		05.33		20.18
					Krambit		05.45		20.05
		B/60		B/59	KUALA LIPIS		06.05		19.20
					Padang Tungku		06.35		19.08
SINGAPORE	dep	20.00	arr	06.25	Chegar Perah		07.00		18.45
JOHOR BAHRU		20.27		05.21	Merapoh		07.31		18.11
Kulai		21.38		04.47	GUA MUSANG		07.52		17.44
Sedenak		21.50			Bertam Baru		08.28		17.08
Layang-Layang		22.04		04.23	Dabong		09.00		16.36
Rengam		22.17		04.10	Bukit ABu		09.13		
KLUANG		22.39		03.44	KRAI		09.55		15.44
Niyor		22.54			Tanah Merah		10.31		15.08
Chamek		23.04		03.24	PASIR MAS		11.00		14.41
Paloh		23.16		03.12	Wakaf Bharu		11.15		14.26
Bekok		23.34		02.55	TUMPAT	arr	11.40	dep	14.15
Labis		23.54		02.36					
Tenang				02.23					
SEGAMAT		00.27		01.38					
Batu Anam		00.50		01.22					
GEMAS	arr	01.03	dep	01.15					

Kedah Line Services					
Butterworth — Arau — Butterworth					
Type/Train No	**B/72**	**B/74**		**B/73**	**B/75**
	am	**pm**		**pm**	**pm**
BUTTERWORTH	06.10	14.30		12.40	21.05
Prai B'tolok depart	06.13	14.32	Tiba arrive	12.30	20.54
Bukit Tengah	06.20	14.38		12.23	20.28
BT MERTAJAM	06.27	14.45		11.54	20.17
Penanti	06.44	14.56		11.46	20.09
Tasek Glugor	06.53	15.04		11.37	20.00
K Menerong	06.57	15.08		11.32	19.53
P Tunggal	07.05	15.16		11.27	19.48
SUNGEI PETANI	07.16	15.27		11.14	19.34
Bedong	07.29	15.40		11.03	19.23
Gurun	07.40	15.51		10.52	19.12
Junun	07.51	16.02		10.41	19.01
B Pinang	07.56	16.07		10.35	18.55
Kobah	08.03	16.14		10.29	18.49
Tokai	08.11	16.22		10.21	18.40
Alor Belat	08.17	16.28		10.15	18.34
ALOR STAR	08.23	16.35		10.05	18.23
Anak Bukit	08.31	16.44		09.59	18.17
Sungei Korok	08.38	16.51		09.53	18.10
Tunjang	08.44	16.57		09.47	18.04
Megat Dewa	08.50	17.03		09.41	17.57
Kodiang	08.58	17.11	B'tolak	09.34	17.50
ARAU Tiba arrive	09.10	17.25	depart	09.30	17.45

Gemas-Kluang-Singapore-Gemas						
Type/Train No		965	967		966	968
		am	pm		am	pm
Gemas	B'tolak depart	06.35		Tiba		20.35
Batu Anam		06.43		arrive		20.19
Segamat		06.57				20.04
Genuang		07.06				19.55
Tenang		07.14				19.45
Labis		07.25				19.32
Lenek		07.34				19.23
Bekok		07.41				18.57
Jagoh		07.48				18.48
Beradin		07.54				18.43
Paloh		08.00				18.37
B. Ridan		08.06				18.32
Chamek		08.11				18.27
Niyor		08.18				18.19
KLUANG		08.26	13.45		13.25	18.09
Mengkibol		08.34	13.49		13.12	18.01
Rengam		08.45	14.01		13.00	17.50
Layang-Layang		09.09	14.12		12.30	17.38
Sedenak		09.21	14.24		12.18	17.27
Kulai		09.30	14.33		12.03	17.06
Kempas Bharu		10.00	14.51		11.53	16.51
Tampoi		10.05	14.55		11.48	16.45
Holiday Plaza		10.09	14.59		11.44	16.42
JOHOR BHARU	Tiba arrive	10.14	15.05	B'tolak	11.38	16.28
SINGAPORE		10.55	16.00	Depart	11.20	16.10

International Express Schedule Butterworth-Padang Besar-Had Yai/Bangkok- Butterworth		
Type/Train No	**ISE/48**	**ISE/49**
Butterworth	13.45	12.25
Bukit Mertajam	13.53	12.05
Sungei Petani	14.24	11.37
Alor Star	15.12	-
Arau	15.43	-
Padang Besar	16.15	-
	-	09.00
Had Yai	16.40	07.20
	16.55	07.05
Bangkok	08.35	15.15
(Thai time; for Malaysia time add 60 minutes)		

Passenger fares between principal stations									
Single journey fare ($)									
	Butterworth			Kuala Lumpur			Singapore		
	1	2	3	1	2	3	1	2	3
Padang Besar	23.80	9.80	6.10	75.40	31.00	19.10	129.90	53.40	32.90
Arau	20.30	8.40	5.20	71.20	29.30	18.10	127.10	52.30	32.20
Alor Setar	14.30	5.90	3.70	64.70	27.00	16.60	121.50	50.00	30.80
Butterworth	-	-	-	54.50	22.40	13.60	110.30	45.40	27.50
Bt Mertajam	1.70	0.70	0.50	53.10	21.90	13.60	108.90	44.80	27.60
Taiping	13.50	5.60	3.40	41.90	17.30	10.60	96.40	39.70	24.40
Ipoh	25.90	10.70	6.80	29.40	12.10	7.50	85.20	35.10	21.60
Tapah Road	33.60	13.80	8.50	21.70	8.90	5.50	78.20	32.20	19.80
Kuala Lumpur	54.50	22.40	13.80	-	-	-	55.90	23.00	14.20
Seremban	54.70	27.00	16.60	10.40	4.30	2.70	46.10	19.00	11.70
Tampin	71.20	29.30	18.10	17.50	7.20	4.50	39.10	16.10	8.50
Gemas	79.60	32.80	20.20	25.20	10.40	6.40	32.20	13.30	8.50
Segamat	82.40	33.90	20.90	29.40	12.10	7.50	28.00	11.50	7.10
Kluang	95.00	39.10	24.10	40.50	16.70	10.30	16.10	6.70	4.10
Johor Bharu	106.10	43.70	26.90	51.70	21.30	19.10	4.00	1.70	1.00
Singapore	110.30	45.40	27.90	55.90	23.00	14.20	-	-	-
Kuala Lipis	110.30	45.40	27.90	57.30	23.60	14.50	62.90	25.90	15.90
Krai	141.00	58.00	35.70	86.60	35.60	21.90	93.60	38.50	23.70
Wakai Bharu	150.80	62.00	38.20	96.40	39.70	24.40	103.40	42.50	26.20
Tumpat	152.20	62.60	36.50	99.20	40.80	25.10	104.70	43.10	26.50
Had Yai	32.00	13.50	-	83.60	34.70	-	138.10	57.10	-
Bangkok	91.10	41.00	-	142.70	62.20	-	197.20	84.60	-

Note: Children between the ages of 4 and 12 are charged half the adult fare while children under 4 years travel free of charge.

Passenger fares between principal stations									
Express train fare ($)									
	Butterworth			Kuala Lumpur			Singapore		
	AFC 1	ASC 2	TC 3	AFC 1	ASC 2	TC 3	AFC 1	ASC 2	TC 3
Arau	29.00	17.00	10.00	80.00	38.00	23.00	136.00	61.00	37.00
Alor Setar	23.00	14.00	8.00	74.00	35.00	21.00	130.00	58.00	35.00
Sungai Patani	15.00	11.00	8.00	66.00	32.00	19.00	122.00	55.00	33.00
Butterworth	-	-	-	63.00	31.00	18.00	119.00	54.00	32.00
Bt Mertajam	10.00	9.00	5.00	62.00	30.00	18.00	117.00	53.00	32.00
Parit Buntar	14.00	11.00	6.00	57.00	29.00	17.00	113.00	52.00	31.00
Taiping	22.00	14.00	8.00	50.00	26.00	15.00	105.00	48.00	29.00
K Kangsar	27.00	16.00	9.00	46.00	24.00	14.00	101.00	46.00	25.00
Ipoh	34.00	19.00	11.00	38.00	21.00	12.00	94.00	44.00	26.00
Batu Gajah	36.00	20.00	12.00	36.00	20.00	11.00	91.00	42.00	25.00
Kampar	39.00	21.00	12.00	32.00	18.00	11.00	88.00	41.00	25.00
Tapah Road	42.00	22.00	13.00	30.00	17.00	10.00	87.00	41.00	24.00
Kuala Lumpur	63.00	31.00	18.00	-	-	-	64.00	31.00	19.00
Seremban	74.00	35.00	21.00	19.00	13.00	7.00	55.00	27.00	16.00
Tampin	80.00	38.00	23.00	26.00	16.00	9.00	48.00	25.00	14.00
Gemas	88.00	41.00	25.00	34.00	19.00	11.00	41.00	22.00	13.00
Segamat	91.00	42.00	25.00	38.00	21.00	12.00	36.00	20.00	12.00
Kluang	103.00	48.00	29.00	49.00	25.00	15.00	25.00	15.00	9.00
Johor Bharu	115.00	52.00	31.00	60.00	30.00	18.00	12.00	10.00	5.00
Singapore	119.00	54.00	32.00	64.00	31.00	19.00	-	-	-

Note: Children between the ages of 4 and 12 are charged half the adult fare while children under 4 years travel free of charge.

INFORMATION INTERNATIONAL SPECIAL EXPRESS BERTH CHARGES		
1st class	$22.60 air-conditioned	
2nd class	$13.60 lower	
2nd class	$9.10 upper	
2nd class	$22.60 lower air-conditioned	
2nd class	$18.10 upper air-conditioned	
Express Train charges:	Thailand:	$4.60
	Malaysia:	$8.00 air-conditioned
		$4.00 non air-conditioned

KTM BERTH CHARGES	
1st class	$25.00 air-conditioned
1st class	$12.50 ordinary
2nd class	$10.00 lower
2nd class	$7.50 upper

Telephone numbers	
Station	**Number**
Padang Besar	04-750231
Arau	04-961225
Pulau Pinang	04-610290
Butterworth	04-347962
Bukit Mertajam	04-592660
Alor Star	04-714045
Taiping	05-825584
Ipoh	05-510072
Kuala Lumpur	
Pertanyaan/	03-2747435
Enquiry	03-7247422
	03-2747443
Sungai Buloh	03-6561930
Sentul	03-4417620
Ampang	03-4579313
Petaling	03-7929231
Subang Jaya	03-7341677
Sungai Way	03-7760672
Pelabuhan Klang	03-3698239
Seremban	06-711708
Tampin	06-411034
Gemas	07-981047
Tumpat	09-757232
Kuala Lipis	09-311341
Krai	09-966224
Wakaf Bharu	09-796986
Kluang	07-710954
Johor Bharu	07-234727
Singapore	
Enquiry	02-2225165

INDEX OF PLACE NAMES